WILD ONCE

Dr Vivianne Crowley is an internationally renowned Wiccan priestess, worldwide go-to authority on Wicca culture, a psychologist and bestselling author. Formerly Lecturer in Psychology of Religion at King's College, University of London, she is now a professor in the Faculty of Pastoral Counseling, Cherry Hill Seminary, South Carolina. Her many books have been translated around the world.

ALSO BY VIVIANNE CROWLEY

Wicca: A Comprehensive Guide to the Old Religion in the Modern World
Phoenix from the Flame: Pagan Spirituality in the Western World

Principles of Paganism
Principles of Wicca
Principles of Jungian Spirituality
Celtic Wisdom: Seasonal Festivals and Rituals
The Goddess Book of Days

Vivianne Crowley

WILD ONCE

C
CENTURY

1 3 5 7 9 10 8 6 4 2

Century
20 Vauxhall Bridge Road
London SW1V 2SA

Century is part of the Penguin Random House group of companies
whose addresses can be found at global.penguinrandomhouse.com.

First published by Century in 2022

www.penguin.co.uk

A CIP catalogue record for this book is available from the British Library.

ISBN 9781529124897

Typeset in 12.5/15.5 pt Bembo Std
by Integra Software Services Pvt. Ltd, Pondicherry

Printed and bound in Great Britain by Clays Ltd, Elcograf S.p.A.

The authorised representative in the EEA is Penguin Random House Ireland,
Morrison Chambers, 32 Nassau Street, Dublin D02 YH68.

Penguin Random House is committed to a sustainable future for
our business, our readers and our planet. This book is made from
Forest Stewardship Council® certified paper.

To all who walk the hidden paths

Contents

Acknowledgements

This book is the result of my journeying and interactions with many people around the world. Some of my friends are open about their interest in the mystical and the magical. If you work in the arts, exotic spiritual interests are almost obligatory. If you work in IT, or even in academia, unusual spiritual interests are not so unusual. My friends who are in the corporate world, and those who are doctors, accountants or lawyers, mostly prefer to keep their professional and spiritual lives apart. Where in the book I refer to well-known authors and public figures, I have named them in full. For people who are not in the public eye, I give only first names, and some names have been changed.

Some of you who read this book will recognise experiences that we have shared. For reasons of privacy, there are details I leave out and some I have altered. I hope you feel that what I describe captures the profound nature of those experiences.

None of us travels alone, and those whom we meet and who share the different stages of our life's journey help to shape us. Sometimes they take us in life-changing directions without even noticing. I offer my gratitude and deepest thanks to those with whom I have been privileged to walk the ways of spirituality and magic. Some are alive still. Many others have joined their ancestors in the realms beyond and to these especially I send loving thanks – Alex Sanders, Arthur Eaglen, Barbara Somers, Ian Gordon-Brown, Ivy Northage, Joan and Reyn Swallow, Madge Worthington, Margaret Bain, Marjorie Aarons and Stein Jarving.

And I send loving thanks to the living, to those with whom I walk the pathways into the uncharted territories of the spirit and the wild places of the forest, and especially to my beloved husband, Chris, without whom I might not have journeyed so far along the roads less travelled.

To my editor, Zennor Compton, and my agent, Laetitia Rutherford of Watson Little, who inspired me to write this book, my deepest thanks for guiding me through the creative process on this journey into the realms of wild magic.

May all our voyages of the spirit be full of love, laughter and illumination.

An Invitation

Supposing you had experiences from an early age that people labelled psychic or magical and you decided to hold on to them, to stay with them, to see where they led? How might you live, and how might that be? This book is about that journey. It is about reclaiming wildness and magic, but most of all *Wild Once* is about a quest to connect with the deeper authentic self. Perhaps this is your quest too?

My quest has taken me through many of the world's spiritual traditions. Wicca with its veneration of the Goddess and of nature remains my core spirituality, but aspects of Buddhism, Kabbalah and many other traditions are woven into my personal practice. What I have found most important, though, is what lies behind all these traditions; for the greatest mystery is found not in temples, churches, mosques, or in witches' circles. We can experience mystery and magic in each waking breath and each dawn of a new day. What lies at the heart of all true spirituality is the joy that comes from realising that in the depths of our being we are connected to one another, to our biosphere and, beyond that, to the living universe – an interconnection of consciousness that unites us all.

Wild Once is the product of a life lived on the inside arc of the magical world, a world that for many is intriguing, mysterious, arcane and alluring. If this world is unfamiliar to you, it may seem surprising that people practise magic in the twenty-first century at all. These are practices that for many people are archaic and strange, but for some of us they are a part of everyday life, much as they were for our ancestors.

Magic is familiar yet new, and not so easy to ignore or suppress. It is in our cells, in our DNA, in blood and bone. Human memories for millennia upon millennia were based in a magical world. If we follow the path of magic, it takes us on a voyage into the older, wilder, more primitive parts of the brain; into the hidden depths of the unconscious, into the highways and byways of the spirit, into the realms of human imagination and dream that lead to the well-springs of our being.

Some of you will be on your own spiritual and magical path. You may be taking your first steps or, like me, have been on your path for decades. Some of you may not have consciously experienced magic in your lives but are curious about it – about what draws people to it and what it has to offer. Perhaps you have children or friends who use crystals, read the tarot or practise manifestation. Maybe you have been a guest at a handfasting, a Pagan wedding, and were moved by the ritual. Maybe friends or relatives practise Wicca, Druidry or other nature-based spirituality, and you want to understand more about it.

A magical spirituality is not for everyone, but some of its essence is – its cultivation of the intuition, its recognition that within us is a deeper self that is connected to the Divine, its veneration of the natural world, and its love of life and of the gift of consciousness. So too is the overall message – that we can all live our lives as journeys of joyful discovery that honour what is good, whole and true in the human spirit, and seek to manifest it in ourselves and in the world.

So, let us begin. Let me invite you to the places of wild magic, to experience what it is to open ourselves to the universe and to the myriad energies that surround us. It is a journey rooted in ancient archetypes, and in the modern imagery of the world wide web. It takes us into the deep magic within us, the magic that stimulates us to new ways of looking at the world. Re-energised, with renewed insight, we can find in magic a state of being that honours the mystical and the extraordinary, and the wonder of the cosmos around us. It is a radical worldview that can become the basis for personal, social, political, spiritual and entrepreneurial action. It inspires us to change the world. And we need the world to be made anew.

I

Throwing Off the Shackles

I always found it difficult to complete that section on job applications where it asks about interests. Usually, I would stick to 'art, classical music, meditation and travel', and leave off 'tarot, talisman-making and wild witchery'. Meditation has crossed the boundary into conventional work worlds, but other esoteric practices still have a way to go. The day jobs on my CV include psychologist, management consultant, research director and university lecturer. It was only in the liberal academic university environment that it felt comfortable to be 'out' as who I was. That is partly due to my age. The twentieth century was less open to diversity and difference than the twenty-first.

Thirty years after the publication of my book *Wicca*,[1] magic has come out of the broom closet. I reflect on this one snowy February, as I sit with Ronald Hutton, Professor of History at the University of Bristol, and Philip Carr-Gomm, Chosen Chief of the Order of Bards, Ovates and Druids, on the stage of the British Library's lecture theatre as experts in a panel discussion on contemporary magic. The event is sold out. It is part of the library's most successful exhibition ever, *Harry Potter: A History of Magic.* Magic is now part of the mainstream, the audience's questions interesting and deep.

Magic means different things to different people. We tell a friend about an exciting concert and say it was magical. A footballer scores unexpectedly – it was magic. Something extraordinary happens and we say it happened almost by magic. There is stage magic, black magic, white magic, green magic, wild magic. What do I mean by 'magic'? For me, it is all those things that are just on the edge of science – the wishes that come true, the premonitions that manifest, the chance encounters that change our lives, the spells that work, the tarot reader who knows exactly what we are planning to ask. Magic is the unexpected, the exciting – that which takes us out of our ordinary state of consciousness and into some other, older, deeper, wilder place. Magic implies wildness and wonder; the archaic, mysterious and inexplicable.

Synchronicity, clairvoyance, premonitions, intuitive leaps, close encounters of the supernatural kind – all these are experiences that some people have all of the time, most people have some of the time, and a few, just a few, never experience at all. We might think they are beyond science, but they are only beyond the science of now. Magic encompasses that whole in-between realm of experiences that are in the process of crossing the boundary between the inexplicable and the explicable. Most of what today we think of as science – everything from medicine to agriculture to cosmology – was once seen as magical. Each year our scientific understanding grows, but there is more, so much more, that we have yet to discover. To say that magic is ultimately explicable, even if not in our own lifetimes, does not make magic mundane. Most of us would benefit from a little more magic in our lives.

Magic begins in the wild places, and in our bedrooms when we cast our first spells. If we continue on a magical path and go beyond simple spells, we discover that magic is less about achieving material change directly than about something subtler – changing ourselves so that we can change the world around us. It removes the unconscious obstacles and conditioning that make us self-sabotage our efforts. Just like when we put on a suit, or make-up and perfume, magic changes how we feel about ourselves and this influences how others react to us, which in turn influences how we react back. It helps us to create the right conditions to attract what we need.

But magic is also more profound than this. If we think of a teenager performing a money spell, then magic might seem purely material, but it is also a spiritual practice. Dion Fortune, the twentieth century's most famous female magician, and one of the first Freudian analysts in London who was not also a medical doctor, famously defined magic in 1934 as 'the art of causing changes to take place in consciousness in accordance with will.'[2] As we go deeper into magic, we discover its radical claim that it can change the way we experience our world. Magic becomes a path of self-transformation; a way of opening our consciousness, of expanding the boundaries of who we are, of allowing the spirit to soar to new creative heights. It is this that keeps people on a magical path long after interest in simple spells has faded.

In thinking about the magical, we do not turn our backs on science; for magic is science as well as a creative art. For a long time, Western science taught us to see body and mind as separate, with only the most tenuous of linkages – then along came quantum mechanics, disrupting old models of mind, consciousness and matter.

Since the 1990s, developments in other newer sciences are challenging long-accepted paradigms too. The new cognitive sciences are exciting because they are opening the way to discoveries that recognise that body, mind and brain are enmeshed, and interact with whole networks of other bodies, minds and brains. Most cognitive scientists stop at the level of human interaction. Others go further and speculate that all biological life forms – and inorganic matter too – interact and communicate in a vast web of interconnected energies, a return to a view of reality shared by indigenous peoples and magical traditions. It is a view that helped magicians adapt readily to technological advances in interconnectivity to become innovators in and early adopters of computer-based technology, and they have a disproportionate presence on the world wide web. In fact, it was magicians Zachary Cox and John Kennedy who set up one of London's first software houses in the 1960s. The thinking needed to invent new ways of encoding and communicating information came readily to those used to the symbolic thinking of the magical world.

Complex ideas about body, brain and consciousness were not what I was thinking about at the beginning of my journey. What I was searching for in my teens was how to label that longing, that yearning, that sense that something lay behind and beyond the everyday world that I saw around me. It was as though this world was an outer coating. Reality was hidden somewhere behind this surface. We enjoy sci-fi films that explore this idea because on an intuitive level we sense that the space-time parameters rooting us in everyday reality are just that – parameters. They help us navigate our day-to-day world, but they do not represent all of reality. What we see around us is not how things ultimately are. A deeper part of us senses that the world that we have been educated and programmed to conform to from our earliest days is artificial, even slightly insane.

Our brains have become lopsided in the process of creating all the technological marvels that surround us. It is as though we are hopping along on one leg because we have been told that the other one is not needed. It becomes normal to hop and not to walk or run or climb. We are taught from birth to cut off parts of our psyches in order to develop others. We are taught to value logic over intuition, and materialism over loving kindness. We are socialised into constraining our lives, into living within the prescribed parameters set out for us by patriarchy and corporate capitalism. And this is a problem, because it just does not work. The world that we create when we live this way kills the spirit.

Do we want our lives to be dedicated to producing and consuming useless objects and unnecessary services, or are we better than that? Is there something we can do with our lives that is truly meaningful and worthwhile? Each of us must find our own answer to this question, our own truth, our own way of being, but we need to inspire one another to move forward, to hope and to dream, to see a new vision for humankind.

And within us is something that protests. It protests at being socialised into spending our time looking at other people's lives on social media, so that advertisers can thrust their products at us. It wants to find a deeper self – a natural, creative, wilder biological self. This is the self that is in touch with the realms of sensation and feeling, the self we find when we listen to the wisdom of the body and the values of the heart.

Much of our deeper being is hidden, and lies below the threshold of everyday awareness. The reality is that we are full of hidden potential. Within each one of us is a wilder, freer, more imaginative and creative self that is closely connected to the untamed wildness within us, that part of us which revels in the joy and the magic of being a conscious entity in an extraordinary cosmos. To find this inner joy, we must embrace the whole of our being – the deeper, animal self that rejoices in life in the body, and the untamed spirit and vast imagination that allow our vision to soar to the highest of heights.

To begin, we must liberate ourselves from the prison of social expectation and of trying to be the person that others want us to be. Yes, we need to be socialised into how to navigate the complex demands of our world; but, no, this is not the end of the story. We must each create our own story, our own narrative, about what it is to be 'me', one that inspires us to seek the best of ourselves and what we can give of that to the world. But how do we find a personal narrative? Once, we would have found inspiration in the stories and myths of our people as we sat by the fire, its flickering flames giving life and movement to the animal paintings on the walls of our cave home. Now we have no meta-narratives to live by; in our complex, urban multi-cultural societies, we must make our own.

In my own life, the narrative that spoke to me was one of inner spiritual quest. We have motifs for such a quest. Influenced by Carl Jung's work on archetypes, in 1949 the mythographer Joseph Campbell produced a book, *The Hero with a Thousand Faces*[3], that explored thousands of the world's myths to extrapolate an underlying archetypal pattern. This was that of the hero who is called upon – often against his will – to go on a quest with many trials and tribulations to save his people from a great threat. The book would become a major influence in Hollywood and has shaped screenplay after screenplay; for example, George Lucas used it to create the storylines for *Star Wars*. Brilliant though Joseph Campbell's work was, he wrote as a man of his time. While he accepted that women could be heroes, his hero myth is related from the perspective of a man; leaving a gap that, as a man, he could not fill.

That gap was addressed in 1992 by Dr Clarissa Pinkola Estés, a Jungian analyst, storyteller and poet, with the publication of her famous book *Women Who Run with the Wolves*.[4] She plunged into the depths of cultures worldwide to analyse myths, fairy tales and folk tales from a feminist perspective and discovered the Wild Woman archetype – an archetype rooted in nature and a time when we still lived close to our deepest instincts and our pre-civilised selves. Thousands upon thousands of women identified with the Wild Woman archetype and Clarissa Pinkola Estés became the first Latina to have a book on the *New York Times* bestseller list. Her idea resonated because it addressed an important message – one of connection.

Joseph Campbell's hero was a lone individual. The Wild Woman within us flourishes through connection with others – human, animal, plant, spirit; all of sentient nature. All of us, regardless of gender, need this Wild Woman archetype in our lives – an archetype that is closely related to that of the magic worker, the witch. She is close to our animal self, but an animal self enhanced by the gift of human consciousness, in touch with body, emotions, mind and spirit. She can help us reclaim our dreams and imagination, our feeling and intuition; those parts of our psyche that communicate in symbols and images, not with words. She leads the way to a wilder and greener, a more natural and magical spirituality.

A nature-based spirituality is simple, basic. It returns us to the origins of human spiritual vision. It does not need organisations, buildings, hierarchies, or belief in a patriarchal god. We might call ourselves practitioners of nature spirituality, green spirituality, magical spirituality or Paganism. More and more of us choose not to label ourselves at all, or maybe we think of ourselves as spiritual but not religious. We need not believe in anything beyond the natural world – unless, of course, our own experience tells us otherwise. All we need is a receptiveness to the world around us in its myriad forms, and an openness too to the unexpected and the unexplained, a willingness to explore the highways and byways of the mind.

This does not mean we should reject rationality and science. We should embrace them, but with discernment. Science provides explanations of our universe that work most of the time but not always, and scientific understanding is not static but rather constantly evolving. It makes sense to leave a space, a gap, for the manifestation of the unknown, the wild, the magical and untamed. A space to let in the magic. And to find that magic, we must begin in the wild places.

2

Entranced by Trees

As a small child, the copse on the boundary of the farm where I live is on the edge of England's New Forest. The copse itself seems to me a mighty forest; the stream that runs through it a great river. In summer, I paddle barefoot in the stream's cold waters, and stand near the bank where the soft clay bed lets me sink up to my thighs. Carefully drawing out my legs, I lie on my back on the bank as the clouds sail by above, while my new mud stockings bake dry beneath the sun. Warmed by the sun, I let myself slip deeper into the soil, breathing to the rhythm of the heart-beat of the Earth, at one with what is beneath.

I grow taller and can climb trees. Humans are drawn to trees. They are deep in our archetypal memory. They stir our imagination. They join heaven and earth – their roots reaching deep below the ground, their branches reaching for the sky. They offer shelter and, before we evolved into humans, they were our home. They are places of safety, refuge. They become for me a spiritual home.

Some trees are easy climbs, some more difficult. I develop favourites and wonder whether to give them names, but it feels disrespectful. Any name I can think of seems too trivial for a tree, and what they call themselves I do not know.

There is the tall chestnut where my friend Marilyn of the red-gold ringlets and I can climb up with our lunch packs and sit where two branches intertwine to make an aerial settee above the footpath. If we are silent, no one realises that two small girls are sitting overhead. And if she cannot come out to play, I play the tree nymph. I dress myself in garlands of ivy and climb the split lightning-struck tree to the highest point that can bear my weight. I slip one foot in the split and ride the wind as it blows the tree, my foot trapped until the wind turns and releases me. I find something in that letting go, trusting to tree and wind, which seems important. High up in a tree, riding upon it as it sways in the wind, sometimes a merging takes place of seeing and hearing, as though the leaves become sparkling crystals of light – a light that sings. And sometimes my consciousness merges with the tree, with its water-hungry roots, its rising sap, its rustling leaves; my blood no longer red, but green.

Have you ever felt that you are looking for something, but you do not know what it is? You can find no words to name or describe it, but you sense it is something you briefly experienced and then lost, like a dream half-remembered that leaves a nameless longing for some inner state of being. If we ask people where they most often experience a sense of mystery, awe or unity with the wider cosmos, it is not in religious settings, but outside in nature. Most of us have experienced moments of fusion and communion with nature, but we may not have the vocabulary to describe them. Older men in particular may find it difficult to express these deep feelings of connectedness, because they have not been taught that these are things to share. But this does not mean they do not experience them. One of the most beautiful descriptions of merging and feeling at one with nature I ever heard was from a London cab driver. He was taking me home after I had given an evening seminar. He asked me about my day, and I asked him how long he had been on the road.

He liked to start very early, he replied, so he could get to the centre of London before the traffic built up. Every morning he got up just before sunrise to make a cup of tea, listen to the singing of the birds and watch the dawn. 'It's a special feeling,' he said, 'when you see it all like that. Like it's bigger than me, but I'm part of it. It's ...'

He struggled to find a word for it for a while, then gave up. Tentatively, I offered, 'Holy?'

'That's it – holy! Not that I'm one for churches or any of that stuff. But yes, it's like ... holy.' It was this daily experience that sustained him throughout the stresses of his day.

We do not have to be mystical or magical to experience profound states of consciousness that we find difficult to describe or name. Perhaps you have experienced in nature one of those moments of pure ecstasy, or peace, where the boundaries that separate us from the world around us dissolve? We become one with the movement of the wind, the smell of the earth, the heat of the sun, the song of the birds. Our sense of 'I' flows outwards, beyond the body, into a timeless zone; our consciousness moving like the waves of the sea, ebbing and flowing between self and other, as though there is a permeable membrane between us and the world. In such states of consciousness, we may enter into a world of pure experience that is not analysed, judged or categorised; a perception of reality that seems timeless and that experiences everything as an interconnecting whole. We may experience then a sense of empathy and kinship with other people, other species, with the biosphere itself; an empathy that can become an overwhelming feeling of love, bliss and ecstasy.

Perhaps like me you have also had an experience where the usual divisions between the senses break down, when sound and light – what we hear and what we see – fuse? These experiences are more than an interesting novelty. They can be extraordinarily powerful revelations; breakthroughs in consciousness in which we experience for ourselves how our perception of reality is conditioned by the body. We discover that the world as we experience it is artificial. Reality is so much more than our limited sensory apparatus can detect and process.

Moments in nature, when the boundaries of self and not-self soften, when there is a flowing in consciousness between tree and me, I would now call sacred. As a child, the natural world became my temple, my church, my place of religion. My experiences in nature became the books of my inner library, my reference points, keys, clues, glimpses and gateways to understanding the universe around me. Decades afterwards, that same feeling has never left me. It was the beginning for me of coming into my own view of the universe, one I would later learn to call Pagan, pantheist or panentheist. Another insight came not from the outer world of nature, but from the inner world of dreams.

Have you ever dreamt you were flying? Perhaps you have had an out-of-the-body experience in which you wake up in the night and realise that you are floating above your body and looking down on yourself? Or maybe an experience of lucid dreaming? You wake up during a dream and know that you are dreaming. Or perhaps you have had a more extreme experience – a bodily trauma, an accident or illness where you had a near-death experience? What these experiences hint to us is that consciousness can exist outside the body. Once we have experienced this, it changes everything.

These experiences are found in all societies and cultures. They formed our early ancestors' ideas of the Otherworld, the spiritual realm that operates outside normal time and space. It exists beyond the physical and beyond the body in a dimension in which other rules apply; a place where we can meet ancestors, deities and animal spirits. Human experiences of the Otherworld are the basis of shamanism, humankind's core spirituality, on which all later religion is built. They convinced our ancestors that there is an afterlife, that death is not the end. The Otherworld would be their final destination, and in the meantime the boundaries between that world and this were fluid. They learned how to enter the Otherworld at will, and how to navigate within it. From their voyaging, they created topographies and myths.

Like most people, I first discovered the Otherworld in dreams. When I was six, an Irish artist called Dominic moved into a caravan on the farm where we lived. He came with his artist's materials and a small tribe of cats. He let me play with his cats while he painted and talked about art. I could understand only a fraction of his ideas, but it made me feel very grown-up to be his audience. In the light summer evenings, he would call up to my window for me to come down and help him feed the cats. But an artist's hours are erratic and sometimes he would call to me well past my bedtime. My mother would not let me go out. Frustrated, I would lie in my bed wishing I was there. And then suddenly one evening – I was. I rose out of my body, floated above the bed, and out through the open window to join Dominic and the cats. I talked to Dominic as normal and played with the cats. Then I flew back in through the bedroom window, hovered over my bed, looked down on myself and re-entered my body. It was a revelation. My body had stayed in the bedroom and whatever 'I' was had not. I had another kind of body, a body that could fly in and out of windows.

The next morning, I climbed up on the high trunk of a fallen oak tree and leapt off, flapping my arms, trying to fly. I spent all morning trying, flapping as fast as I could, but of course it did not work. I could have dismissed the experience as a passing dream, but something about it changed my view of the world around me. By the end of the morning I knew that there is more than one reality. There is the one where we walk on the ground, and the one where human beings can fly. I stumbled into that other reality by accident. I tried to get back there by sheer force of will, but that did not work. I did not yet know the answer, but I sensed that something significant had happened. It was a clue, a hint, that there could be more to life. If I had lived in a shamanic culture, my out-of-the-body experience and others that followed would have been understood and perhaps trained and honed by the adults around me to be useful for my community. As it was, I stored these experiences in my memory, knowing that at some point I would be able to enter at will what I learned later was the shamanic world, but it was many decades before I met a shaman. My childhood world was like the shamanic world in one way, though: my family and I lived in close connection with the animal world.

We lived surrounded by animals: the chickens who ran in and out of the farmhouse; the cows I brought home for milking; a friend's rabbits, which disappeared overnight from the hutches and returned a few days later on the dinner table; working dogs, a tribe of feral cats, and the tamer cats of my artist friend Dominic. 'Do cats go to heaven?' I asked at school. When I was told no, I was devastated. I couldn't understand it. What was the point of a heaven without animals? That was no heaven at all.

Although I loved animals, my friends and I were typical rural children. We prided ourselves on being tough. At home, we often lived on the game that my father's friends shot. My mother was not keen on preparing dead birds, so I took over the plucking and gutting. One day a pheasant was brought in. I was used to plucking cold, dead game birds, but this one was still warm. I plucked out the tail feathers. They were beautiful, but how much more beautiful they would have been if the bird was still alive. I put my hand inside it and pulled out a handful of acorns. It had just eaten its last meal. I was acutely aware as never before of a life destroyed.

Afterwards, I wrote a poem about hare hunting. It was a parody of William Henry Davies' 'Leisure'.[1]

> What is this life if full of care,
> we have no time to hunt the hare?
> To hunt this poor defenceless beast,
> which dares on grains of corn to feast.
>
> The fancy dress, the coats of red,
> they match the blood the hounds will shed ...

I kept the pheasant's tail feathers, and I have them still. Sometimes they decorate my autumn seasonal altar.

Plucking the still-warm pheasant is a defining moment, but I do not realise it at the time. It is not until I am sixteen that I meet someone my own age who is a vegetarian. As soon as I hear the word 'vegetarian', I identify with it. I know that I am one too. 'What do you eat?' I ask her, and she tells me. I go home to explain this to my mother. She copes by cooking me omelettes every day for two years, but it does not put me off. I am beginning to define myself, what is and what is not 'me'. There are choices that we make – often instantly, almost like a religious conversion. They seem to come out of the blue, out of nowhere, but really they build up in the unconscious, sometimes for years, before bursting into consciousness. I have taken the first step towards my adult identity. It is like finding one missing piece of a jigsaw. I just need to find the rest. I need to rediscover my Wild Woman and her witchery.

3

Discovering Witchery

If in your teens you ever tried out a spell, you will remember that mixture of laughter and nervousness as you gave it a go, not really believing but not disbelieving either; a small experiment in playing with the beyond. My experiments start even earlier, in the school playground. They start because I do not like being cold.

British schools of my era are enthusiasts for organised outdoor team sports, the kind played in wide-open windswept spaces, regardless of weather. It never occurs to our teachers to allow us anything as effete as tracksuits. Our blue frozen knees are often shaking with cold, but that does not matter. We still have to run around on waterlogged muddy fields, hitting very hard balls at one another with hockey sticks and the even more scary lacrosse sticks. My father loves cowboy movies, and it is probably on one of our many trips to the cinema that I see a Native American rain dance and have an idea. The next time my friends and I really do not want to go to the playing field, I make a suggestion: 'Shall we see if we can make it rain?' We do, and it does. Afterwards, my friends start to call me 'the witch'. It is not a friendly word and it makes me feel uncomfortable. I stop doing rain dances, but gradually my witchiness makes a comeback.

The route is circuitous, and it begins with Catholicism. I was not initially raised a Catholic. I have no idea I am one until my grandmother visits from Ireland and is horrified at my lack of Catholic education. My parents had me baptised as a baby, but do not practise religion. My grandmother makes an extended visit, teaches me prayers and hauls us all off to mass. I take up Catholicism. I like the Latin, the smells and the bells. It does not produce the ecstatic experiences I feel in nature, but there is something powerful in the beauty of the ritual, in the singing, in the statues of the Virgin Mary – and declaring myself a Catholic at school has big advantages. I become one of the envied group of pupils – Catholics and those from strange non-conformist sects – who are excused from religious education lessons. Instead, we sit silently in another classroom reading our books and bonding. We attend one another's parties and marvel at the different restrictions our religions bring. We don't eat meat on Fridays. They're not allowed to celebrate Christmas, but they can have Bonfire Night. Something in the back of my mind tells me that all these rules and regulations are vaguely ridiculous.

My new Catholic friends are Italian. There is a whole Italian community nearby in which the men were formerly prisoners of war in England. I start going to Latin mass with them. My parents encourage this, I now suspect, because it leaves them alone for sex in bed on Sunday mornings. My bus journey home from mass takes me into new spiritual territory. It takes forty minutes and I need something to read. The bus stop is by a newsagent and I start buying American sci-fi comics. Then, one week, I notice the shelf with the Sunday tabloids and *Tit-Bits*, a cross between a tabloid newspaper and a downmarket *Hello!* magazine. *Tit-Bits* and the tabloids thrive on titillating exposés of witches in all senses of the word. The editors specialise in photographs of bare-breasted women in witchy regalia brandishing ritual knives. I am transfixed and I buy anything with images of witches, along with the sci-fi magazines. I go to mass and then travel home looking at evocative images of witchy women such as Eleanor Bone. Maybe I too am a witch? Suddenly, the word seems alluring, less scary. Maybe it describes the something in me that feels different.

The traditional image of magic is as occult, a hidden and secret tradition, a practice of the night carried out in the shadows. The symbolism of magic is almost a love affair with the dark. The core grimoire of Wicca is even called the *Book of Shadows*, and witchcraft in particular is a challenge to notions of propriety, religion and 'goodness'. People engage with magic for myriad reasons but, however we rationalise it, in the beginning magic appeals because, despite its current popularity and normalisation, magic is wildly transgressive. It touches on something within us that preceded all the veneer of human civilisation. It comes from a time when we sat by the fire and shamans told us stories of the origins of our people; a time when the night-time world was mysterious, terrifying and potentially lethal. Who knew what creatures of the night – predators natural or supernatural – were out there lurking, waiting for us if we left the protective circle of the fire?

Magic is joyous and fun; wild, exciting and strange. It touches on something archaic within us that responds to the beat of the shaman's drum. We feel its vibrations, our blood rushes, our hearts beat with its rhythm; our feet want to dance, around the fire, under the moon and stars; for magic is about the unexpected, the exciting. It takes us out of our ordinary state of consciousness and into some other, older, deeper, wilder place. It implies wildness and wonder; the mysterious and inexplicable. It creates a frisson of excitement and perhaps a little fear. The same kind of spine-tingling fear that we get from a really good ghost story told by firelight on a dark and windy night; or from a Hollywood movie when, against all advice, the new homeowner descends the staircase to the basement alone. We enjoy being excited and a bit afraid.

I start my first coven at school when I am twelve. I am at a girls' school, and by now we are fans of all things witchy. One of the articles I read describes an initiation rite, so I copy this for our coven. I stand with my legs apart and my arms upstretched to the sky, and the first girl crawls through my legs to be reborn. She stands behind me as we rebirth the next girl and so on, until there are thirteen of us in our school uniforms – our coven. It is short-lived. We meet at the secluded area at the bottom of the school grounds, but our headmistress receives a complaint from a rather grand house that backs onto the school. Fortunately, the neighbours are not complaining about us being witches. What they object to is our noisy chanting. The headmistress assumes we are being over-boisterous rather than spell-casting, so we are simply told not to play near the neighbours' fences again. This inhibits our witch experiments – the rest of the grounds are not private enough. I close the coven and set up an illicit lunchtime hairdressing salon instead. My witchiness goes dormant as I hit puberty and teenage angst. I direct my energies instead into persuading my mother that I need high-heel shoes and shorter skirts.

Venturing into magic ends here for many would-be witches, but for me it does not. To quote the disparaging phrase about Senator Elizabeth Warren now subverted into a feminist rallying call, 'Nevertheless, she persisted.' I might not have persisted though, were it not for our family's move to London.

We have left the farm, but nature is still for me my source, my wellspring, my place of sustenance. Then, in my early teens, my father's job means a move to London. I am traumatised. We arrive in the summer, when cities stink. The air is full of dirt and fumes and the smell of car exhausts. The roads and pavements radiate heat. I feel trapped, hemmed in. By day, it is impossible to see the horizon, or a sunrise or sunset. At night, it is never truly dark, so I cannot see the stars. I feel like an uprooted plant, torn up from the earth and imprisoned in a pot. It is a spiritual rupture. My psyche is reeling. I find some contact with nature in London's parks, but this is nature that is tamed and constrained. It is not enough to feed my spirit. The sense of loss is not just about losing clean air, physical beauty and bird song. I had not realised how much I was nurtured by tree and earth and sky and wind. Now I need other food for mind, heart and spirit.

I start to look without knowing where to look, or even how to name what I am looking for. It feels like a quest. I read avidly: books from the library, now within easy walking distance rather than a bus ride away; books from the second-hand book stalls of London's markets. I find a copy of the mystical novelist Charles Williams's *War in Heaven*, in which the forces of good and evil engage in spiritual battle for possession of the Holy Grail.[1] His is a very Christian magic, but the book's imagery speaks to me. I decide to call my spiritual search 'the quest for the Holy Grail', but I am not looking for the Christian cup of the Last Supper. I am searching for this nameless thing I have experienced within me, the state of being that brings us into unity with nature and the universe beyond.

I find the key in the surprising location of the book racks at the back of a Catholic church, where the edifying publications of the Catholic Truth Society are for sale. Most are about the lives of saints, how to pray, how to receive the sacraments, the obligations of marriage – all the topics that the Church likes to pronounce upon. But one booklet is different. Its title is *Witchcraft: A Warning.*[2] Its author is Aloysius Mullins, a Dominican priest whose order for centuries were the dreaded leaders of the Inquisition against Jews, heretics, Cathars and witches. They burned some of my favourite people. The booklet is a description based on what the author has read, including the experiences of a fellow Dominican who joins a coven, but falls victim to a News of the World exposé and is 'now in retirement somewhere safe'.[3] It describes a religion in which the Divine is Goddess as well as God, men and women are equal, woman is priestess just as man is priest, women are accorded knowledge and power, and nature is venerated. What's not to like? Whatever the author's conscious intentions, the booklet makes witchcraft sound amazingly attractive. I am determined to join. There are witches out there somewhere, but where and how do I find them?

I begin to discover the answer through one of those serendipitous occurrences when we open a book at random, hear something on the radio, or see an image and gasp. Something speaks directly to us. It is exactly what we are looking for. One day I switch on the television randomly in the midst of an interview with two people dressed in robes. Their names are Alex and Maxine Sanders, and they say that they are the King and Queen of the Witches. They are describing what I read in the Catholic booklet – witchcraft is a spiritual tradition that worships the Horned God and the Great Mother Goddess, and helps people to develop their innate psychic and magical powers and use them to help others.

What they are describing ticks every box. I must get in touch with them, but how? I go to my local library looking for witchy books and find a contact address in a book by June Johns.[4] I write an enthusiastic letter. I am only sixteen, I say, and I know that I have to be eighteen to join, but in the meantime could they give me some advice on how to be ready? I wait one week, two, and no reply comes – then, disappointment. The letter is returned, the words 'no longer at this address' written across the envelope.

In the meantime, I need a way out of the sterility of concrete and tarmac. Now I am separated from nature, where in London can I find spiritual nourishment? I start with art galleries. I am fortunate that my love of art came early to me. I was entranced when at the age of six I visited my first gallery, Southampton City Art Gallery, which has southern England's largest collection of modern art. In Britain, major galleries like the National Gallery and the Tate are free, ideal for an impoverished teenager. I can go in them whenever I want, just to sit and look at a single painting. Art opens doors into other realms. I grow to love the Impressionists, who by working outdoors in nature and painting light, create a magical vision, a way of seeing the world anew. I am fascinated by the Surrealists, but I have yet to read André Breton's 1924 *Manifestoes of Surrealism*.[5] The only manifesto I know at this point is the Communist one. It is now the late 1960s, the era of Vietnam, anti-war protests and the heady world of student demonstrations. Moving to London has shut me off from nature, but has awakened my political awareness. The true horrors of the Cultural Revolution have not yet made themselves manifest and I am the proud owner of Chairman Mao Tse-tung's *Little Red Book*. I am a fan of 'letting a hundred flowers blossom and a hundred schools of thought contend'.[6]

I am looking for people who can connect me with the world of magic but I have no idea where to start. If I hang out around paintings that seem magical, looking vaguely like a Pre-Raphaelite maiden, which is not too much of a challenge for a teenager with long dresses and wavy almost-waist length hair, maybe I can find other people that the paintings speak to, people of like mind? I meet all manner of interesting people and fend off some nerdy would-be boyfriends, but no one appears who seems a likely teacher of an aspiring magician's apprentice. The galleries do however refine my appreciation of art and feed my spirit while I am looking. I also prepare myself for a future magical encounter by honing my skills in the arts magical by casting horoscopes, reading cards, using Ouija boards and practising Buddhist meditation.

Once I am eighteen, I try again. I know my way around London now – which bookshops have esoteric books, which shop staff are helpful to young seekers of the occult and the mysterious. I find an address, a contact, and my Wiccan life begins. I join first the coven of the people I saw on television. Years later, I discover that the second coven I join is the one which had initiated the Dominican priest mentioned in *Witchcraft: A Warning*. These are the strange links and spirals that emerge when we set out to find our heart's path.

You may have come across Wicca in *The Craft*, *Practical Magic*, *Buffy the Vampire Slayer* or *Motherland: Fort Salem*, or in countless other television series and movies from the 1990s onwards. You may have passed by a magical supplies store window, full of cauldrons, cobwebs and black cats.

Throughout my teens and twenties, I revel in the dark ambiance of popular witchcraft. I embrace the romance of its night-time world. I wear long black clothing and dye my long hair deepest red. I acquire multiple tarot packs, candlesticks, candles, incense, wands, swords, cauldrons and other witchy artefacts, but as the paraphernalia accumulates so my understanding evolves. I join a Wiccan group because I am attracted to the idea of developing psychic and magical powers, but what I discover is that, beyond its popular media face, Wicca is so much more. What I find is an affirmation of my values and an affirmation of my womanhood. Beneath all the dark imagery and artefacts is an ethos and a value system that is shared across all magical spirituality. It is a rejection of patriarchal religion, and a reclaiming of individual expression.

One sure way of being burned at the stake if you were a woman during the centuries of witch persecutions was to wear men's clothing. Indeed, this was one of the accusations levelled at Joan of Arc, the only woman ever burned as a witch and then canonised as a Catholic saint. Joan dared to flout the gender essentialism of the fifteenth century. She put on armour and created her own army to rid her beloved France of its English occupiers.

History shows me that women who subvert the patriarchy and the narrow roles carved out for them are persecuted and vilified. Women are seen as less than fully human; an inferior creation subject to the power of men. Delightful though my father and his friends can be, there is nothing in my life to suggest that being subject to men is safe. Nor do I think I am defined by the body I inhabit; but as a child, every religion I read about tells me the opposite, and so too does my schooling and every institution I encounter. Girls wear dresses and play with dolls. I am a girl who plays with teddy bears and footballs. I like beautiful dresses and climbing trees. My friends are boys and girls.

As a teen, I do not fit in with the large, scary butch girls of the lacrosse team, nor with the boyfriend-obsessed girl crew who wear as much forbidden make-up to school as they can without the teachers noticing. I am interested in the mystical and magical, in art, music and politics, in fashionable clothes, civil engineering, agriculture and forming my own views. I am betwixt and between.

I start to read books on psychology, but they are of no help in understanding what it means to be a woman.

Firstly, I find Sigmund Freud. All women, he preaches, suffer from 'penis envy'.[7] What is he thinking of? Never in my life have I longed for a floppy dangly thing stuck on at the front. Carl Jung's gender ideas are flawed, but I find his work more female-friendly, which is why so many women trained with him, including many who were lesbian. I find two books that help me to integrate my love of psychology with Goddess-based spirituality – Dr Esther Harding's *The Way of All Women* and *Women's Mysteries*.[8] She and her partner, Dr Eleanor Bertine, a physician and feminist activist, were two of the prime movers in establishing Jungian analysis in the United States. Jungian psychology gives equal value to the feminine and the masculine and teaches that our psyches are inherently bisexual – not in the sense of sexual orientation, but in terms of our inner potential. Deep within, we are not limited by society's ideas of 'male' or 'female'. At the deepest levels of our psyches we are androgynous; we are both. It is only when we realise the whole of our being, when we embrace qualities that we have unconsciously suppressed because society has taught us that they do not fit the stereotype of masculine or feminine, that we can become truly individuated, truly whole.

What my Wiccan practice teaches me is that fundamental to magical thinking is the idea that we are all sovereign, autonomous individuals with the right to own the whole of our being – body and spirit – and to discover who and what we truly are. This is an ethos that rejects all that oppresses and enslaves others; an ethos that wants to create societies in which all have the opportunity to live fulfilling lives that meet the needs of the spirit as well as the body. In other words, when we discover the magical, we also discover the political.

I encounter the magically political first in a book that was one of the inspirations for contemporary Wicca. I find it in the Atlantis Bookshop, London's oldest esoteric bookstore, in one of those quaint narrow streets near the British Museum. Atlantis becomes my go-to place for magical books.

Atlantis is one of those wonderfully quirky shops that look like they should be in a Harry Potter movie. To this day it remains a family business, with the third and fourth generations of the Beskin family now at the helm. Its magical history stretches back a hundred years. William Butler Yeats, Aleister Crowley, Gerald Gardner, Dion Fortune, Israel Regardie and Doreen Valiente are just some of the magical great and good – and sometimes not so good – who have shopped, held their author signings, and met there with others to exchange magical gossip and perform rituals in the basement.

The book I discover at Atlantis is a new edition of an obscure text by the larger-than-life nineteenth-century American journalist, folklorist, antiquarian and traveller Charles Godfrey Leland – *Aradia, or the Gospel of the Witches.* Charles Leland was one of those people gifted with a flamboyant Leo charisma that made people of all creeds, colours and classes tell him their stories.

Aradia is the fruit of his 1886 meeting with an Italian fortune teller and witch from Florence, known as Maddalena. Her family, she tells him, are descended from the mysterious Etruscans, the people who inhabited central Italy before the Romans, and they have secret esoteric knowledge of ancient spells and rituals passed down for generations. A friendship grows between them, and eventually Maddalena shares the secrets of the Italian Witch tradition, known by the witches as *la Vecchia Religione* (the Old Religion). Italian witches are not only practitioners of the magical arts, she explains – *la Vecchia Religione* predates Christianity and is still practised in secret as a subversive alternative worldview, in which goddesses and not gods created the universe.

I find *Aradia* interesting as a magical text and a piece of folklore, but it is also a political manifesto. Aradia is a saviour goddess, a Messiah figure who will overthrow the wicked rulers and oppressive Church to liberate the people. Leland in his appendix writes that, regardless of whether or not we believe in magic, the witch symbolises rebellion, a rebelliousness open to all women: 'For every woman is at heart a witch.'[9] The act of magic itself is an assertion of individuality, empowerment, and an overturning of societal norms that oppress women.

As I read the words of Aradia, I find in this ancient forgotten goddess inspiration and empowerment. Nowadays I might see in her the Wild Woman archetype. Hers is the call to the wild places, to the woods and groves, the hills and mountains. 'Whenever ye have need of anything,' she tells us, 'once in the month, and when the moon is full, ye shall assemble' – and there the mother of Aradia, the goddess Diana herself, will be present in the hearts of her worshippers to teach us 'all things unknown'.[10]

This is a way of magic and mystery and of finding true knowledge of the self in the lonely deserted places and the depths of the forest – in nature's green heart. I feel empowered by my worship of the Goddess, but she is not the only deity who calls me.

4

Dreaming of the Horned God

'Do you ever dream of the Horned God?' our twenty-year-old intern, Duncan, asks me one morning.

The question jerks me out of my analysis of research data. I am not 'out' as a witch in my work as a Cabinet Office psychologist, and in these pre-internet days, it is possible to keep much more of one's private life to oneself. I give him the psychologist's standard response: 'Why do you ask that?'

'I dreamt last night of the Horned God, and I felt I should tell you about it.'

We talk about his dream and I suggest what he can read to find out more about the Horned God. His intuition has led him to the right place. Through my study of Carl Jung's writings and my experiences of magic, I can help him interpret his dream, for I too have dreamt of the Horned God.

The Horned God comes from the earliest human time, when we lived by hunting. He is deep in our ancestry. We find his representation in cave paintings, a figure dressed in skins, tail and horns – the deity who brings the hunted to the hunter, who ensures the survival of the tribe. It was the famous cave painting in the Cavern of the Trois Frères in Ariège in south-west France that inspired the anthropologist and Egyptologist Dr Margaret Murray to make the intuitive leap that became a major inspiration for the witchcraft revival. The witches persecuted for centuries as Devil worshippers were not Satanists after all, she argued, but secret adherents of the Pagan horned deity worshipped as goat-headed Pan in the ancient Mediterranean world, in Britain as the stag-headed Herne the Hunter, leader of the Wild Hunt, and as Cernunnos by the Celts of continental Europe; for *hern* and *cern* come from a common root word for 'horn'.[1]

I know none of this when I first encounter the Horned God as a child. It begins for me when I find a stone. I am six years old and returning tired one summer afternoon from the woods, walking up the hill to the farm. Haze shimmers on the hot tarmac and I feel the heat of the road through my sandals. Then I notice something shining on the grassy verge, shimmering in the sunlight like glass or metal. I bend down and see that it looks like an egg. I pick it up. It is warm and heavy in my hand; not an egg but a brown-speckled, egg-shaped stone. Then I turn it over and there is that heart-stopping moment when something important happens, when we see the one we are to love, or when there is great danger. On the other side of the stone, its natural markings have created the face of a goat.

There is something magical about the stone, so I take it home. I do not show it to my mother. It feels like something special, something just for me; a sacred object, a thing of power. I make an altar for it in my bedroom. I cover a cardboard box with a cloth and go out to pick a bunch of wild flowers, which I put in a vase beside the stone. It fascinates me. I sit and look at it until it is evening. I cannot understand its power, but something in it is nudging at my consciousness. I know the image is important, although I cannot say why or how. Then, a few weeks later, one morning I find something strange in the woods – a circle of white stones about five metres or so in diameter that was not there when I went home the evening before. In the centre is a firepit and the embers of a fire. It could be from an overnight hiker, but it does not look like a campsite. It feels as though something strange and mysterious must have happened here. Years later, I discover that witches gather in the New Forest. Perhaps I found one of their ritual sites?

A couple of years pass and I read an extraordinary children's book, *Princess Charming* by Katherine Oldmeadow.[2] Ostensibly, the book is a boarding school adventure story, but it reads as a Pagan propaganda novel with strong lesbian undertones that I recognise as different even as a child. This is less surprising now Katherine Oldmeadow has been identified as one of the women likely to have been a member of the New Forest coven that gave birth to contemporary Wicca.[3] The girls in the story turn to venerating Pan and dance for him in the moonlight. One of them even seems for a moment to become the god himself. This is a religion I can relate to, where girls are allowed to dance in the moonlight to honour a goat-headed god. The wild call of Pan entrances me. I understand now the appeal of the image on my goat-faced stone. Could it be that, somewhere out there in the forest, girls like me still dance for Pan?

Whatever religion we do or do not profess, each of us has our own spirituality. It comes to us step by step, synthesised from our family's religious culture, from traditions we encounter in adult life, and from our life experiences, to create a worldview – values and ideas that make life worth living. The psychotherapist, mystic and former monk Thomas Moore explores this beautifully in *A Religion of One's Own*.[4] Whatever label we choose to give it – or maybe we do not label it at all – our personal spirituality is a tapestry that we continue to weave for our entire lifetime, unpicking some threads, substituting others, evolving the design and its colours.

I begin to weave my spirituality out of my childhood experiences in nature and the images – powerful archetypal images – that come into my dreams and visions. At first I have no map to this territory, no framework to explain the images' power. When I discover the deities of ancient Greece, I begin a journey into the realms of myth, to gods forgotten, ruined temples and standing stones. When I am twelve, I persuade my mother to take me to the druid Midsummer ceremony at Stonehenge. There are only some white-robed druids, my mother and I, and a German tourist who has camped overnight. He is still snoring when we arrive, so we wake him up so he does not miss the sunrise. The ceremony is interesting, but it does not move me. The druids' white robes and headgear, and their matching white rubber boots for the vagaries of an English summer, seem quaint – more comic than profound. The singing of the birds that sit on top of the stones seems more spiritual than the ceremony. I sense that there is power and energy in this place. It is just that they do not know how to switch it on.

The experiences that each of us has on our spiritual journey are like pearls on a thread. One by one, we add our experiences to the thread of our life – our store of memories – and from these we create patterns of interpretation and meaning. The archetypal symbol of the Horned God that has such resonance and power for me comes from the oldest time, the time of caves and hunting. It comes from the beginning of humankind's journey into dream and mystery. It comes from the wildest part of our being, when our species first wakened from our animal state into consciousness, and with an awareness of individuality could say, 'I am.'

In my mid-teens, I write a poem. I call it 'The Pipes of Pan':

> In caverns deep, the old gods sleep
> but the trees still know their Lord
> and it's the Pipes of Pan that call the tune
> in the twilight in the wood.
> The leaves they dance to the Goat-God's tune
> and whisper his name to the winds
> and the oak tree dreams of a god with horns
> and knows no other king.

The poem comes straight out of the pen, straight from the unconscious. When I read the poem I want to cry. It is for me a poem of mourning and loss, of grief for the natural world systematically ravaged by humankind. It is a keening for a natural spirituality destroyed by religions that separate us from nature and set human beings apart from the species around us. I feel that we have lost our souls. How can we find our way back to what we have lost?

One rainy lunchtime a few years later, I take refuge in Foyles bookshop in Charing Cross Road, in the heart of London's bookshop quarter, and I discover part of the answer in Carl Jung's book *Modern Man in Search of a Soul.*[5] The chapters are a heady mix of psychology, Gnosticism, theosophy, Eastern spirituality and dream analysis. They point to the psychological and spiritual challenges of each stage of life, and the need for transformation within the human psyche. I understand about a tenth of it, but it is enough. It convinces me that the study of the human psyche interests me much more than the Victorian novels and Restoration dramas that are the required reading for my English degree. I take a break from university and reapply for psychology. Much to my disappointment, the University of London's science-based psychology curriculum makes only passing reference to Sigmund Freud and almost none to Carl Jung. I persist and gain a B.Sc. and a Ph.D., but this type of psychology does not make my heart sing.

Carl Jung's psychology became a bridge for me between the academic world and the magical world, the urban and the natural, the civilised and the untamed. He was a master interpreter of symbols, and of primordial archetypal images that have been with us since the dawn of humankind. Symbols are elusive, many-layered and mysterious. They stimulate the psyche because they tantalise, hovering just at the threshold of our understanding. They conveyed our species' deepest longings and spiritual aspirations long before we developed the written languages that enable us to communicate our inner thoughts and feelings in words.

Archetypal images and ideas are shaped by our culture and environment, but the human ability to produce them comes from what Carl Jung termed 'the collective unconscious', the inherited level of the psyche shared by all of humankind. Our personal unconscious is a gateway to the collective unconscious – which exists beyond the body and beyond even time and space. It is an awareness that we glimpse and then lose, and then glimpse again. Figures such as the Wise Old Woman, the Child Saviour, the Sacrificial King, the Wise Fool, the Sage, the Priestess, the Great Mother and the Horned God that appear in the myths, stories and spiritual imaginings of culture after culture, arise from the collective into the personal unconscious through the dreams of our current generations too.

Our intern Duncan's dream came from deep within the collective, and he felt that I was a person who would understand it. Talking to him, he seemed like an old soul, wise beyond his years. One morning a few weeks after he asked me about the Horned God, he came into my office clutching a leaflet. When he saw it, he told me, he thought he should bring me a copy because 'It looked like something you'd be interested in.' I intuited I should take notice.

Esoteric traditions talk much about angels, but they are not necessarily otherworldly beings with wings. The word 'angel' is based on the Greek word for 'messenger', and we can listen to and understand messages most easily when they are transmitted to us by other human beings. We all act as angels to one another from time to time, bringing the message that takes someone's life forward in a new direction. To hear our human angels, we need to listen, really listen, to what people are saying to us, and be open to messages arriving from all manner of unlikely sources. Duncan became my angel that day.

The leaflet did indeed describe something I was interested in. It was a series of workshops run by Ian Gordon-Brown, Barbara Somers and Joan and Reynold Swallow, of the Centre for Transpersonal Psychology. I had seen the leaflet before in the library of the College of Psychic Studies in South Kensington, but had not got around to taking it further. I doubt that I would have done. It took a small nudge from the universe to get me to explore an option that ultimately was of major importance to me. I took the leaflet home and showed it to my husband Chris, and we decided that this was something we would enjoy exploring together. We attended the introductory series of workshops and then applied to train as therapists. What we learned benefited us professionally, but more importantly it helped to illumine our spiritual and magical paths, and later our teaching. We became accredited teachers of the Centre for Transpersonal Psychology, and we still teach this spiritual approach under the title of Spiritual Psychology.

The Centre for Transpersonal Psychology's approach to the psyche is based on an underlying principle that resonates with me. Within each of us is a spiritual centre, a deeper self that connects us with the Divine. We can strengthen our connection to the self through work with guided visualisation, imagery, myth and dream. The Centre's theoretical basis includes the work of Carl Jung and the group of powerful women that were his collaborators – his wife Emma, Marie-Louise von Franz, Esther Harding and Toni Wolff. They were pioneers in mapping the journey of spiritual transformation. Their lives overlapped with the heyday of the magical revival, as did many of their aims and ambitions. Carl Jung in particular was heavily influenced by esoteric, spiritual and magical teachings of the West and East. Alchemy, mysticism, Kabbalah, tantric yoga and Buddhism became rich pools of inspiration for his theories as increasingly the people who came to him for help were not psychologically ill. They had apparently successful lives, but their inner lives were barren and spiritually impoverished. They had discovered the age-old truth that material success alone will not bring happiness and meaning into our lives. We can find meaning only through our own spiritual quest, a quest that begins with our inner world, with ourselves; for the first maxim of the spiritual path, long ago carved in ancient Greece in the forecourt of the oracular Temple of Apollo at Delphi, is *gnothi seauton*, 'know thyself'.[6]

Have you ever dreamt of finding new rooms in your house that you did not know existed? This is a classic dream of self-discovery that signifies that our psyche is opening up; a new part of us wants to emerge into consciousness. Often the new rooms are welcoming and represent new talents, qualities and possibilities that we can joyfully embrace. Sometimes we are more reluctant to explore. The new rooms are threatening – dark, dank cellars whose doors we are afraid to open; attic rooms that can be reached only up rickety and unsafe stairs. But whether we like our new rooms or not, these are positive and important dreams.

They are a signal from the deeper self that is urging us to grow. It wants us to go into the new rooms, to explore, to allow all that is hidden within us to be revealed.

This is challenging, because it means discovering within us aspects of ourselves that do not please us at all. Knowing ourselves means looking behind the mask of the persona, the face that we put on to meet the faces that we meet. It means opening ourselves to all those aspects of ourselves that we have suppressed and buried because we have been taught that 'real men don't do this', 'girls can't do that'; all those aspects of ourselves that are not part of the gender role that we live out in everyday life – the animus, the repressed inner masculine, and the anima, the repressed inner feminine.

Most challenging of all, it means opening ourselves to the shadow – all the qualities within us that we do not want to acknowledge because 'it's not nice to think that way'. One of Carl Jung's greatest contributions to spiritual psychology was his understanding of the darker side of the human psyche. The shadow represents all those parts of our nature that we try to suppress and hide, even from ourselves. We aim to bury them so deep that we forget all about them; but there they lurk within us, waiting to burst forth. It is like in one of those movies where a house is built on a graveyard of malevolent undead, who are just waiting for their chance to erupt into the newly decorated basement.

It takes courage to recognise and admit the shadow; to open the doors and windows in the psyche that allow us to know ourselves. This is the task not of light workers but of shadow workers, those who acknowledge the dark impulses that lurk within us all and are part of our human condition. Carl Jung wrote, it is 'disagreeable and therefore not popular' but we do not 'become enlightened by imagining figures of light, but by making the darkness conscious'.[7] It is only by acknowledging our own shadow and the human collective shadow that we become more able to transform it.

The magical path shares many of the growth aims of the spiritually oriented psychologies; in particular the idea that our inner connection with the Divine is not made with a 'higher' self so much as a deeper and more authentic self. This is the self that accepts the reality of the shadow of repressed negativity as well as of our unrealised potential.

If we are to embrace our inner potential, we must be willing to step into the unknown, into the darkness. We must become the master or mistress of our inner domain. We must open the doors to all the rooms in our inner house, so we can walk about freely and unafraid, treating with kindness and respect what we find there. This is not easy. It means self-acceptance – a true self-acceptance that can come about only through self-compassion. It comes from recognising, accepting and befriending all the disparate parts of our psyche that are seeking to evolve and to grow.

Compassion meditation as taught in mindfulness training can be of great help here. In such meditations, we focus first on sending loving-kindness or compassion to ourselves, then we move on to others. This makes good psychological sense. If we cannot love ourselves, we cannot truly love others. If we are perfectionists who beat ourselves up psychologically for every mistake, we will not tolerate the failings of others. Meditating by sending thoughts of love and compassion to others affects our emotional state. This in turn impacts on our health and well-being. Compassion meditation activates brain areas involved in emotional processing and empathy, areas that help us deal better with negative emotions.[8] Creating these loving connections releases blockages in the psyche that trap us in our own inner world isolated from others.

The process of acceptance of those buried aspects of our psyche that we at first perceive as 'other' and 'not me' leads ultimately to integration in a new centre of consciousness that accesses all our being – a process that Carl Jung called 'individuation', of becoming the unique individual that we were always meant to be.[9] It is the first major goal of the spiritual quest; part of what in magic is called 'The Great Work', the spiritual transformation of the individual that leads ultimately to the spiritual transformation of humankind.

We can achieve inner change in many different ways. Much of it comes about through the experiences we gain in everyday life, as we mature into adulthood and form relationships with others as friends, partners, colleagues and parents; and as we learn to take responsibility for others. An active spiritual and magical life can accelerate the process of individuation, if we allow ourselves time to commune with our inner world, our deepest psyche, the source of vision and inspiration. Meditation, artwork, creative writing, dream recording, ritual – all these are routes into the unconscious to connect with our deeper self.

We do not pursue the path for ourselves alone. Magical thinking teaches us that, in opening ourselves to the depths of our being, we increase our human collective awareness. Our species is in its infancy, but the baby steps that each of us takes evolves the collective psyche of all humankind. Nor are we alone on our journey. As we draw closer to the unconscious, we come into contact with archaic archetypal god-forms, such as the Great Mother Goddess, the Horned God, the Wise One and the Sun Child, that rest deep within the human psyche waiting to help us. They remind us of our need to reconnect to instinct, to feeling, to the realm of the senses, for in these we find deep wisdom, the wisdom of blood and bone, of tree and leaf, of stone and flower, of wind and water.

But inwards is not the only direction of travel on the quest; for as well as opening ourselves to what is within we must also turn outward. We must become aware of the nudges of the universe; aware of those helping hands that are there all the time, if we turn our ears to hear, our eyes to see.

5

Opening Ourselves to the Universe

I exist because my father got on the wrong train. When he realised, he asked the nearest passenger where the train was going. That passenger was my mother. Hers was the next station, and he decided to get off the train there and go back to central London. Once they were on the platform, on impulse he asked my mother if she would like to go for a drink. My mother was not the sort of lady who went drinking in pubs with strange men she met on trains, but my father was wearing a red tie. She considered this such a lapse in good taste (this was the 1950s) that she felt sorry for him, so she said yes. Six months later they were married.

Maybe it is my personal history, maybe my impulsive Irish genes, but for whatever reason, I embrace being open to the nudges of the universe. Magic is about taking notice of nudges. It overlaps with what Richard Wiseman, Professor of the Public Understanding of Psychology at the University of Hertfordshire calls 'the luck factor'.[1] If we open ourselves to the universe, we may find a little magic in the world. The mythographer Joseph Campbell had another term for it. To him it was being helped by 'hidden hands' to find our sense of purpose, our vocation – what he called 'your bliss'. If we follow our bliss we find that doors open, and we put ourselves 'on a kind of track that has been there all the while'.[2] We discover our path, the life we were always meant to live. It is like the dreams where we discover new rooms in our house. The rooms were always there. We just had to open the doors.

To make truly rational judgements, we must take account of the information given to us by intuition as well as that from linear thought. Intuition is a way of knowing that sees wholes and patterns that go beyond what the conscious mind knows. It draws on unconscious knowledge, some of which is forgotten or suppressed, and some of which leaps forward into the future to see what does not yet exist. When we have to make life-changing decisions, there may be so many possibilities and factors to weigh up that there is no 'logical' choice. Logic works well with a known and finite set of facts, but when we make major life choices, we are operating against the background of the unknown future. We can never know all the facts, so trusting our intuition, which operates outside everyday time and space, becomes the most rational course of action.

Intuition is the foundation of all creative thought, whether in the arts or the sciences. In 1925, the Nobel Prize–winning theoretical physicist Erwin Schrödinger first published his book *Meine Weltansicht*, translated four decades later as *My View of the World*.[3] At the time he held a post at the University of Zürich, and was on the threshold of the breakthrough of the Schrödinger equation – a foundation of quantum mechanics. The inspiration for his equation came not only from his scientific calculations, but also from his study of the Indian philosophy and spirituality of Vedanta.

An idea shared by Vedanta and Western magic is that we human beings are not separate and isolated, for at the very deepest level of consciousness, the whole cosmos is a unified whole. It is as though each of us is a cell in the cosmic brain. All our thoughts, feelings, sensations and experiences flow into the vast reservoir of the cosmic mind. We pass through life largely unaware of this deep connection between ourselves and all the other consciousnesses on our planet and beyond. It is only in intense momentary breakthroughs, when what is usually outside our everyday awareness becomes conscious, that we know that we are part of a greater whole. Carl Jung's idea of the collective unconscious is similar. This level of the psyche existed in our species long before we developed language. We become aware of its contents through dream and symbol, through our ability to use our imagination, and when we learn to listen to intuition, the voice within.

Some kinds of intuition make themselves known through ideas, image or words that just pop into the head; but there is another kind of intuition that is not of the head. It originates in the body, from within our deepest muscles and oldest senses. It is related to our instinctive reactions. If we learn to take more notice of our body's reactions, we will become better at interpreting the signals it is sending us. We can enhance this awareness through practices such as meditative body scans, Yoga, and other forms of body work that put us more in touch with our bodies, and of how they are responding to our emotions and to the world around us.

We do not have to presuppose that anything supernatural occurs when we talk to people and something 'smells fishy'. When our species' sense of smell was better developed, we would have been aware of smelling what each other was feeling, just as animals do. Nowadays, this system operates below our conscious awareness, but we still subliminally smell other people's stress and fear. We may also subliminally see and register their physical tension. Muscle tension can be contagious. If we subliminally notice it in others, we will tense in response.

Other intuitions come from what we hear and see. How often have you had the experience of listening to someone and not believing a word of it? It might be a boss explaining why she cannot afford to give you a raise, an employee phoning in sick on the day of a big match, a sales rep telling you that this is the best product ever, or a debtor telling you that the cheque really is in the post. We do not believe them because their underlying thoughts leak out in their voice and their body language. Even if we are not consciously aware of what is going on, our unconscious is registering these contradictory messages and trying to nudge us into awareness.

This type of intuition takes us away from the cerebral cortex to the limbic system, a deeper and older part of our brain that is closer to our wilder, more animalistic self. Animals, including the human animal, have primitive instincts that warn them of danger. We can often rationalise why – for instance, animals know an earthquake is coming because they can sense the minute earth tremors that precede its arrival. But some of our reactions cannot be simply rationalised away. During the course of any day, we will have countless intuitions about how things are going to turn out. We know something to be so, even though our conscious minds have no information to go on. It is as though some other sensory mechanism is operating – a sixth sense that warns us that a particular course of action is a bad one. It was this that was operating on Saturday, 17 December 1983, when I decided not to get off the train at Knightsbridge to go Christmas shopping at Harrods and right into an IRA bomb.

Some people listen to their intuition, others ignore it. Sometimes what we experience are not true intuitions at all, but fears, worries and anxieties that undermine us into thinking that something is bound to go wrong. But once we start to take better notice of our reactions, we can learn to distinguish the intuitions that come to us from a deeper place than our everyday anxieties and doubts.

We can learn to trust our intuition more by acting on it in small ways at first, and then building up to bigger decisions as our confidence grows. Like any activity, from sport to music, the more we practise the better we are likely to get. Professor Richard Wiseman's research on the luck factor shows that people who follow their intuition are lucky. They make better decisions about important life issues such as relationships and careers.[4]

Trusting our intuition is easier for some of us than for others, but even if we were not born with strong intuition, we can develop it by learning to embrace the hints and nudges of the universe and becoming more open to the experiences it offers.

Most psychological models of personality are based on the 'Big Five' factors of the acronym OCEAN – Openness to experience, Conscientiousness, Extraversion, Agreeableness and Neuroticism. The most important dimension for magic is openness to experience, an orientation essential also for creativity, innovation and invention. It is this mindset that allows us to try out new things – ideas, jobs, food, places to visit. It allows us to bring change into our lives and accepts change as fun and an enjoyable challenge. It also encourages us to experiment, which means opening ourselves to the idea of failing as well as succeeding. We don't always have to be right. It is an orientation essential for creating new products, new enterprises, new trends in fashion and art, new political movements and new spiritual vision. Openness to the new is important too in another way. It leads to tolerance of difference, an essential building block for diverse and multicultural societies.

On a deeper level, openness to experience aligns us to a way of viewing the world that takes us beyond psychological assessment and the type of personality inventory that we might complete as part of a job application. The more we open ourselves to the world around us, the more we can embrace adventure, exploration and change rather than clinging to certainty. This is important, because there is no certainty. The longer we live, the more we discover that we must always expect the unexpected; whether it is Covid-19, 9/11, the Holocaust or the Spanish Inquisition. Uncertainty is not something newly thrust upon us by unforeseen pandemics and disasters, but part of the fundamental nature of reality. If we accept impermanence and change as natural, and embrace them rather than resisting them, we can open ourselves to view life as an adventurous exploration of discovery, of trying new things and of daring to be different. We can open ourselves to being challengers of conventional wisdom, and catalysts for political, social and spiritual transformation. Our openness can stimulate the disruptive thinking that can change the world.

Perhaps you are thinking, *This isn't me. I am not open like this.* Not all of us are – in fact, most of us are not – but this can be our direction of travel. We *can* change. Psychologists often write about personality as though it is fixed, but this is not necessarily so. Personality describes tendencies and what we have done in the past. If we become more attuned to our automatic reactions, more acute observers of ourselves, we can choose not to go with our past programming. We can choose to make other choices. We can learn to be more open. Openness is a mindset and a habit. If we train ourselves to be more open in small ways, we begin to behave differently. When we behave differently, we rewire the brain into new habits, and gradually we change.

Extraversion and introversion mediate our intuitive experiences. If we are introverted, then developing a little extraversion helps us to actively seek out new experiences and interactions with others that create lucky interconnections. If we are extraverted, taking time to slow down, and listen to others rather than talking at them, will give our unconscious the opportunity to register and bring into consciousness the hints that the universe is trying to give us. We need both modes of being to navigate life successfully – listening to others, and listening to ourselves.

In my teens, after hanging out in art galleries waiting for a passing magician to make contact fails to work, I decide to become more extravert. I know it will be easier that way. I want to understand and to integrate the psychic and spiritual experiences that began in my childhood. I am becoming a spiritual explorer, and I know the answers to what I am seeking will not be found in books – though they do help. To meet others of like mind, I must reach out.

Introversion can be a prison, and inside many introverts is a suppressed extravert trying to escape. I walk out of my self-imposed cell and start talking to people on buses, at demonstrations, and in the strange, mainly male crowds of political activists, spiritual preachers and ufologists that gather at Speakers' Corner in London's Hyde Park, where anyone and everyone can stand on a box and pitch their particular solution to the world's ills. My opening conversation gambit of 'Hello, I'm Vivianne and I'm looking for the Holy Grail' is a good conversation starter, and I have some interesting encounters. I meet no enlightened spiritual masters at Speakers' Corner, but through being open to talking to people, I do find my way into a Wiccan coven and eventually to a teacher of Kabbalistic magic, whom I discover sitting next to me on the number 73 bus from Stoke Newington to Oxford Street.

Not everyone feels comfortable with such proactive openness, but if we open ourselves, even a little, to new experiences and we engage with the people we meet, they may become our angels. We may meet that one person, perhaps someone we never see again, who makes the key connection for us. We may begin a chance conversation with someone who inspires us with a new idea, or even a new direction for our lives. Clues and hints from the universe can come from anywhere, which is why I always tell my students to talk to the people they find themselves standing next to in coffee and lunch queues at conferences and events. 'You never know who you might meet.'

Sometimes, intuition comes unbidden and direct. We need no intermediaries, no angels, no external conversations to prompt us. An idea comes into the mind fully formed.

I am working as a management recruiter while waiting to start my psychology degree. It is ten in the morning. We are waiting for a new staff member to arrive. He has been recruited to replace me. He walks into the office and a voice in my head says, *That's the man I'm going to marry.* This is awkward; I am engaged to someone else. There is a ruby and diamond ring on my finger. I have no intention of breaking my engagement.

I find myself crossing the office to where he is standing by his new desk. I offer him my hand to shake, and before I can stop myself, I am saying, 'Hello, I'm Vivianne. Are you divorced?' He manages to look only slightly disconcerted. I ignore the fact that mine is not the normal greeting on the first day of a new job in an open-plan office. Part of me is waiting to hear his answer. Another part of my brain is rationalising. He looks older than me, more conventional, more established in everyday life. He must be married, but maybe no longer? In any event, it is not a problem. He is happily single. Three months later we start our relationship. My former fiancé finds himself a new love and they head out together on the hippie trail to India.

After another three months, I decide one Saturday morning that it is time to mention the 'w' word. 'I wonder if you've realised that I'm a witch, and so are most of my friends?' He takes the news well. He is never very awake in the mornings. He grunts, rolls over and tells me, 'That's fine. As long as I don't have to join.' A few weeks later, we start doing candle magic together. He has never explored the magical world before and in his early teens rejected all organised religion, but his creative side responds to the aesthetics of magic and he has an instinctive veneration for nature. Soon he joins me in my Wiccan practice, and the following year we are married. Would this have happened if I ignored the voice that predicted my future? Perhaps, but by listening to it Chris and I could begin a life of magical adventures together a little bit more quickly and smoothly. Our adventures take us to the realms of the dead.

6

Healing Spirit

Most of the twentieth century was an era where talking to the beyond was common. It was even entertainment. Out would come the Ouija board or a glass on a flat table surrounded by letters and numbers. 'Is there anybody there?' we would ask. The glass would move, or the board would shift, and off we went, communicating with dead relatives, spirit guides or disincarnate spiritual masters. It was as simple as accessing the internet and sending messages flying across the ether is today. In my teens, my friends and I established a dialogue with a spirit that called himself Ramakrishna. Even then, we were not naive enough to be convinced that he was the esteemed Hindu saint, but he did provide surprisingly accurate and precognitive information. It whetted my appetite to know more.

A lack of enthusiasm for dead people when I am in my twenties means that I never take up a career as a spiritualist medium, but I do the training. My university Ph.D. research develops my thinking function, but analysing non-parametric statistics and conducting qualitative research interviews do not make my heart sing. My Wiccan and magical training strengthens my intuition, but I want to improve it, to make it more accurate. I would like more training, but finding an education in intuition is not easy. The conventional education system focuses on logical sequential thought, to the exclusion of almost everything else. The only places I find that offer teaching that develops intuition are spiritualist training groups, which is why I decide to enrol in the Ivy Northage School of Mediumship.

Chris and I are fairly new in our marriage, which in fact took place in a spiritualist church, and I persuade him to come along too. He does not really think that mediumship will be his thing but he is open to exploring, so one autumn evening he agrees to leave his rather grand Thames-side office at a City management consultancy, and comes along in his pinstriped suit and shiny shoes to the shabby gentility of the College of Psychic Studies to see if we can pass the entrance exam. This involves having our auras scrutinised to see if we are sufficiently psychic.

It is not too great an ordeal. We have already had our auras scrutinised in order to get married. We married in a spiritualist church because there are few organisations in England at this time that are authorised to perform marriages and will create a service that is inclusive enough to make our guest list of Irish Catholics, English Protestants, Jews, Hindus, Muslims, magicians, witches, feminist activists and others feel welcome. The London Spiritual Mission would only marry us if the officiating medium thought we were spiritually compatible, though. Fortunately, we passed the auric compatibility test, and now we pass the test to join the beginner's class in mediumship.

The famous medium Ivy Northage turns out to be a redoubtable, no-nonsense lady with some books to her name, a headmistressy manner and very high standards for her trainees.[1] The training she and her brilliant and caring assistant Janet Orman provide proves excellent. The whole process takes about five years, and its focus is platform mediumship. This is the type of mediumship practised in the Sunday services of spiritualist churches and in the theatres of seaside resorts. If you want a wonderfully subversive account of mediumship, you can read Hilary Mantel. Before she ever wrote about Thomas Cromwell, she published a brilliant but underrated novel called *Beyond Black,* set in the subculture of psychics, tarot readers and mediums in southern England.[2]

Chris and I find ourselves the youngest people in the class and, as a heterosexual couple, unusual. Most of our fellow students are middle-aged women or gay men. Chris completes parts one and two of the training but decides that this is really not for him. I persist and find that I can open my psyche to get impressions of people's dead relatives and can convey enough convincingly detailed messages to be promoted to the next level of training.

The rationale for mediumship is that dead people want to communicate to their friends and relatives that they have survived death. The great upsurge in membership of spiritualist churches in the twentieth century was in the wake of the massacres of World War One. Grieving parents and wives flocked to hear messages from their dead menfolk, assuring them that all was well in the life beyond.

I have no dead people I want to communicate with, so I do not feel the same level of commitment to spiritualism as my colleagues. Sometimes it feels as though we are establishing channels of communication with people's dead loved ones, but I am not so convinced that there are hordes of dead people hovering about just waiting for a communication channel to open. Often mediumship seems more a matter of empathy and telepathy than supernatural intervention. We develop an intuitive awareness of what grieving relatives and friends need to hear and reflect this back to them. The messages offer comfort and emotional healing, rather than proof of survival after death.

Mediums have spirit guides, usually advanced and esteemed spiritual teachers who act as gatekeepers, providing access to the medium for the dead people who want to communicate. I am told I have spirit guides, and different mediums on different occasions describe some similar beings to me, including an Indian woman in a white sari. I even have a chalk drawing of her by the psychic artist Coral Polge. I accept that when mediums gaze into my aura that this is what they see, but it feels to me like a projection of something within me rather than an external reality.

The classes also teach us how to open the throat chakra and do inspirational speaking or channelling, important skills for mediums in spiritualist churches. The idea is to let go of conscious control and to allow our guides to take over, and then to speak whatever comes – assurances of universal love, wisdom, forgiveness, the reality of an afterlife in which we are reunited with those we love. The content is usually spiritually uplifting, sometimes even beautiful and inspiring, but the words that we are told are channelled from our spirit guides seem to me to come from a nearer source. For me, it is a surrendering of the conscious mind, a letting go of the ego to connect with the deeper self that is in empathic communion with those around us. This tells us what people need to hear at that time and place in their lives.

It is a powerful technique, but I am not convinced that I am channelling the thoughts of a wise Native American elder, a Tibetan master, or any of the other exotic partnerships that mediums lay claim to. Carl Jung recommended that for creative thought we should talk with and listen to our inner muse – the female anima for a man, and male animus for a woman.[3] We can find creative and spiritual inspiration from these hidden aspects of ourselves, if we allow them a channel to speak.

The guides of female mediums are often male and the more I learn about Jungian psychology, the more it seems to me that spiritualist women are giving voice to the animus, the internalised image of the male within that holds for women raised in patriarchal societies all the unrealised qualities that society has tried to crush. Madame Blavatsky had her secret Tibetan masters who lived in the fastness of the Himalayas; the work of the pioneering abstract painter Hilma af Klint was inspired by her communication with the 'High Ones'; the magician Dion Fortune communicated with 'Master Jesus', and rather more prosaically Lord Erskine, the former Lord Chancellor of England. Given the financial donations she received, the latter proved useful. By channelling a male voice, the mainly female mediums can permit themselves to speak with an authority that they might not otherwise feel they possessed.

I may have doubts about the rationale of mediumship, but not about the effectiveness of the training. I have taken a post as a psychologist at a rehabilitation centre and am working as part of an interdisciplinary team with medical, social work and other staff. The mediumship training begins to seep into my work as a psychologist. It is something I have to learn to control.

There is a wonderful scene in Lewis Carroll's book *Alice Through the Looking-Glass And What Alice Found There* that Carl Jung used when explaining synchronicity. In it, the White Queen tells Alice that she lives backwards. 'There's one great advantage in it,' she says to poor Alice, who is very confused by this concept. 'One's memory works both ways.'

Alice replies that she is sure that hers works only one way. 'I can't remember things before they happen.'

'It's a poor sort of memory that only works backwards,' the White Queen replies.[4]

Spiritualist and magical training do not teach us the secret of living backwards, but I find they do create a permeable membrane in my psyche. Past and future are not always separate. This can be awkward, and sometimes I make mistakes. Usually I can cover for them, but one day in a case conference to discuss a new client who is coming to us for psychological assessment, I say, 'Oh, yes, the one who's been in prison.'

There is a frosty silence around the table. The head of unit looks at me angrily. 'Who told you that? It's supposed to be confidential!'

The problem is that nobody told me. I assume I read the information in the case notes, but when I look again, it is not there. What to say? 'I must have sensed it,' is all I can think of, but she is distant with me afterwards. I learn to be more careful about knowing what I should not know.

Gradually, I resolve the problem. My brain learns to compartmentalise. When I interview clients and there are things that I know that are not in the case notes, I provide leads, openings, routes for them to tell me. My intuition helps speed up the process rather than being a source of embarrassment. It is helpful in my work, but I want to find other ways to use it.

The Wiccan group that I joined initiated me as a priestess – one who is in service to the gods – and as a witch, a maker of magic. The priestess is more akin to the medium, a channel through which the gods can speak, a performer of the rituals that give comfort to others. The witch is a worker with energies; one who creates change in the world. The two roles reinforce aspects of my identity, the parts of me that do not fit conventionality. They begin to integrate the psychism inherited from my mother, the spirituality inherited from my grandmother, a wildness in the blood that comes from my father, and something from outside all this genetic inheritance – a sense of connection to older traditions of spirituality, to a time when priestesses once served at the temples of goddesses and gods.

When people find the spiritual tradition that speaks to their heart, they often have a feeling of 'coming home'. It is as though what should be unknown and unfamiliar is known and familiar. It is like remembering something buried deep within the unconscious; what was forgotten is now unforgotten. This is what I find as I begin to work ritual in Wicca and to act as a priestess in the rites. They come naturally to me, instinctively. The ritual actions are like enacted mandalas based on archetypal patterns rooted deep in the unconscious, patterns that have beauty and meaning. They represent our species' ability to recreate our world through the power of imagination. We dare to dream and to enact our dreams, through symbolic ritualistic actions that help us better focus on and understand our goals, desires and motivations. They are springboards that give us a vision for the future.

I sense that being a priestess is a calling, a vocation, something I have been in the past. Some places that Chris and I visit trigger memories. The ancient Greek Temple of Apollo at Didyma in Turkey, at the beginning of the Christian era – when the visitors to the oracle are becoming merely a trickle. The ways of the old gods are dying, as people turn to the new religion. We visit the Asclepion on the island of Kos, the temple of the deified physician Asclepius – once the medical centre of Greece, a place of peace and memories. Images of this ancient world come to me. The tourists fade away and I see instead the hordes of patients, queuing as I take bookings for the incubation rooms where pilgrims sleep overnight and dream true dreams for interpretation by the priesthood.

I have no way to verify these images, but such memories are more important for what they tell us about our life now, than for what they tell us about the past. The memories show me two ways of using the powers of intuition. Do I wish to become the modern equivalent of an oracular priestess, a conveyor of messages from the gods; or should I follow the path of healing? Behind the prosaic world of twentieth-century spiritualist mediumship lies an older tradition, still practised by priests, priestesses and shamans in indigenous communities. We give ourselves to the voice of the unconscious, sinking deeply into the collective psyche, stepping out of time and into the timeless zone where past, present and future co-exist – the realm of gods and spirits – to bring back knowledge. But in this era, this is not for me. I choose the path that fits best with my training as a psychologist. I choose the way of the Asclepion, the path of healing.

The spiritualist training teaches me to see auras, the halos of light that appear around people's bodies and show much of what we are thinking and feeling. Some people have the innate ability to see auras; others of us can learn to see them. Is it an objective type of seeing, like seeing the hand in front of one's face, or a subjective impression? It is not easy to explain, but once you start to see auras they look physically real. I notice auras at first in the mediumship classes and then in special situations – when in meditation groups or group rituals – but over time I find I can see them in everyday situations too. I see them around people I am interviewing at work, particularly when they become emotional or enthusiastic. I see auras around speakers at conferences, when they are passionate about what they are saying and speaking their truth.

Many of the people in my Wiccan group practise healing, directing energy to those in need. From working with them and from my spiritualist training, I learn how to examine someone's aura to notice the gaps, thinness and discoloration that indicate ill health and distress. I begin to practise spiritual healing on friends, then I approach a healer at another of London's wonderful

Victorian institutions, the Spiritualist Association of Great Britain – famously supported by Sherlock Holmes author Sir Arthur Conan Doyle – and located then in an imposing house in Belgravia, London's upmarket embassy district. After another aura-scrutinising interview I am taken on as an apprentice by Marjorie Aarons, leader of the Wednesday healing clinic and author of a book of teachings of the trance medium Lilian Bailey.[5] After some months, I am let loose to channel energy, and to soothe and heal the procession of people and ailments that turn up at the clinic. As a healer I never cure cancer or perform great miracles, though a few small ones happen along the way – bulging discs in spinal columns cease to bulge, asthma and psoriasis disappear, long-standing migraines are banished, sleeplessness is resolved, women become pregnant. I can see that the healing techniques I practise reduce stress and affect the autoimmune system, bringing it into a more harmonious relationship with the body. The healing speeds recovery and often people come to me as an adjunct to their cancer treatment because they want to prevent its recurrence.

Most of my healer colleagues are much older than me and believe they are healing with the assistance of dead physicians, ancient healers or angels, or sometimes a multidisciplinary team of all these. I experience no supernatural others while healing. Perhaps if I had been born a generation earlier, I too would have an ancient Chinese doctor by my side, but what I feel is happening as I heal is a consciousness change. I notice that I experience physical sensations during healing. Some sensations are in the solar plexus, a chakra centre long associated with healing energy.

Others are in my brain and from what my patients tell me something is happening in their brains too.

Technological advances have enabled research using functional magnetic resonance imaging (fMRI) that gives us clues as to what happens in the brain when we experience healing. In their research in a hospital in Hawai'i, Dr Jeanne Achterberg and her colleagues conducted experiments in which people were placed in an MRI scanner that recorded changes in brain activity. Eleven healers participated in the research using a variety of distant healing techniques, such as reiki, in which the patient and healer do not need to be in the same room, or even the same country. In this case, a healer sat in a separate room and directed healing thoughts and energy to a patient in the scanner in random two-minute periods in a sequence chosen by a toss of a coin. Although those in the scanner had no way of knowing when healing was being transmitted, their scans showed highly significant changes in brain function during the two-minute periods of healing. Analysis of the scans shows that receiving healing activates those areas of our brains that are involved in decision making, resting consciousness, self-reflection and the relief of pain.[6] But how?

The research team could find no known biological processes to account for the results. What Jeanne Achterberg and her colleagues offer is a more complex and intriguing interpretation based on quantum entanglement. This is an aspect of quantum mechanics that suggests that acting on a particle in one place can instantly influence another particle, regardless of whether it is near or far away. Quantum entanglement has been demonstrated between photons, molecules, human neurons and bacteria, and there is speculation that some highly organised physiological systems, such as the human brain, are capable of this too.[7] Distant healing is a form of quantum entanglement that fits with an idea on the interface of physics and neuroscience that consciousness is not localised in the brain or even the whole body, but can operate outside our everyday understanding of space and time to affect not only our own body but also the bodies of others.[8] And it is not just human others. There is evidence that distant healing works for animals and plants too.[9]

As I develop my abilities as a healer, I find that one of my greatest skills is in alleviating pain. The techniques that I learned help me to take people into a state of consciousness where they can cut down or even give up their pain medication. For chronic conditions this is a life bonus, but sometimes the healing is not about life but about death. For a few years, my practice is almost all people who are terminally ill with cancer. The practice grows by word of mouth. The local hairdresser's, where women chat and exchange information, becomes a major referral route. I start to follow people's journey from outpatient treatment through to hospice bed. I would love to reverse their cancer, but I do not have that power. The power I do have is to make illness more bearable, to soften the edges of pain and to take away the fear that intensifies it. The healing begins as alleviating pain and progresses into release from the body.

Death, illness, loss – these are human experiences we all share. Thinking magically does not exclude us from sharing in these realities, which are the fate of all biological beings like ourselves. How we experience them is, however, more under our control. The Dalai Lama often uses the phrase 'emotional disarmament' to convey the idea of seeing reality clearly as it is, rather than through the distorted lens of our hopes and fears.[10] This is difficult, but most spiritual paths try to help us do exactly that. The language will vary between traditions, cultures and historical periods, but the aim is to stand in the eye of the storm – to stand at the centre, like a magician in a ritual circle – and from that vantage point in consciousness, to see all that is around us. And if we can do that, what do we see? We see the rising of the sun and the setting of the stars; we see the others around us; we see the above and below and the cycle of the seasons. If our vision is not made narrow by fear, desire and longing, and if we open ourselves to the myriad possibilities that the universe has to offer, then our range of reaction is greater. We keep our flexibility, our ability to find the most creative and adaptive solutions to the problems that face us.

In my teens, I wanted to change the world through magic. As an adult I develop smaller ambitions. Magic is something that can make life just that little bit better. The healing acts that my terminally ill patients and I do together reduce their need for morphine. They remain conscious for longer. Their brains can function instead of being befuddled. There is more time and coherence to talk with relatives and to prepare themselves for the end. I find myself helping priests give the last rites, for my patients are of all faiths. Some, though, have moved beyond conventional religion, or never had it, and they need spiritual assistance of a priestess, as well as healing.

Once every culture had its maps for the death journey. Some of those from literate cultures have survived. *The*

Tibetan Book of the Dead and *The Egyptian Book of the Dead*, for example, were after-death manuals, guide books on how to navigate the afterlife. Now we must create our own maps. Often my patients have no fixed beliefs, so I work with them in the ancient way, visualising with them the journey that will take them out of the body. Rehearsing it, we meditate and visualise their rising up from the bed and moving forward into light and into the realms of ancient myths, with me there to give them confidence as a guide and friend. I become a priestess of death. I help the spirit to fly free, to open to the possibilities of new life, no longer in this body but perhaps in another.

I sit in awe at the threshold between life and death, and watch as a profound change comes over people as they make that mysterious transition from one state to another. I find within me the strength and rootedness of the trees of my childhood. I sit as the spirit hovers outside the body and then there is that moment when it is gone. The light goes out; a life comes to an end in this reality, and begins its journey to another.

To be with someone at this time requires an interior stillness and an openness to another's mind and heart. The empathy is strengthened by my experiences in Wicca. The interior stillness comes from another source.

7

Magic in Mind

'*Om mani padme hum*' – Hail jewel in the lotus. The mantra echoes around the commune as we sit in meditation, the smell of joss sticks and patchouli oil pervading the room.

My family's move to London in my mid-teens takes me into magic, but it also brings me to the exciting world of London's hippie culture. I make an older hippie friend – he must be at least eighteen. Lion is a Londoner, and he takes me to visit his even older friends and their alternative life-styles, people in their twenties who live in communes and squats. They smoke marijuana and sit around, sometimes naked, eating brown rice and seaweed with chopsticks. They burn joss sticks on Shiva shrines, and have Buddhist thankas and Victorian silk shawls hung on their walls. I rummage through Camden Antiques Market and the shops of Portobello Road in Notting Hill to adopt their aesthetic of Afghan coats, velvet trousers and vintage dresses. Suitably attired, I head out for rock concerts, jazz cafés and night-long parties. The whole of hippiedom is in love with the mystic East. My new friends introduce me to the *Bhagavad-gītā* and *The Tibetan Book of the Dead*. I become their go-to tarot reader and resident mystic. We hitchhike to rock festivals and they make overland trips to sit at the feet of Indian gurus. Their world is a revelation and I embrace it joyfully. I never knew that such wondrously exotic people existed.

Eventually, Lion takes me to his Buddhist class. I begin to practise meditation with Sangharakshita, leader of the Friends of the Western Buddhist Order. The incense, cushions and Buddhist images appeal, as does Sangharakshita's quiet charisma. His work in India to convert Untouchables to Buddhism and free them from the shackles of the Hindu caste system impresses and moves me. But I notice that Sangharakshita is much more interested in the male students, and something about it makes me uneasy. His classes and patriarchal guru-based system are not for me. Decades later, he is exposed for having pressured male students into sexual relationships, supposedly to further their spiritual progress.[1]

Meditation helps me through my teenage anxieties and becomes a bedrock of my adult life, but the patriarchal hierarchies of Buddhism do not attract and I do not want to become a scholar of Sanskrit, Pali or Tibetan in order to understand the traditions more deeply. I want to find something just as mystical and magical in London. This makes me an oddity among my friends. They return from India dressed in orange, beaded necklaces with the Bhagwan Shree Rajneesh's portrait around their necks, an exotic set of new sexual experiences to recount, and new names, such as Premananda. Meantime, I stay in the West and find I need go no further than Stoke Newington to discover that meditation is just as important in the magical traditions as it is in Eastern-inspired practices. When in addition to a Wiccan group I join a group teaching Kabbalistic magic, I am expecting erudite revelations. But first I must practise concentrative meditation.

Some forms of meditation involve focused attention on a particular chosen object, such as a sacred statue, a mandala, a sacred phrase – a mantra – or simply focusing on the breath. I am told to visualise something neutral that triggers no emotional or symbolic associations – a pink cube. I visualise it flying alongside me, outside the upstairs window of the bright red London bus that I take to work. I visualise it floating around the office and hovering above my bed. I understand the principle of what I am doing. Concentration is an essential part of magical practice.

I learn the symbolism of the Kabbalistic Tree of Life, a whole encyclopaedia of images and symbols that magicians call correspondences. Each area of the Tree of Life is associated with particular deities, angels, spirits, spiritual practices, animals, plants, perfumes, colours, gemstones, planets and myriad other phenomena.

I use these to create pathworkings, complex visualisations containing whole landscapes and journeys. I learn how to act as an astral tour guide, to take others into these visualisations and to dialogue and learn from the deities, spirits and other beings we encounter in them. In my therapy training, I discover that the magical pathworking techniques taught by the Kabbalists overlap with what Carl Jung called 'active imagination'. He used it to dialogue with the figures he encountered spontaneously in his dreams and visions, including his 'inner guru' Philemon. Magical visualisations take this a step further, and intentionally create symbolic landscapes that trigger specific experiences.

If I think magically, the deities I encounter in the pathworkings have an objective reality. If I view these exercises as a psychologist, I feel that I am dialoguing with aspects of my own being – shadow, animus, anima, the deeper self. In practice, I discover it is helpful to let the two framings live side by side. Their ultimate nature may be beyond our human understanding and, regardless of their metaphysical reality, life works better if we just treat gods as gods. Psychologising all of it is hubris, reducing the images of the collective psyche to our personal reality. I respect that the inner landscapes create pathways into communion with consciousnesses that are not me, not mine; they come from a deeper place.

I discover in the pathworkings that there are roads more and less well-travelled. Sometimes the way is wide and open, as many have opened this part of the psyche before. Sometimes the way becomes narrower, the effort harder the air thinner, the altitude higher, the dizziness greater. Sometimes we reach an inner state of being and can feel no other human consciousness there at all. But once one of us has hacked a path through the jungle of the psyche, it becomes easier and easier for others to follow. And having once trod a path, we can take others there too. This is what we are doing, we voyagers in time, space and consciousness – artists, poets, writers, musicians, mystics, magicians, all those who use the power of intuition harnessed to intellect.

Concentrative meditation teaches us to narrow our attention and focus on a particular object, visualisation or train of thought. The meditative practices I learn in my teens and twenties become a bedrock that sustains me as I move from my Ph.D. fieldwork into the bugbear of all Ph.D. students – the writing up – it helps me focus on what needs to be done. I find I can write for long hours uninterrupted. In my meditation practice, I move on to another type of meditation – the cultivation of an open awareness. This type of awareness is what is taught now in secular mindfulness training. It requires a wide lens instead of a narrow one. It involves becoming aware of everything around and within us rather than focusing down. When we learn to practise open awareness, it takes us not just outward to what is around us in the external world, but also into the inner world of body, mind and emotions. Time spent daily in meditation allows our intuitions to come into consciousness; so too does recording our dreams, for these are another route through which the deeper self can communicate.

Meditation and mindfulness may seem a long way from magic, but both give space for intuition to flourish. This has practical as well as spiritual benefits. Richard Wiseman's research on the luck factor shows that those of us who use our intuition well spend more time on activities that still the conscious mind and allow us to draw closer to the unconscious.[2] Often intuition comes to us unbidden in dreams, or something just pops into our heads as we go about our daily life, but we can access our intuition more if we set aside time and space to listen to the voice of wisdom within; times when we deliberately take a break from the busy, frenetic world of doing – to simply stop and be. This allows us to hear the voice of intuition, but it also has another profound effect. It opens a space in the psyche, from which we can better exercise choice.

Meditation, walking in nature, ritual, these can all provide moments of pure experience that help us still the noise in the system, the competing voices and advice of others. If we set aside for a time the clutter in our brains, it is like decluttering our homes. Suddenly there is room to breathe, to spread out, to enjoy the space; and to see what is there and if we really need it.

There is a phrase that for many of us who practise meditation resonates with the force of a revelation: 'Thoughts are not facts.' It is one of those stunningly simple ideas that can make us stop in our tracks as we realise the blindingly obvious. Just because we have a particular thought, this does not make it true. Most of us waste time in fruitless speculation and worry about things that will never happen, creating negative fantasies and the worst-case scenario our imagination can possibly construct. We fret about what other people are doing, thinking or saying – none of which we have any control over. Social media amplifies and exacerbates this. By observing the mind and its workings, machinations and meanderings, we start to notice how these negative narratives begin. Once we notice, we have the option to step back, to try new approaches, to explore new goals, to do things in ways that we have never done them before; to experiment, to try and to fail and to try again.

If we learn to be more aware of what is happening within us, we have the potential to create a gap, a space, between our emotions, sensations, thoughts and experiences and how we react to them. Instead of labelling everything that comes into our minds as good, bad, right or wrong and reacting to it, we allow ourselves to become aware of the impressions that we receive without immediately making judgements. This standing back is important for the development of magical will. As I learn through my therapy training, it is also a vital underpinning of the work of one of the most important theorists and practitioners of transpersonal psychology, Dr Roberto Assagioli, founder of the psychological method of psychosynthesis.[3]

'Will' can sound forceful, macho even; an effortful straining of muscles in an uphill struggle to make it so. But magical will is not like that. It is about exercising choice, rather than being pushed this way and that by the thoughts and emotions that swirl around within us. Meditation can help us become aware of what is within. We can then exercise our will to make conscious choices about what we want to do and wholeheartedly focus our energies on pursuing that choice. When we fully commit ourselves, and are not internally divided, will is no longer an effortful striving. Psychologists speak of 'being in the flow'; athletes might call it 'being in the zone'. Long-distance swimmers know this state when they become part of the sea, as though the waves are propelling them to their destination. Runners know it when muscles, limbs, breathing and blood move into a synchronous flow in which they feel they could run forever. When we can exercise choice, we can change ourselves and our world.

Along my life's journey, I have met many inspiring people. One of them was Olivia Durdin-Robertson, co-founder with her brother Laurence, Lord Strathloch, and his wife, Pamela, of the international goddess-worshipping movement the Fellowship of Isis. She lived to the age of ninety-six, sustained by daily meditation and draughts from the well in the underground temple complex of her ancestral home, Huntington Castle in County Carlow, Ireland. She expressed very clearly the way we want our minds to work when she said that the only moment that is truly real is *now.* 'The past is a phantom world unalterably fixed which is skipping away from us, and the future, until it becomes the time for present action, has no existence.'[4] It is the ever-becoming *now* that we can change.

Often we associate the mind with imagery of sky or of air. We have 'blue sky' thinking and 'blowing away the cobwebs', but the mind can also be like the element of water – pure crystal mountain streams, fresh wells in the desert, a great sea that connects all things. We love to add water features to our gardens because water is an antidote to all the overly busy, bustling thoughts that are competing for attention from our brain. Water soothes us, which is why some dentists place fish tanks in their waiting areas.[5] Research shows that when we cannot be near water, just seeing images of it can alleviate stress and bring feelings of calm and peace.[6]

A few years ago, when I was on a meditation retreat a poem came into my mind:

> My thoughts are like fish –
> big ones, little ones,
> lone fish and shoals,
> friendly and threatening:
> I am the ocean.

Down in the depths swim the lurksome ones,
those that know not humankind,
some are blind.
Occasionally an electric eel –
beautiful, unexpected, it wakes me up,
and the great whales in their pods,
intelligent, wise, purposeful thoughts.

In the dark stillness, all these I see,
but they have no need of *me* to be.

We can best observe our thoughts if we give ourselves time to enter the water, to swim in the sea of our minds, and to experience what is there. Instead of being tossed about by waves of mental and emotional reactions until we feel we are drowning, we can find areas of still, calm water in the psyche where we can make choices. We can follow a particular shoal of thought-fish on their journey, or we can stay floating where we are.

In this resting and holding back, there is wisdom and peace. It gives us precious time to hear and see something deeper than the everyday parade of thoughts, emotions and activities. We come to a point of stillness, a place of silence, where we can listen to the voice of intuition and wisdom within us, the voice that becomes ever stronger the more we listen to it. It this mode of being that I learn to enter as I refine my skills at divination.

8

Dialoguing with Oracles

Patricia twirls her wine glass round and round by the stem, looking tense. Her facial muscles are a clue, as is her posture, hunched up on the edge of the sofa, and the slightly high, tight pitch to her voice. 'He's driving me crazy.'

'What's the matter?'

'You know that stuff you do?'

Which particular 'stuff' does she mean, I wonder?

'Reading the tarot and all that.'

'Yes.'

'Could you do a reading for me?'

'OK. Do you want to know something specific, or just a general reading?'

'I want to know how to convince the obstructive bastard to do what everyone knows we need to do.'

'Ah.' The 'obstructive bastard' is how she describes her boss.

'It's obvious that we need to move out of Italy, we're losing money hand over fist, but he's set dead against. It was his acquisition and he'd lose too much face.'

Face, I guess, would be important to Patricia's Hong Kong Chinese male boss. 'What is it you want to know?'

'How can I persuade him to listen?'

I'm wondering whether what she needs is a spell rather than a divination, but Patricia is a very rational finance director and she is not in the habit of asking her friends for tarot readings, never mind spells.

Intuition comes into play when interpreting divinations, but it can also help us decide what divination system to use. An image comes to me. I am not seeing the tarot, but the Chinese divination oracle the I Ching. Is it because Patricia has told me before that her boss is Chinese, or would the I Ching be better in this case? There is a subtlety in using intuition. It is easy to get steered into a tangent by latching on to random associations. I clear my mind. I am still seeing the I Ching.

Sometimes once we learn to listen to our intuition, knowledge comes like a bolt from the blue. We meet our life partner and know at once that they are the one. Sometimes we can find answers to life's problems in our dreams. Sometimes we need just a little more help. And it is not just individuals. Corporations spend millions of pounds trying to do that most ancient of magical practices of predicting the future. Economists, marketing experts, political analysts and strategists are all trying to get the answers. Economists mathematically model nations' economies, and organisations employ strategic forecasters. Forecasting is big business.

Inevitably, forecasters must make predictions based on the patterns of the past. Often, though, the future is not a logical progression from the past. This is particularly true when new disruptive technology comes onto the scene. I have worked on future forecasting myself. We run our computer programs and produce our charts, then everything changes. A random factor slips in – a freak hurricane, a terrorist attack, a pandemic, a panic run on a currency sparked by an inaccurate rumour – and the models fall apart. We have to find a way to engage with the 'new normal', to deprogramme ourselves from the past, and prepare ourselves to do something different.

Oracles and divination systems have always stepped in at such moments. If we do not know what to do, then looking at symbolic patterns can inspire us to find a new way forward. The patterns may have meaning, or they may just be a random set of numbers or symbols, but as our brains play with this new data, new connections are formed. Our synapses start to fire and make imaginative leaps and creativity flows. The patterns of the divination become a form of meditation that helps us escape from the trap of old ways of thinking, and to see a situation from a new perspective. I have experimented with many different systems and everyone must find what works best for them. For some, it is the tarot, or simple playing cards; for others, the pattern of a progressed astrological chart; for some the runes, and for others the shells of Santeria. My preferences are the tarot and the I Ching.

I spread out a cloth on the floor and explain to Patricia how the I Ching works and a little of the background. I also explain that it is widely used in the Chinese business community. I can see that she finds the idea reassuring. And a system that involves diagrams and numbers feels much more her thing than the vivid images of the tarot.

I Ching can be translated as 'Book of Changes'. The philosophy behind it is primarily Taoist, but one that a scientist would recognise. Nothing in the universe is stable. Everything is in the process of transition and change. An I Ching divination is a snapshot in time that shows us where we are now and the direction in which we are moving.

The traditional method of doing an I Ching reading is with specially prepared dried stalks of the yarrow plant, but a simpler way is to use three coins. Some people prefer to use old Chinese coins, but three coins of the same denomination of any currency work just as well. The three coins are shaken in the hand, then thrown down on a flat surface six times. Beforehand, one side of the coins is assigned the value three, the other the value two. Depending on which sides fall uppermost, each throw of the coins totals a value between six and nine. The totals indicate either a yin receptive energy or a yang active energy, and whether that energy is stable or is in the process of changing to its opposite. The different combinations of yin and yang energies are drawn as different types of line, and a complete set of six lines is known as a hexagram. There are sixty-four possible hexagrams, each one accompanied by flowery poetic interpretation of the hexagram and additional interpretations specific to any of the lines that are changing from yin to yang or vice versa.

I take Patricia through a brief meditation to still our minds, then ask her to clasp the coins in her hands and focus on her question.

'Don't think about possible answers, just focus on the question with a spirit of openness to whatever comes. Shake the coins in your hands. Now throw them down on the cloth.'

I take a pen and note the number of the first throw, then the second and so on until the sixth.

'Now we have the hexagram. Let's see which one it is.'

The answer is Hexagram 34, *Ta Chuang*, the Power of the Great.[1]

'Is that good?' she asks.

We turn to the text and read it together, looking for clues to help her in her situation. The interpretation is encouraging. We read that 'perseverance furthers'.

'Your boss is stubborn,' I say, 'but if you persevere, you will get a result.'

Then there is something that strikes me as a very important part of the interpretation: 'The superior man does not tread upon paths that do not accord with established order.'

I would not say that Patricia is oblivious to conventions, rules and restrictions, but she is not what I would call over-conscientious about them either. She has a habit of ignoring protocol and can be very outspoken, which is unlikely to go down well with her boss.

'The superior man in this case is not a man,' I explain. 'Here, you are the superior man. The superior man means a person of wisdom – in this case you, because you are the person taking the wise course of consulting the oracle.

'Within the hexagram are two trigrams or patterns of three lines,' I explain. 'The top one is the symbol for thunder, which is a noisy, arousing energy. Underneath is the symbol for creative energy. So what do we know so far? There is a lot of energy in this situation, but it is a positive creative energy, the kind that goes places. There will be lots of noise – discussion, maybe even aggressive discussion, conflicting opinions, and it is very important that you phrase things in the right way, "in accord with established order". I think you need to make sure you use the proper communication channels and that you communicate clearly, but courteously. Whatever everyone else does, keep your cool, keep control. Do things by the book – this book, in fact – and you are likely to be successful.'

Patricia has one of the changing lines. The translation reads: 'A goat butts against a hedge and gets its horns entangled.'

The I Ching has a sense of humour. Patricia is a Capricorn with Aries rising.

'Goats are active animals,' I say, 'and they butt their horns where they will. They are no respecters of other people's boundaries. The main message here is that you have a lot of power. Respect those you are negotiating with and do not go in horns first. Be powerful but restrained. Don't act the goat. Don't get stuck in an untenable position. You have power, but you need to be quick on your feet and able to find compromises.'

I write all this down and give it to Patricia, and she goes away to do her preparation for the major stakeholder meeting that will decide the issues. She prepares her PowerPoints and rational arguments, briefs her team and follows the behavioural advice of the I Ching. Patricia wins through. The board is convinced, and her boss puts on a brave face and agrees to her strategy. Not long after, Patricia leaves for a better-paid job. She has got what she wanted and it gives her the confidence to move on.

Most of the time, if we learn to think magically, we do not need divination. If we open ourselves to the universe and listen to our intuition, often we find the answers that we seek. They come to us through the unplanned encounter, the book that falls off the shelf into our hands, the mis-directed email. Carl Jung coined the term 'synchronicity' to describe those moments when such coincidences occur.[2] His collaborator Marie-Louise von Franz developed his ideas further in her book on synchronicity and divination.[3]

Synchronistic occurrences are 'meaningful arrangements', serendipitous events not consciously bidden.[4] Some seem trivial; others alter the course of our lives. Sometimes, over a short period of time, we experience a whole series of synchronistic events. It is as though the universe is trying to tell us something, signalling that we should take notice. The archetypes are moving the furniture in the rooms of the psyche, and we are entering a period of profound inner change. The more we take notice of our dreams, the more we will notice that synchronistic events occur. If the deeper self within the unconscious thinks we are listening to it, it will try to communicate what we need to know.

Sometimes, though, no clues come. There are situations where we gather all the facts about a life choice we need to make, but somehow we cannot come to a decision. It may be that we need more information that is not available. It may be that logic leads us to a decision that does not feel right. Sometimes we think we want to do something, but an inner voice is saying, 'No, no, no!' This might just be a fear of the unknown. Our species loves to explore, to see what is just beyond the horizon. This has made human-kind the dominant species on the planet. The dilemma is that we also love security and safety and sticking to what we know. Our personality and our moods will lead us to prefer one over another. If we are depressed and anxious, we are more likely to cling to the safety of what we know. When we feel confident, we feel more in control and able to take risks – to tread boldly into the unknown. And sometimes, as they say, 'it's complicated'. We experience a feeling of 'decentredness', of not being at ease with ourselves and our lives. Something needs to change, but we are not sure what it is. This is when divination can help.

When we do magic, we manufacture synchronicity to create meaningful arrangements. We make a Jupiter talisman to find investors for our new business (Jupiter being the planet associated with prosperity). By 'coincidence', a jovial investor appears and offers us the finance that we need. Divination is another means of creating and then interpreting synchronicity. It involves deliberately setting up situations in which we can detect and listen to our intuition, using techniques practised for aeons by shamans, prophets, priests, priestesses, magicians, astrologers, cunning men and witches. It works on the principle that, behind the apparent random chaos of everyday life, there is a discernible pattern to events and to the way the future is unfolding. This implies that there is a meaningful connection between the answer to a divination and a question that we want answered.

The idea that a divination mirrors events in the external world is based on the ancient magical principle that the macrocosm is reflected in the microcosm. Everything is a cell in the cosmic body. If we examine the condition of one cell, it indicates something about the condition of the whole. A tarot spread or an I Ching hexagram acts like a symbol or a code. The conscious mind struggles to interpret it until, like the grit in an oyster shell, it produces the pearl of wisdom, the key to what we need.

Detached openness is the essential basis of all magical and spiritual pursuits, hence the emphasis in magical training on open awareness, on perceiving without prejudgement. For divination to work well, we must be genuinely trying to find useful advice and the best way of moving forward. Divination is particularly useful when we want to discern more about what is really going on beneath the surface of a situation. Perhaps we sense there are hidden tensions, energies or activities that are influencing events, but we do not know what they are. It is also useful for exploring options and possibilities. Maybe we want to find a better way of achieving our goals, or we want to know the implications of a decision we are planning to take. We are not looking for pronouncements of how things will be, but indications of how events are evolving and how best to act in response to them. What we will have at the end of a divination is an indication of likely trends, and often some hints about what to avoid that we can use to guide us.

The divination will tell us partly what we consciously know, partly what we know unconsciously but is not yet in conscious awareness, plus an element of information about events and influences that are completely unknown to us and are part of the pattern of the future. On a psychological level, we can interpret what happens like this: if we approach a divination in a calm and meditative state, with an attitude of openness and a willingness to see whatever it is that comes, then the symbol system reveals to us unconscious concerns and emotions that are influencing our behaviour. We will become aware of information that we have registered subliminally, just below the level of conscious awareness. We may have noticed other people's body language, verbal signals or other 'leaked' information, all of which is part of a data set that we can use in order to make decisions. A divination can help us combine what we already know with unconsciously absorbed information, to anticipate how events will unfold. And sometimes, of course, we discover things that we could never know by any other means.

We can do divination for ourselves, but skilled interpreters of a particular divination system will help us to see what we might otherwise miss. Diviners have skills that overlap with psychotherapists, as they help us to discover what is hidden within us, but there can be another element too. If their psychic perception is highly developed, they may see things for us that we would never otherwise see.

Usually the I Ching does not provide direct answers to our dilemmas, but it helps us see our problems in new ways. Sometimes, though, the answers are startlingly literal.

One winter, a scientist friend visits from the University of Copenhagen. Would I do an I Ching reading for him? I am surprised. He has never asked me to do anything like this before. I am about to ask if he has a particular question in mind, when I have an intuition – *don't*. I sense he will accept the divination more if I do not know his problem.

The result is Hexagram 44, *Kuo*, Coming to Meet. 'The maiden is powerful. One should not marry such a maiden.'[5] He tells me his question: should he propose to his girlfriend? The relationship is news to me. I did not know he even had a girlfriend. He goes back to Copenhagen and does not marry the maiden. The oracle brought out his underlying doubts.

If we do not like the first answer an oracle gives, it is tempting to try again. The received wisdom is that this is a very bad idea but, like everyone else, in my early days with the I Ching, I do it. The first time I get a reading I do not like, I try again. My second reading is Hexagram 4, *Mêng*, Youthful Folly. I consult the text. 'It is not I who seek the young fool; the young fool seeks me.' Yes, this true. 'At the first oracle I inform him.' I have indeed been informed, but I do not like the answer. I read on. 'If he asks two or three times, it is importunity. If he importunes, I give him no information.'[6] I get the message. I now call it the 'go away fool and do not bother the oracle again' hexagram. I just go with answer number one.

Divination can help us change our behaviour and attitudes to meet the demands that life throws at us. We make a slight shift in how we deal with the world, and it is like making a miniscule turn of an old-fashioned kaleidoscope – a completely new pattern emerges. Ancient divination systems still flourish today because, although societies and civilisations may have evolved, we still have the same need as did our ancestors to cope with change and the unknown. In ancient times we would happily have consulted an oracle through a priest, priestess or shaman with a hotline to the collective psyche, and they would dream for us, go into a trance to give us messages, or use a symbol system to perform a divination. Some of us are happy to consult ancient oracles still, but for those for whom the I Ching or tarot are a bridge too far, there is a twenty-first-century solution. It is called Street Wisdom, and it is the brainchild of the multi-talented singer, performer and writer David Pearl and entrepreneur Chris Baréz-Brown.[7] They describe it as a method of walking-based problem-solving. I describe it as secular divination. It creates an artificial situation that allows the unconscious to speak.

It is why on a June afternoon in 2017, thirty-five of us are gathering in a backstreet behind the Strand, one of London's major thoroughfares. Three of us, coordinators of the Royal Society of Arts Mindfulness Network, are acting as 'Street Wizards' to facilitate a Street Wisdom event.

We brief the group about the purpose of Street Wisdom, which is to find inspiration to answer a question in our lives that we want to address. The instructions are for participants to walk for ten minutes on their own wherever they want, allowing themselves to be drawn to whatever attracts them, then to return for the next instruction. We dispatch the group on three more ten-minute excursions after the first. For the second, we ask them to walk again, but to slow right down. For the third, to notice patterns in the environment around them as they walk. The instruction for the fourth walk is to see the beauty in everything. These first forty minutes or so give them time to let go of their normal preoccupations and free up the brain.

Then we read out the final instruction, which is just to set off and wander to the agreed rendezvous point, but with a specific question in mind. The idea is to look around us and to notice anything that might be relevant to the question. It could be a book title in a store window, a smell that triggers a memory, a line of a song from a street musician. If we open our minds, then the universe will give us the clues we need to find the answer.

At this point I realise that I have no question of my own. Since I need to walk to the rendezvous point anyway, I decide to try Street Wisdom for myself. It has been fourteen years or so since I have written a book. My writing in recent years has been research reports and academic articles. What pops into my mind is whether to write another book. Halfway along the Strand, just before Charing Cross station, I see coming towards me a Buddhist monk in his saffron robes, a brown cloth bag crossed over his shoulder. He stops and says hello, then he rummages in his bag and brings out a golden card with a picture of the goddess Guan Yin, a Bodhisattva of compassion. 'I would like to give you this,' he says.

Guan Yin is meaningful to me. She is one of the deities I venerate. At home, I have a beautiful green-bronze statue of her riding upon a sea monster, with her phial of healing in her hands. It is only when I am a few hundred yards down the street that I turn the card over and see that on the other side there is a message: 'Work smoothly. Lifetime peace.'

So I work smoothly now on this book – the golden card on my desk, my statue of Guan Yin in the next room, my house a place of peace. As I write this section, an email comes pinging into my inbox. It is, of course, from Street Wisdom. 'Dear Vivianne …'

The universe likes its little jokes.

9

Making Magic

I often say that people come to magic seeking power and stay for the love. But people become involved in magic for many reasons – spiritual growth, reconnection with nature, to develop spiritual or magical powers, to find what other traditions lack. Some find what they are seeking and stay; others move on elsewhere. One of the reasons many of us stay is because we find something that we were not expecting – a sense of deep connection. The bonds we form with others on the path are a source of joy. When we are joyful, we see the world in a new way. The glass is now half-full, not half-empty. We appreciate and value the world around us, and those with whom we share it. From joy, we develop a sense of thankfulness.

Magical groups come in all shapes and sizes – covens, groves, lodges, communities, networks, or simply a group of friends. The first magical group I join is the Wiccan coven founded by the witches Alex and Maxine Sanders. When I first meet the group, I find them unusual. They are creative, artistic, caring and psychic. They strike me as different, but not strange. They are different in the same way I am different, and I feel a sense of kinship. Even from the first, I know I have found my tribe.

We are a young group, most of us in our late teens or early twenties. The late-twenty-somethings among us seem old and wise indeed. We have moved beyond teen-witch love spells and are looking for a magical spirituality, one that allows space for the inner wild self that wants to reconnect with nature and for the magical self that wants to reconnect with the powers of our earliest ancestors. We are seeking too that buzz and exhilaration that come from breaking out of the constraints of ordinary everyday consciousness. For we discover in magic and witchery the world of night, mystery, the moon, the cave, the hidden place of initiation lit by torches, a place of transformation that enables us to open up to all that we are and all that we can ever be.

Many of us revel in a witchy persona of long hair, black velvet robes and large metal pentagrams. We embrace dark imagery, rejecting stereotypical notions that equate spiritual growth with light, and evil with darkness. We are idealistic, well-read, and some of us are university drop-outs. The allure of magic is much stronger than the mundane world of academic study. Some of us will go on to become full-time tarot readers, astrologers or spiritual teachers, but most of us will re-engage with study and careers.

I am grateful to have found a group that will take people in their late teens. There is an esoteric tradition that young people should be told to go away and to come back when they are thirty. One Kabbalistic group I contacted in my search for a magical group told me just that, but for an eighteen-year-old, twelve years is two-thirds of one's life. I could not wait that long. In order to move forward in my life, I need first to know my spiritual direction.

Magic is intimate. It involves opening our psyches to one another so that we can feel one another's energies and emotions. We share hopes, fears, traumas, ideas, thoughts, feelings and psychic experiences. And we form bonds, on a deep unconscious level – bonds of empathy that are subtle but strong. We dream something and find that the other members of our group have dreamt it too. We sense that one of us is troubled, so we ring up to find out. If we do magic with others over a long period of time, we enter into the type of deep connection that we have with family, partners, children, childhood friends, or friends we room with in our teens and twenties. At its best, a magical group is a set of allies, a chosen family, who support and encourage us in everyday life, as well as on our spiritual path. Its members become our long-term friends, people with whom we feel free to be ourselves. They are people with whom we can discuss our inner journeying, our soul's longings, and all those weird and wonderful experiences we have along the way that we don't feel we can discuss when our colleagues ask us, 'How was your weekend?'

As an author on the sci-fi and fantasy book circuit in the 1990s and 2000s, I overlapped occasionally with Terry Pratchett, author of the Discworld series. He was an excellent person to share a gig with, adept at talking the organisers into upgrading our food, drink and rooms. For someone who disclaimed being a magical practitioner, he was also extraordinarily and suspiciously knowledgeable about the mundane realities of the arts magical. His books about witches are full of humorous details that only someone with access to the inside arc would know. My favourite is his description of a coven meeting in *Witches Abroad.* By the light of a flickering fire, the witches come together on a dark moonlit night for magic and after-spell snacks. As they unpack their contributions, one of the witches exclaims, 'You mean everyone brought potato salad?'[1]

As Terry observed, magical groups evolve a group mind whereby members often do have the same idea – and the gods do like their little jokes. Sometimes everyone really does turn up clutching potato salad, or pizza, or chocolate gateau. But besides amusing moments of mundane synchronicity, there are more profound manifestations of the coming together of minds, hearts and spirits in effective magical groups. There is the deep stage of meditation, ritual or spell-casting, when the sense of separation between ourselves and others dissolves. We go back to a time when human beings were in touch with the dream world, the sources of imagination and myth, and in touch with our biological being – smell, taste, sound, instinct, intuition, emotions, as well as thought. We go back to a time when we were not so imprisoned by our individual egos, to a time when we were in a state of consciousness that enabled us to think as one; for mind to communicate with mind, heart to communicate with heart. This is what I learned when I entered the world of magic.

It was not just our reasoning ability and opposable thumbs that enabled us humans to evolve from our ape ancestors. Just as important was our ability to imagine that which we have never seen, to envisage how things might be different, as this gave us the power to change the status quo and to create what did not exist before. Animals can innovate – apes can learn to use tools, birds can learn new songs – but our human ability to imagine, and to create what we have imagined, distinguishes us from the other species around us. It is no coincidence that many scientific breakthroughs from the sixteenth century onwards were made by scientists who were also magicians or voyagers in the imagination. Science has never progressed without imaginative leaps that challenge accepted wisdom. The hours spent over a laboratory bench or at a blackboard puzzling over mathematical equations are the foundations of advances in science, but to break through into new paradigms we need what the ancients always turned to when they needed to know something – the realm of imagination and dream.

The physicist Albert Einstein's theory of relativity was inspired by a dream he had around about his early teens. In it he was on a sledge at night, sliding faster and faster down a slope – so fast, in fact, that his sledge was approaching the speed of light. He looked up at the sky and saw that the appearance of the stars was changing. When he woke up, he knew that this dream was important, a clue. He meditated on it and later produced his revolutionary equation $E = mc^2$, energy equals mass times the speed of light squared. In other words, energy and matter are different forms of the same thing. Under the right conditions, matter can become energy and energy can become matter, which takes us back to the insights that magic has had all along.

Magic presupposes that there is a whole realm of unseen and unmeasurable energies behind the physical world that we experience every day with our bodily senses. In ritual and other magical acts, we choose to believe, at least for a time, that symbolic actions can harness these energies and result in effects that manifest in the material world. Maybe we think it is something that one day science will be able to explain, maybe not. At different stages in our magical journey, our beliefs will shift, our interpretation will change.

In my first decade in Wiccan groups, we did a lot of practical magic for ourselves and for others – finding new jobs and places to live, finding a partner, getting over relationship break ups, selling houses, healing – all the needs of everyday life. Our magical intentions had to pass strict tests. They must be to help and not to harm; to heal and not to curse.

But magic is complicated. It does not happen in a void. It depends on us laying the groundwork, creating the right material conditions for something to occur. Often people ask for magic, but they do not really know what they want. Or maybe they are conflicted – one part of them wants something and another does not. Sometimes we ask for something, while doing everything we can in the realm of everyday life to sabotage our efforts. Sometimes we want magical help to create a change in our lives; yet at the same time we are afraid of what that change will bring, so we put off doing what we need to do on a practical level to bring it about because change is difficult. We know that change is the reality of all existence, but at the same time we want certainty, stability, something to cling to. What our world crises teach us is that clinging on is not possible. We have to evolve and move forward, whether we want to or not.

Over time, most of us do less and less practical magic. We learn to rely on our intuition instead. If we want a new job, we let our intuition guide us to where to look, whom to ask. We put ourselves into a positive mindset so people respond to us positively and help us to our goal. But sometimes this is not enough.

Spells bring to mind the elaborate and exotic, the eye of newt and toe of frog that the witches of *Macbeth* threw into their cauldron. Most spells are much simpler and none needs involve animal parts. Some rely on sympathetic magic, and crystals, herbs or other substances with traditional magical properties. Others involve no physical medium. They require us to enter a special state of consciousness. Magical consciousness is an extension of meditative consciousness. When we meditate, our inner state of being is the goal of the process. When we enter magical consciousness, we have additional aims in mind. Often the aims are spiritual – to connect with a particular deity or to gain insights and knowledge – but sometimes we need something more material. We may do some magic on our own, but there are occasions when we will need extra impetus – a push, a shove, a helping hand. If we are magical practitioners, we can turn to our magical group.

If you have practised meditation with an experienced teacher or group, you may have noticed that your meditation goes deeper than when you practise alone. There is a subtle qualitative shift; the energy in the room changes and there is a sense that spiritual presence and power are present. It is similar when working magic with an experienced group. Visualisation and meditation in a group focused on a magical purpose can take us to a much deeper place than if we do this on our own.

This is why one spring evening in London, Chris and I are sitting on the floor on a circle of cushions in a candlelit room. Our group has come together to do a job spell. We begin the meditation. We let go of the concerns of the day and focus on the breath. Unconsciously, we allow our breathing to synchronise and our heart rate to slow to a rhythm that allows us to enter a light trance. We are holding hands. This simple gesture helps us fuse into a single group mind. Touch between one person and another helps us to synchronise our brain patterns and have shared visions. We focus on our goal – that Vanessa will find a new job. Vanessa is a long-term member of our group and we know her well. She is proud, reserved and rarely discusses her emotions or personal problems. She does not like to ask for help, but now she has been unemployed for five months and is becoming depressed. We are sufficiently worried to ask her if she would like some magic to help her in her job hunting. She is sufficiently worried to agree.

We begin a chant, a simple chant that Chris and I created decades before. It has been repeated over and over again. The words are not important in themselves, but they set the context for what we are doing. They are to keep our brains focused on the problem that we are trying to solve. 'Circle spiral, circle spin, bring the right job for Vanessa in.' Most traditional spells are doggerel. They are like children's nursery rhymes, with rhythms that are loved because we know them so well. We created the chant in the early

1980s, the first time one of our group needed some job magic, but we are now on version 1.1. On the first occasion, our friend was a computer programmer. He was offered a job cleaning railway carriages. It was a recession and work was particularly hard to find where he lived, and it did tide him over at a particularly bleak time, but it definitely was not his dream job. The next time, we added the word 'right'. We want Vanessa to find the right job for her. This is not so easy. She is very fussy.

Magic is a way of re-envisaging the world. It works with parts of the brain that pre-existed human dependence on language and the written word; the parts involved in visual imagery, creativity and dream. As we chant, we focus together on an image that represents the outcome of the magic. We have agreed on an image that is not too specific. We do not know what kind of job Vanessa will find or where, so we visualise her walking to work feeling happy and content.

There comes a point when I sense we have focused as long we need, and we say a phrase that is traditionally used to end a group spell: 'As we do will, so mote it be!' *Mote* is an interesting Old English verb. It can mean 'must' or 'may'. In my own mind, I feel it is 'may'. It may be, or it may not be. We are not trying to compel events, but to steer them. Magic is like cutting back the undergrowth that blocks the path, removing the debris that blocks the stream. We are creating a free flow of energy, a channel along which something may manifest – for Vanessa, a job. We share what we experienced during the visualisation – how we felt, what we noticed, our sensory impressions, words and images that came to us. Each of us has experienced something different, but there is a common denominator. Most of us have a sense that Vanessa's new job will have something to do with advertising. Vanessa is unimpressed, very unimpressed. She worked in advertising in her first job after graduating. It was the kind of job that most people would die for, but she hated the advertising business and thinks it the spawn of Satan – unethical, a prostitution of her talents, the wrong place for her to be. 'Supposing they wanted me to work on an ad for meat? Or dairy farming? Or big pharma?' She shudders with horror.

We persist – gently. Magic cannot force people to let down their barriers, but we all feel this is the way forward, something she should at least explore. 'Why don't you see if there are any agencies that specialise in working for not-for-profits?' Jane asks. There's a resonance in what she says, a sense that she has hit the target.

'That's a really good idea,' I say. 'Why don't you check it out?'

I can see that Luke, another group member, has registered what I have – the look of resistance on Vanessa's face. She has Mercury in Taurus and is as stubborn as a mule. She has no intention of taking our advice.

We bring the session to an end, but there is unspoken agreement. We will not leave it there. Vanessa really needs a job soon. The next day, Luke gets googling and comes up with three agencies that specialise in work for environmental charities. Vanessa has the track record and credibility to apply – she is a long-term activist with a couple of near-arrests at the edgy end of demonstrations. She contacts the agencies, but they have nothing suitable just then. We encourage her to make a speculative application to a climate change organisation. She gets an interview. They are interested, they say, but there is currently no free role. Disappointed, but now with the bit between her teeth, Vanessa makes a similar speculative approach to two other organisations. It is while she is waiting to hear back from them that the first organisation comes back. There is a job coming up in digital advertising. It is for maternity leave cover only, but she takes it. Four years later, she is still there and promoted.

We can have all the insights and nudges in the right direction in the world, but to make use of them we need to act. Often we lack the courage or the conviction to try to explore the possibilities that magical intuition throws our way. When we have the emotional support of those who are rooting for us and who wish us well, just knowing that our tribe is behind us and that others are willing to give their time and energy to help, gives us the confidence to move forward. It inspires the energy and conviction we need to overcome the inertia that can occur when we have tried and failed. The support of others can help us to develop courage, to see that success and failure are just part of life's pattern, that the wheel will turn and new opportunities will arise, that every ending is truly a beginning, and that sometimes what appears to be a mistake or even a disaster can be the gateway to a whole new life.

Our spell to get Vanessa a job worked, but what really happens when we ask someone to perform a magical spell for us? Three things are at play. Firstly, most of us ask because we are running out of options. We have got stuck, and feel we need an outside boost to find a new way forward. A whole series of things has gone wrong in our lives and we need to turn the tide. When we perform a spell together, we substitute a new narrative, a voice that tells us things will go right. We just have to open our inner ears to hear it.

Secondly, when we ask for help from others, we break out of our isolation. There is a wise-old-granny saying, 'If you don't ask, you don't get.' This is often true in everyday life and it is especially true in magical life. If we do not ask for help, we are much less likely to get it. By asking for help, we are acknowledging that we live in an interconnected web of other people, other ideas and other energies. We step outside our self-imposed boundaries to reach out to others who may be able to help us find solutions to our problem.

Thirdly, we open ourselves up to the possibility of the unexpected, the new, the previously unthought-of. In Vanessa's case, the answer to her job search seemed obvious, once she thought about it. The problem is that when we get stuck in a rut, or in a spiral of negative thinking, we no longer see the obvious. In fact, we no longer really look at all. We need something to jolt us out of our immersion in negative thoughts and give us a new approach. To solve a tricky problem, we need an open but disciplined mind that can look for and then integrate new concepts, inspirations and information. By breaking out of our habitual mode of thought, we engage in a process of divergent thinking to generate new ideas and avenues of activity.

In asking her magical group for help, Vanessa was gathering together a collection of minds in a kind of magical brainstorming. When we discuss the ideas that a spellworking visualisation throws up, many will be logical and obvious, but sometimes insights come from a deeper and more mysterious place. Often during a magical working, we experience what seem to be random thoughts and images. These can seem fleeting, ephemeral, not worth mentioning; but these vague smoke signals are often major clues and it is important to notice them.

Towards the end of Vanessa's spellworking, an image had floated into Dan's mind. He had glimpsed the inside of an office building and there was something distinctive about it. 'Everything was blue,' said Dan. 'The walls, chairs, flooring.' The insight did not help Vanessa with her initial applications, but it did help when she walked into the reception area before her first interview at the climate change organisation and found herself surrounded by blue. They had started work on a sea clean-up campaign, and the decor was to make people think of the ocean. Vanessa's confidence had taken a nosedive as her unemployment dragged on, and Dan's image made her feel more confident. When we are confident, people respond to us more positively. By sharing his insight, Dan helped Vanessa to succeed.

10

Naturally Mindful

We love to read stories of people who sell up their homes, buy a camper van, and head off into the sunset with children and dog to roam the world, immersing themselves in nature and having adventures. We love to read these stories because most of us cannot do this ourselves, and because deep down we know that the novelty of the nomad life might soon wane. We are not lions bred in captivity who can be returned to the wild, but there is a sense in which we do need a spiritual rewilding.

Have you ever felt a craving, a thirst for greenness, for flower and grass and tree? Scientists have created a term for this – nature deficit disorder. Our bodies and minds are shaped by millions of years of evolution, in which we lived in small groups surrounded by nature. The concentration of huge masses of us in cities is unnatural. Even if we bury our discomfort in our deepest unconscious, we sense that this way of being is alienating. We need an antidote, and there is one.

Have you noticed that you feel happier when you look out of the window and see trees and plants? You might not even have noticed, but have unconsciously accepted that it is natural to feel this way. Nature is beautiful. The veins of a skeletal leaf have an exquisite intricacy that even the most artistic of us can never surpass. Our eyes and ears are soothed and refreshed by nature's greenness; our minds and hearts awakened. Research supports what we know instinctively – time spent in nature is therapeutic and healing.[1] It brings renewal, creativity and new energy to give to others.

Beneath all the constraints of civilisation, there is within us a more natural and untamed self – a wild, magical, ecological self that is close to our animal origins, but close too to our spiritual core. This wilder self takes us away from the superficiality of contemporary life, towards something older and deeper. It takes us deep down into the unconscious to our species' earliest beginnings, a time when we were free to roam under sun, moon and star, to walk naked and proud without need of adornment.

The images in the tarot that are most akin to these feelings are those of the Sun and the Star, the sun child and the star woman who are naked and unafraid, at ease with themselves and the natural world around them. They represent what we lose as we leave childhood behind and enter adult life, but also what we need most to regain if we are to integrate all the disparate aspects of our being into an authentic whole. We human beings cannot live divorced from the natural world around us without paying a price in terms of health, well-being and the destruction of what our species most needs in order to survive.

It is easy to lose touch with the natural world. Many of us live caught up in dreams, memories and regrets. We are not really aware of what is around us, and more importantly of the possibilities that the universe offers us. We go around in a kind of daze with earphones plugged in, shut in with our own thoughts and fantasies, our minds scarcely registering the input that our senses provide. We use music to block out other sounds, so we do not hear the birds sing. We travel on our daily commute without noticing anything about the route we take. Only if something really unusual happens do we 'come to' and realise exactly where we are.

The human brain thrives on novelty and needs the stimulation of the new. A difference between our brains as children and as adults is that every day for a child is a new learning experience. As children, our brains are constantly developing. We are in a continual state of learning and stimulation, always processing and integrating new experiences. The intensity of learning is such that a day seems to last forever.

It is easy as adults to lose our sense of wonder and our engagement with the world. Our vision becomes glazed. Our minds cease to see clearly the world around us, or our inner world. And when we cease to see, we cease to question. We accept things as they are, and we lack the imagination to change them.

The idea that the true potential of the psyche is latent, and asleep in a kind of waking dream, is common across spiritual traditions. The aim of many spiritual practices is to teach us to wake up to what is around us. If we can do this, we can start to live fully, in the moment, extracting from it all that it has to offer. We can be truly alive. We can aim to cultivate newness of mind, openness, curiosity and a lack of preconceptions. Instead of wandering blindly through our world not seeing, we can learn to walk through it seeing in a way that feeds the brain.

The Japanese Buddhist monk Shunryū Suzuki, who became one of the most famous Zen masters in the West, taught: 'In the beginner's mind there are many possibilities, but in the expert's there are few.'[2] Close your eyes for a moment and imagine you are a child once more. Each morning you waken to a new adventure in living. Can you remember your emotions the first time that you saw a rainbow, or snow, or the sea?

As adults, we can recapture that sense of wonder. We can learn to notice more and to appreciate more of what is around us if we take short breaks, even if it is just once a day, to be totally present and to savour the experience of the moment, as a wine taster savours a fine wine. We can do this for a few minutes anywhere, but one of the magical exercises that I teach people who come on my courses is to choose a nearby tree to visit daily, or a particular view from the window, for those lucky enough to look out over a garden or a landscape, where it is possible to see the seasons change. If, every day, we take some time to observe what is around us, we will notice that the scene is never exactly the same. Each day there are subtle shifts.

What do I see if I look, really look, at the world outside my window now? The morning sky is full of grey clouds tinged with light. The birch tree in the garden is snowy white against the greyness. It is an unusual tree, a beautiful Himalayan birch. It is a deciduous tree and each day there is change. Gradually its green leaves dry out, turn yellow, then brown, then fall. The falling is spasmodic. Some days leaves cascade down in wind or heavy rain. Some days are still, and hardly a leaf falls. As leaves strip away from the branches, the view behind is revealed. In late summer I cannot see through the leaves. In autumn, gaps appear in the foliage. Behind the birch tree, the bare branches of taller trees weave a latticework against the sky. In early winter, I start to see the hills beyond the garden. At midwinter, the trunk changes. Strips of bark peel away. They make wonderful parchment for writing magical intentions. The ground below the tree is covered with leaves that are home to worms. The birds in the tree become startlingly visible, hidden no longer by the leaf canopy. The growth of a new year comes early. By late January there are catkins, a sign that the sap within the tree is rising and awakening to begin the year's cycle again.

When we look at these sequences within nature, we see a symbolic message that life is endlessly renewing in cycles of growth and decline. This is a message that in the darkest hour can bring hope and can make each day a revelation.

Experiences of communion with nature can open us to what the philosopher and sustainability expert Professor Glenn Albrecht calls *eutierria* – 'a good and positive feeling of oneness with the earth and its life forces'.[3] The word is strange, neo-scientific, even alien; a combination of *eu*, which in Greek means 'good', with *tierra* (the earth) and *ia* (a condition of). Eutierria is what we experience when we enter into the right relationship with our planet. The boundaries between nature and self can dissolve, bringing a renewed sense of peace and connectedness.

We do not have to label ourselves spiritual or magical to experience a sense of oneness with nature. We do not have to be poets, mystics or psychics. This sense of connectedness is hard-wired into the human brain, part of our wild animal self. It can be felt by anyone. There are many ways to reconnect with the world of nature, some more physical and some more symbolic. Walking, camping, gardening, meditating on the natural world, celebrating the seasonal cycle with rituals – all these can be routes to greater empathy with the non-human world. Through meditation and imagination, we can extend our minds to feel how it is to be a tree, a bird, an animal, even a whole forest.

As adults, we find our way back into these experiences during any activity that gives us time just to be with trees, birds and the landscape, and to listen, smell and see what is around us. A few years ago, when I walked in the sequoia forests of California, the feeling was the same as that I had as a child. There was that same sense of the sacred, of the power and wisdom of trees and of their long memory; a feeling that once we humans have gone away for the night, then the real life of the forest can begin.

What might happen if we open ourselves to nature and our natural wilder self? Will we be more receptive to *eutierria*, oneness with nature – with plants, fungi, insects, birds, animals, the creatures of the sea, with all creation? Might this change our relationship to the Earth? If we mindfully walk to work each day, will we notice more the subtle changes that bring the procession of the seasons, and feel a need to take time to honour these seasonal tides? If we stand outside at night to look up and out into the cosmos, might we find more joy in the gift of being alive? If we attune to the Earth and all her changes, will we better connect our human actions with what happens to her?

We find the sacred in nature because our deeper self is an ecological self. When we come into connection with the deeper self, we transcend our individual separateness to connect not just with our collective human consciousness, but with the consciousness of our biosphere, of our planet, of the Earth, of Gaia herself. This radical re-centring of our human sense of self can change our worldview profoundly.

Meditation does not have to be practised by sitting cross-legged on cushions in meditation halls, because not all meditative practices require stillness. Meditation can take us back to the wild places, to our more natural selves, for where better to develop awareness of what is around us than in nature? Mindful walking in nature – or, for those of us who feel the need to be more physically active, rhythmic exercise such as running or swimming – is an active way of engaging the body, freeing the unconscious from the grip of the conscious mind, and allowing ourselves to go into the zone where we are not consciously thinking.

Newer branches of science such as ecopsychology recognise what magical teaching has long accepted – that our psyches are deeply connected to and affected by the world of nature. We can see the evidence of this all around us. Our moods are affected by the amount of daylight we are exposed to. In winter, we can succumb to seasonal affective disorder (SAD); but when it is sunny and our muscles are warm and relaxed, we feel happier. Human yearnings to be outside in the light and to reconnect with the land and with nature are strong, but when our lives are pulled in so many competing directions, these feelings are easy to ignore or to suppress. Day after day we can find ourselves leaving our centrally heated houses to climb into our air-conditioned cars, park in underground garages and take lifts to air-conditioned offices without ever having contact with the natural world.

With the Covid-19 crisis, millions of us stopped doing a daily commute and stayed at home. For some, this meant job loss and economic disaster; but the luckier among us discovered, as did our employers, that we could be just as productive when working remotely. We could adapt our day. We could walk at lunchtime rather than eating a sandwich at our desk. We could open ourselves to nature once more and, with reduced traffic and planes, we could hear the birds sing.

Walking is beneficial for body, mind and spirit, but where we walk is also important. We are happier, less stressed and ruminate less after walking in a forest than if we walk for the same amount of time in a city.[4] 'Rumination' is a psychological term for those soul-destroying moments when we find ourselves going over and over negative thoughts and memories – past wrongs done to us, guilt and shame about things we have done, regrets about what we have failed to do, fears and phobias – endless downward spirals that can trap us in self-loathing and hate, unable to escape our pessimism about ourselves and the world around us.

Neuroimaging shows that our brains react differently when walking in a city and walking in nature. If we walk in nature, the neural activity in the subgenual prefrontal cortex – the area of the brain associated with an increased risk of developing mental illness – decreases. Walking in the city does not give us this same effect.[5] If we think about it, it is easy to understand why. When we walk in nature, the focus of our attention switches outwards, to what is around us. We are drawn into the beauty and sensory experiences of nature – its sights, sounds and smells. In the city, we instinctively protect ourselves by ignoring much of what we see – the dirt, the garbage, the graffiti, the homelessness. Instead, we focus inward, which draws us back into any negative spiral of thought going on in our heads. Just twenty minutes a day spent walking outside in nature makes a difference to our sense of well-being. Many of us must make do with city parks rather than rolling green hills, but even the constrained nature of urban gardens and squares can help to reduce stress.[6]

Nature gives us a sense of perspective on our lives. Thoughts, emotions, anxieties and fears that preoccupy us can dissolve when we contemplate the beauty of a bird's flight, a flower's bloom, the sea's ceaseless rhythm, the vastness of the sky. Time spent in nature helps our thinking processes too. Our memory works better after we have been walking in woodland.[7] Our creative problem-solving ability increases significantly if we spend a few days hiking outdoors.[8] And if we cannot get out, if we are confined indoors for whatever reason, there is another way. We can look at images of nature. This too reduces stress and promotes recovery from illness.[9]

What the Covid-19 pandemic and enforced staying at home gave some of us was the luxury of having time to just to 'be'. We humans are complex creatures, with complex needs that pull us in different directions. In recent centuries, the idea of taking time out to just be was not valued. In countries all over the world, the Protestant work ethic has been embraced to such an extent that we are encouraged to spend all our waking hours working and earning money in order to consume, and then working to earn more money to consume more. This dysfunctional, unsustainable spiral pushes our planet to the edge – to the tipping point beyond which it may no longer be able to sustain biological life – and we who are trapped in the cycle are being pushed closer to the edge too.

This does not mean that we should pretend we are 1960s hippies about to tune in and drop out. The world needs us to engage rather than disengage, to address problems rather than opting out, but we can function much better and make much saner choices if we make time to stop and digest our experiences; to reflect and remind ourselves of what really matters to us – our values, and what brings us joy. This means focusing on the spiritual as well as the material; on 'being' as much as doing.

Paradoxically, taking time out to be does not waste time, nor use up time that we would otherwise use productively. It gives us more time. Replenished, refreshed from drinking at the well of being, we can do so much more than when we are stressed, exhausted and burned out. If we take a few minutes each day to be mindfully aware of where we are, what is around us, and what is important to us, our horizons widen and our minds open to new possibilities. This is important for both psychological and spiritual health. Ten minutes a day spent in open mindful awareness changes our perception and allows us to see the world with fresh eyes – the eyes of a child who is newly discovering existence. Practising a little longer – twenty minutes instead of ten each day – has a longer-term effect. Neuroscience research shows that mindfulness practice changes our brain's physiology, and hence our future experience of the world.[10] And if we change our experience, we change who we are.

Scientists and philosophers are now telling us what mystics and magicians, hikers, campers, naturalists and indigenous peoples have known all along. Concrete does not soothe. It impoverishes the spirit. In my own life, it was only when my family moved to London and I was torn from nature that I realised just what I'd had and what I had lost and what I needed to regain.

11

Reaching the Peaks

The first sixteen years of my magickal life were private and personal until one morning when I am writing an article for a management magazine on psychological stress, I look down and see that my fingers have started to type something else. Somehow my brain has switched mode and made an inner shift. Instead of writing about what is in my head I am writing what is in my heart. I am experiencing one of those moments that the Surrealist painters called autonomism. A word, a phrase, an image, even a taste or a smell flicks an on-switch in our brains. The synapses activate and bridge gaps to connect and integrate our thoughts, even before we know we are thinking them. Energy starts to flow, the hand starts to move, and we gaze in surprise at what is pouring out from the pen. Artists experience this when they paint as though in a frenzy to record a vision that has come to them. Musicians experience it when they find themselves hearing new songs, or even whole symphonies, in their heads and rush to write them down before they lose them.

I have been awarded my PhD. I have developed an expertise on the psychological impact of social policies and am increasingly being invited to write articles for journals and to speak at conferences. Now I have produced a three-page synopsis for a book about Wicca. I send it off and, much to my shock, a letter comes back expressing interest, quickly followed by a contract and an advance. It seems that the book is exactly what the publishers were looking for and they want it as soon as possible. I persuade my boss to give me a six-month sabbatical and start thinking about what to write.

I make the mistake of taking on a part-time lecturing post as well. Two months in, the term is coming to an end and I haven't managed to write a word of the book. I have that agonising panic that would-be writers have when faced with a ream of blank paper. A Christmas card comes from Ivy Northage and Janet Orman. I have not told them about the book, but they write, 'Love from Janet and Ivy – remember us when you are famous.' It gives me confidence that I have something to say. I visit one of my Wiccan teachers, Alex Sanders, and he makes me a talisman to help with the book. In symbolic language it shows ideas streaming in from the collective unconscious.

I often think in pictures and symbols rather than words, and for me paintings can be gateways to new experiences in consciousness. Ian Gordon-Brown of the Centre for Transpersonal Psychology shows me reproductions of the paintings of the Russian mystic Nicholas Roerich. They act as gateways to new ideas, just as did the paintings I saw in art galleries in my childhood and teens. I feel I have a whole tribe rooting for me as I synthesise all my experiences so far into my own interpretation of Wicca.

The ideas begin to flow from brain to hand to pen and then to keyboard and screen. In these pre-internet days, the text is written on one of the earliest cheap PCs – an Amstrad. The file capacity is so small that I have to break each chapter into two files, and the publishers cannot take the text on disks. I have to print it out and post it. It is a scary moment, I feel the book will change the lives of thousands of people. I take a deep breath and push the envelope through the letterbox, the first stage of its journey into the world.

With the book finished, the copy-editing done and a few months until publication, Chris and I take the opportunity to make the trip that I never managed in my teens and twenties, and we fly to India. We travel on buses and trains, in villages and cities, in the Himalayas and on the plains. It becomes a spiritual odyssey. I drum around the Shiva lingham in a small temple in Udaipur. I sit meditating by the sacred lake in the beautiful city of Pushkar, and marvel at the Jagatpita Brahma Mandir, the most important of the few temples in India dedicated to the creator-god Brahma. Chris and I meander round the competing guru ashrams of Rishikesh, and stand on the burning ghats of the Ganges at Varanasi. We meditate at one of the holiest Buddhist sites in the world, Sarnath, where the Buddha preached his first sermon – a place of beauty and peace. The plains and cities are fascinating but tiring. We long for space, tranquillity, coolness. We do what the Brits of the Raj did in the summer – we go north. We take an internal flight to the Kullu Valley in Himachal Pradesh, in the foothills of the Himalayas. Delhi's airport teems with people. Guards at the doors prevent anyone who is not flying from entering, which is a relief – however many people there are inside, there are thousands more outside.

We are not heading to Kullu for the scenery alone, although it is well worth it for that. We are on a pilgrimage to visit the house of the painter Nicholas Roerich and his wife, in the ancient town of Naggar, the home of the gods of the Kullu Valley and once the seats of its kings. Now, we will be able to see the originals of some of the paintings that Ian Gordon-Brown showed me to help me write my book.

Our backpackers' Bible, the *Lonely Planet* guide, tells us that the old royal castle at Naggar is now a hotel and it is possible to stay there, but it warns us that there are only three rooms. We try ringing the phone number listed but this goes to the local tourist office. They seem unable or unwilling to tell us whether there are any vacant rooms there. Naggar is only twenty miles from the nearest airport, but over an hour's taxi ride on the mountain roads, and we need to stretch out our finances. A taxi there and back is too expensive – but we want to go. We walk round Delhi airport and I have an idea. Supposing we find someone else here who wants to go to Nicholas Roerich's house? I look around for likely travellers. The airport is packed with thousands of businesspeople, families and countless backpackers. Any of the backpackers could be a candidate, but I hesitate. No one looks quite right. Just then, a couple a little older than us walk by – a tall man with a neat ponytail, and a slim woman. They look Italian or French. They are too stylish to be Brits, too elegant for Americans or Germans, not fair enough for Dutch or Nordics. I approach and hear them talking. They are French.

It is slightly embarrassing to walk up to strangers in Delhi's international airport, hundreds of miles away from the obscure destination of Naggar, to ask of all the hundreds of possible destinations they might be flying to today, of all the possible places they might go to even if they are on the same flight as us, whether they happen to be thinking of getting a taxi to the Naggar Castle hotel. But I decide to give it a go. This is why I decided in my teens that life would be easier as an uninhibited extravert. 'Nothing ventured, nothing gained' is the eternal magical motto.

'*Excusez-moi.*'

The man looks unimpressed by my French. 'Yes.'

'Are you going to Kullu?'

He nods, slightly surprised.

'To visit Nicholas Roerich's house?'

He is beginning to look a bit alarmed.

It is best to move forward swiftly in these situations, so people do not have time to start thinking that this is all slightly weird. 'Could we share a taxi at the other end?'

He looks very unkeen.

'If there's only one room at the hotel, then of course you can have it.'

The frown disappears.

We land at Kullu airport and our new French friends turn out to be expert negotiators. We soon find ourselves in a rickety taxi heading up the narrow mountain roads into the clouds to the hotel, where fortunately there are two rooms.

Naggar is now a popular tourist destination with multiple accommodation options and the renovated Naggar Castle Hotel receives enthusiastic reviews – but this is long in the future. When Chris and I visit, we find the hotel is not quite as romantic as we imagined. In fact, it is seriously eccentric and more fort than castle, more Fawlty Towers than Grand Budapest Hotel. Our room is large, but decaying. We turn back the bed cover and the sheets are stained with mouse urine and droppings. The forty-page menu we are given so we can choose our dinner is mouth-watering to read, but when we order we discover there is only one dish and a choice of three drinks. We can have dhal with rice, dhal without rice, and lemonade, beer or tea. The meal is enough to take away the hunger pangs, just. We pay for it straight away so the staff have enough money to buy more food for tomorrow. At night the wolves howl, but they are outside and we are safely inside. We ignore the scampering and gnawing of the indoor wildlife that seems to be sharing our room. The view is worth it.

We visit the Roerichs' house, now a museum, to see paintings that I have seen only in books and as reproductions. Nicholas and Helena Roerich were inspired by the goddess worship of India and of Tibetan Buddhism. They believed that the twentieth century was ushering in a new era, a renaissance of women that was inspiring women's movements all over the world.[1] I have long loved Nicholas Roerich's painting of the enthroned Goddess as *Mother of the World* in its deep blues and violet, but the paintings I see here are some of his series of the Himalayas. Like the French Impressionists, he was fascinated by painting light, but he chose wilder and rawer places to experiment. He moved to the Himalayas, communicated psychically with disincarnate spiritual teachers, and painted the same mountain scenes over and over again, but always different in the ever-changing light around him.

Nicholas Roerich realised from his paintings that his mood shifted in response to the changing light and colours. Now we stand looking over the peaks, experiencing for ourselves what he was painting. We see how throughout the day, the colours change. As the clouds sweep over the mountain peaks, so shades of green become purple, greys turn to blue. Shadows shift so rocks and crevasses appear on the mountains, where before all looked smooth. The sky changes above, and deep, dark, jagged chasms appear, only to disappear as clouds pass, and once again the light changes. In the skies, blues, violets, greys, pinks, oranges and golds appear and disappear with the changing seasons, weather and passing hours. It is truly wondrous. How could anyone fail to be a mystic here?

And what do I sense in this place where my esoteric predecessors believed they could communicate with Bodhisattvas and Hidden Masters? What do I believe about these mythical beings of Buddhist and esoteric lore? The mountains have always been for human beings places of mystery. How could they not be, when it is only in recent centuries that we have been able to climb their peaks and penetrate their secrets? Our ancestors believed that gods lived on the mountaintops. Now, we may not think of mountains as the homes of holy gods, but they still evoke an emotional response in us as archetypal symbols of aspiration. They resonate with us when our lives are going through periods of transition to rise to new challenges.

Have you ever felt in your own life that you are on the threshold of a transition; that something is propelling you forward in a way that will change your life's direction? At these times, we can find peace and courage in the wild places, places where we can touch on the deeper wilder self and our inner sources of inspiration. Mountains, lakes and seas, forests and wild moorland, these are the places that draw us when we need time to prepare to embrace the future and whatever it may bring.

On our last evening, as Chris and I look across from the terrace to the mountains and the lengthening shadows beyond, I know that this place has been a staging post. I sense that some inner transition has taken place. There is a weaving and an interlacing taking place within me of all I have learned so far. My therapy training at the Centre for Transpersonal Psychology helped me to see how Wicca and other magical practices can bring us into unity with the deeper self, but the therapy training came first from a different impulse – the impulse to heal.

12

Magical Healing

There are eighty of us in a marquee with a wooden floor, the type usually used for weddings. Summer rain is drumming on the canvas roof. The rain has its own rhythm, but soon it will be drowned out by a rhythm of ours. The publication of my book *Wicca* has taken Chris and me from being practitioners of magical traditions in the UK to teaching internationally, and we are working on building supportive networks of like-minded people who can share knowledge and techniques across the barriers of culture and language. Now we have gathered in Germany with teachers and others from across Europe for a week of magical events. We are about to begin a healing ceremony. The rite was created by our friends Julia, Rufus and Paul. We know it can be powerful in a small group where everyone knows one another, but Paul, Chris and I have never brought together a disparate group of this size before. We hope the ceremony will work.

I have my bodhrán ready. Musicians usually play the bodhrán with a wooden beater. I prefer to use my hands. I need to feel the skin of the drum beneath. I ask if anyone would like healing. A young man speaks up. Has a serious chest complaint. This is not the ideal rite for his condition. He will have to lie flat in the centre of a spiral of people, while we cense him with two different incenses that our incense expert Paul has created. One incense has herbs and resins to drive away disease. The other is healing and soothing.

Lying flat while being censed with incense seems as likely to produce a coughing fit as a cure, but now the young man has asked it feels wrong to refuse him. Gently, we lay him down on blankets with a cushion under his head. We stand in a circle holding hands and begin to sing a chant. It was taught to us by a woman who learned it at the Greenham Common women's anti-nuclear protest camp in Berkshire, England. She in turn learned it from women who had been on environmental protests with the American witch and activist Starhawk. Chants like these are used as our ancestors used them. They are simple and repetitive, the beat set by a drum. The women of Greenham were using the chant to give them strength and solidarity during their long protest. Their rhythm was upbeat and fast. For ritual, we use a much slower rhythm. We want to still the mind to a point where we can reach out in empathy to radiate healing and love.

'She changes everything she touches.' Those of us who know the chant sing slowly, hypnotically. Others join in. 'And everything she touches changes.' The 'she' is ambiguous and can have many levels of meaning. 'She' could be a woman, a goddess or our planet Gaia. We might sing it to a woman who needs to change something in her life. We might be singing of Gaia's ability to regenerate herself, or it might be that we are empowering a single woman to act as a priestess, a channel for Divine energy to manifest change in the world. The lines are repeated over and over, until we become at one with the chant, swaying to the rhythm of the drum beat, until our bodies want to move; the swaying to become a dance. I let go of the person to my left and dance inwards and round the circle; then inwards and around again, until our circle of people has become a dancing spiral, as we loop in decreasing arcs until I arrive at the young man who needs our healing. I kneel beside him, and those behind me sit or kneel too. Those of us nearest to him stretch out our hands to the edge of his aura. It is bright and shining now he is the focus of our attention, but the aura is not the whole and symmetrical aura of someone in good health. It is ragged, stronger in some places than others, the outline not clearly defined. It feels as though he is leaking energy.

From the outer edge of the spiral, people are passing the purging incense towards the centre, each of us focusing when we receive the censer on our collective intention – for his body to be rid of illness. Someone begins the chant again, softly, more gently. The pungent scent of the incense intensifies as it draws ever closer to the centre; the mingled notes of myrrh and wormwood. As I reach to take the censer, spontaneously the chant ceases.

There is a pause, a silence. We all sense we have reached the moment of transition, when whatever can be changed can change. We have created a small shift in the multiverse of possibilities, a space, a gap, a potentiality when by will and by choice someone can choose to embrace the healing that triggers the autoimmune system. Those of us near him now focus on drawing the sickness out of his body. We visualise it as a dark, smoky haze. The burning charcoal in the censer is consuming the dark haze, breaking it down, dissolving it. Surprisingly, our recumbent patient has yet to cough, but I sense it is time to withdraw from his aura. I pass the incense back to the person behind me. The chant starts again, this time more a whisper, gentle so as not to disturb the peace of the moment, then fades away and stops. I sense that the incense has left the spiral.

We start the chant again. The censer of healing incense with its heady sweetness of frankincense is now passing around the spiral to the centre. Each of us focuses on loving, healing thoughts for the young man as our turn with the incense comes. Our chant shifts a little higher, faster, lighter. Suddenly, the tent grows brighter. The rain stops. Sunlight is bathing the canvas. The marquee fills up with golden light as the intense smell of frankincense builds. I pass the censer over his body at the edge of his aura. It is brighter, whiter, glowing whole, with none of its former raggedness. I thank the Goddess and we bring the rite to a close. Still he does not cough. We sit for a while bathed in the healing energy and the synchronistic sunlight filtering through the marquee. We take it in turns to hug him and one another. Something has happened, something of love and beauty, a manifestation of some deeper power in the human psyche.

People have gathered to perform similar healing ceremonies for millennia, and they are found still in indigenous communities. The chants will differ, as will the names of the gods or spirits called upon to assist, but the drum rhythms will be similar. Human beings have learned by experience which rhythms excite, which soothe, and which can take us into a trance state where a shift in consciousness occurs and the immune system reboots. Sometimes plant-based medicines are used in healing ceremonies, sometimes not. In our healing ceremony we used an incense with frankincense, which is known to reduce wheezing and shortness of breath. It is a staple of traditional Indian, Arab and Chinese medicine. Research has shown its therapeutic potential in treating pain, asthma, psoriasis and erythematous eczema, multiple sclerosis, osteoarthritis and gingivitis, and potentially cancer too.[1]

Most important, though, is the effect of healing ceremonies, and of similar healing actions such as prayers and spells, on the psyche. In recent centuries, we in the West were taught to view the mind as some abstract, invisible substance separate from the physical body. With mind divorced from matter, medical science underestimated just how much our psychological and spiritual state affects our health. Now the science of psychoneuroimmunology creates bridges to understanding the interactions of body, mind and spirit.

We know that stress damages the immune system and makes us more susceptible to disease. We know conversely that psychological and social support can boost the immune system and promote healing.[2] Part of the process that was happening in our healing ceremony in Germany was that someone who was struggling alone with his illness was surrounded by loving support, but the effect was not just psychological. Ceremonies such as ours trigger the brain to release oxytocin, known as the 'love hormone', and endorphins, the body's own endogenous opioids.[3]

In some countries, conventional medicine is becoming more open to traditional healing methods such as shamanic drumming and communal ceremonies. In the United States, much of this work was carried out initially with patients from Native American and other communities where healing ceremonies are part of traditional culture. Now they are more widely used in clinical settings. One proven use is in the treatment of post-traumatic stress disorder (PTSD) experienced by combat soldiers, firefighters, police officers, and others who are thrust into violent and traumatic situations. Even when shamanic practices are carried out in clinical rather than spiritual settings, people have healing experiences that make a positive impact on their daily lives, bringing them peace, calmness, safety and the ability to think clearly, no longer preoccupied with their past trauma.[4]

Emotions are to magicians what colours are to painters. Magicians need to have an emotional palette – a range of ways of expressing feelings and of 'feeling into' the minds, hearts and experiences of others. This requires empathy, something that people with a strong feeling function can do more readily than those of us who are primarily analytical thinkers. Empathy means understanding how others might feel. What happens in a healing ceremony is that we shift the brain into a state of heightened empathy, and we transmit loving, healing thoughts to someone with whom we make an empathic connection – a connection of love. The strongest links in consciousness are between identical twins, and most people have strong links only with relatives or partners. Healers are people who can create these empathic links with people they have only just met. This is not unique to spiritual healers; it is an important skill for psychotherapists too.

One of the elephants in the consulting room, rarely discussed openly in professional settings, is the extent to which therapists experience telepathic connection or synchronistic events with their clients. Recent research shows that nearly fifty per cent of therapists have such experiences.[5] *Star Trek: The Next Generation* picks up this theme in the character Deanna Troi, who is part way between counsellor and clairvoyant. Her character exemplifies scientific research that shows that empathy and telepathy are indeed closely linked.

Empathy is a basis from which spiritual healers go one stage further – from sensing clients' thoughts and feelings to directing healing intentions. Spiritual healers appear to be consciously entering a changed state of consciousness, whereby they switch on the brain circuit that enables them to connect with the brains of others. A healing ceremony is an enhanced act of empathy. When people are willing to come together to create an elaborate ceremony for us, we feel wanted and valued. The depression that can accompany illness in itself makes us more susceptible to disease. When we feel loved, it helps us harness our own inner healing processes and boosts our immune system. We heal more quickly. A healing ceremony is a gift of love. And it is love – the reaching out between what we sense is 'I' and what we sense is 'not I' – that is at the heart of magic.

In our rite, we honoured the Goddess, the Divine Feminine principle, an energy that is part of each of us but transcends our ordinary, everyday consciousness. We do not need to believe in a supernatural being in order to call upon the Goddess. For me, she is a feeling of deep interconnectivity born in the heart, not the head; born of love, not belief.

Each of us will have our own moments when we have felt this transcendent love. We may sense such a presence in nature, or when we are making love to someone we care about deeply. We might experience it when in a marriage rite we say 'I do' to the one we love. For some, it might come when holding a newly born child or grandchild. For others, it is when a dying person we have sat with passes peacefully out of the body. It might be a special moment in a psychotherapeutic encounter – a critical point of transition in the healing process. We experience a presence, another consciousness above and beyond the people in the room. It is at such moments that we know that the whole is truly greater than the sum of its parts.

To be at the centre of a healing ceremony arouses profound feelings that are difficult to express in words. Some people describe it as a back-to-the-womb feeling of love and peace. To me, it seems more akin to orgasm, but instead of the intensity building in the body, it builds in the psyche and spirit – a spiritual explosion of love and connection with the people in the rite and with the universe beyond. It manifests as zinging sound and golden light, in flows and waves, energy without fixed form, sweeping us up in its embrace. At such moments, we experience the universe as pure Divine love.

13

Invoking by Moonlight

The sky turns to night above us. The full moon has already risen above the horizon. It is a July full moon the deep gold colour of ripened wheat. As it rises higher in the sky, the golden orb turns to white. Silvery light bathes the tall dark pines. The fire in the centre of the clearing begins to crackle and ignites. Flames and sparks leap up into the air. Above, we hear the sound of a police helicopter. It is illegal to light fires in the forest in the summer in Germany, but the Germans among us are familiar with the ways of the forest. The earth pit and the circle of boulders around it will keep the fire secure. One of the German witches is a policeman. He checks that he has his police ID handy, just in case his colleagues decide to investigate further, but the helicopter sweeps up and away.

We sit in a silent circle around the fire, eighty of us – expectant, waiting. We have come from across Europe to exchange magical teachings, and now we are to celebrate the power of nature together. Rustlings in the bushes break the silence as the animals of the forest come nearer, drawn by curiosity to the warmth and light of the fire. The drums begin, ancient, deep, their vibration reverberating in our bodies; our pulses and hearts synchronising to their rhythm and bonding us as one.

We warm the drum skins over the fire to dry out the damp and make them taut. Our drums fuse cultures – a West African djembe with a much-battered Moroccan dumbek, Native American drums and their European frame-drum equivalent, the Irish bodhrán. We begin, tentatively and then more assured, adapting to one another's rhythm. Soon I no longer think about the beat. It is flowing straight into my hands. The drumming grows more intense. It speaks to something older by far than all the disparate cultures that have inspired us. It speaks of the oldest time, when all music began – and older still, perhaps. Our prehuman ancestors would have stomped the ground and drummed the trees like apes and gorillas do today. The rhythms arouse excitement and fear. I feel the fear of hundreds of generations – the fear of the shadows, of powers unknown, of the mists that disguise, of paths overgrown, of predator tracks in the morning dew, of the ever-nearing growl, of the flapping wings of panicking birds scattering between the trees.

Around the circle a chant begins, a chant for the ancient god of the forest, Lord of the Animals, the Stag King. We call upon him as the Horned One, honouring him in all of his many names. My heart thumps louder and louder. A deep and wordless cry comes out of my throat. My palms and wrists grow sore with the drumming. I abandon the bodhrán and begin to dance. I am chanting and dancing for the Lord of the Forest, he of the many names. We call him to come forth, out of the shadows, out of the past, out from the hidden caverns, out from deep within ourselves.

The old gods that are animal, human and divine, they connect us to the reality of the natural world around us. They are not up there, but down here; not apart, but a part of nature and of who and what we are, and of what we can be. For thousands of years, shamans would dress in antlered headdresses and become the Horned God, the Lord of the Animals, to ensure that their people were in a harmonious relationship with the spirits of the animals they sought to hunt. Such relationships are important, both psychologically and ecologically. When we recognise that we exist in relation to other species and are dependent upon them, then we teach our children the behaviours necessary for our and their survival. We learn not to kill the young, the lactating and pregnant mothers, the finest and most virile males. We cull rather than kill, so we and our prey both thrive.

Am I thinking these thoughts as I dance? No, the drumming has intensified, and around the circle many of us have entered the trance that is beyond thought. I pull off my clothes and dance naked, the moonlight reflecting from my white arms as I raise them to the moon's orb. I am dancing the Stag God into being. The chanting is swirling through every cell of my body, in sound and vibration. All is he and he is All. And then he comes – crashing through the undergrowth, his antlers silhouetted against the moon. Tall, impossibly tall, he comes, a leather mask covering his face, his body naked beneath a brown cloak. He cries out, a great cry joining our chanting. I fall to the ground to honour him. From the circle comes a woman's startled but reverent, very English voice: 'My God!' We all sense it. The god has come. The chant becomes a whisper. The drums fall silent. The god speaks. He speaks of his love for all nature and for all of humankind. I sense a feeling of overwhelming love between animal and human, human and the world, between each one of us in the hushed circle listening to his words.

I know his voice. It is my Norwegian friend Stein. With his two metres' height now topped by an antlered head-dress, he really is impossibly tall. In this time and place, deep in the German forest, he holds for a time the energy of a god. In an act of spiritual mediumship – some might call it channelling – the Horned God speaks through him to heart and sinew, to blood and ancestry. He speaks from the time of the first humans, from the deepest dreaming of our species' beginnings.

Somewhere along the way to civilisation, we lost many of the natural qualities that made our species successful. We have become separate from one another and have lost the ability to connect with symbols that could bind us together. The world religions have much wisdom in their teachings, but too often they take us further and further away from ourselves and the natural, the wilder, the simpler – away from our connection with our biological nature. Drumming and chanting take us back to humankind's earliest spirituality, the spirituality of the wild places, of our nature untamed. Music vibrates through us and produces deep emotional resonance. There is some music that we hear that we cannot help but dance to. Dance is one of the great mysteries of humankind, a way of moving the body so that we lose for a time our sense of separateness and individual self. We connect once more to our wilder, preliterate, biological self – the self that is at home in nature.

For thousands of generations our ancestors made music. Long before they first laid paint on a cave wall to create an image, they drummed and danced and made simple flutes in imitation of birdsong. When we respond to the rhythm of the drum, we return to an ancient, archaic part of our being. It is as though all those past generations have bequeathed to us in our DNA the instinct to create songs and music that bind human beings together. We dance in the woodlands, and can hear faint echoes in languages we no longer understand of the stories that became the poetry and then religious myths of our peoples, spoken with rhythm and repetition so all could remember the teachings. When we drum and dance, entranced by rhythm and music, we move into a collective state of consciousness in which our bodily rhythms synchronise with those we are with and our brains secrete 'happiness chemicals' – endorphins and the 'love hormone' oxytocin. In these bodily highs, we experience feelings of connection and love towards one another and to all creation around us.[1]

For a few hours we return to a sense of deep connection with the trees of the protective forest. We slip outside of time. A profound feeling of peace comes over me, as though all my experience so far in this incarnation has blended into a much greater whole: the whole collective memory of humankind. I feel my individuality now merged with something much bigger – with the human beings in the circle around me, with all those who recognise the need for the return of the ancient gods, with all humankind in its stumblings and sufferings, and with all our ancestors linking us back to those first people from whom we all spring. The feeling releases me from the conflicting emotions of everyday existence; from doubts, anxieties, past hurts and pain; from unfulfilled desires and wanting. Everything I need is here, now. Nothing more is needed.

I look up. The vault of heaven is spread out in all its beauty in this place far from light pollution. And way beyond our solar system, beyond our galaxy, perhaps some other conscious being is looking out into the vastness of space, just as I am now, wondering at the magnificence above us.

We feast around the fire and I gaze at the faces around me. The drumming starts up again, this time with sweet chanting and singing. The time of wildness gives way to a different rhythm, as the sky lightens and the moon descends below the treetops. Dawn is coming and we have a deep sense of peace, but the word 'peace' does not fully convey the feeling. It is much more – a sense of gratitude for having been given a profound gift, and a sense of catharsis. Old blockages, wounds, inhibitions and fears no longer matter. We reach a different perspective. We go out beyond the confines of the ego and return feeling more at ease with ourselves, more centred and in control. We human beings spend much of childhood and adolescence learning how to become individual and separate. We need to develop a strong sense of 'I' in order to engage with the world of the everyday. When we engage with wild magic, we learn how to take time out from the 'I'. We let go for a time of the separation between self and other. There is an interaction between subject and object, a dissolving of the barriers that separate us from the world of interconnecting energies around us. 'I' and 'other' become one. We see differently and, inspired by that difference, the everyday 'I' can engage with the world in new ways.

In my childhood I experienced the call of the Horned God and I was not alone. Why did this image prove to be such a powerful archetype for so many people in the nineteenth and twentieth centuries? When an archetype reactivates in the collective unconscious, those who experience it first are those who are close to the unconscious, those who dream and tune into their creativity. Poets, writers, artists, musicians and dancers, as well as makers of magic, have brought the archetype of the Horned God of the wild hills and woodland groves back into our cultural psyche. An archetype wakens when there is something we need to know, something we need to address; when something is lacking in the life of the conscious mind. Consumerism and technology do not feed the soul, our imagination or our natural animal selves. There is something else that we need, something that comes from the past.

The image of the Horned God comes from the natural world, but the reality of our everyday lives is often far removed from nature. Most of us live in cities and towns. Our surroundings are concrete and tarmac. At night, street lighting fades out the stars. One solution is to return to nature; to go back again and again to the world outside the city; to reconnect with our deep longing for greenness. The ancient and old inspires us, but we are not our Pagan ancestors. Yet, in another sense, we are the same. We modern humans evolved into our present form around 300,000 years ago and have changed little since. We are better-nourished and medicine has enhanced our lifespan. Reading has changed the way our brains retain and process information, and now IT changes it further. But our basic desires and longings – for food, sleep, security, shelter, sex, love, to be valued by others, to touch for a moment worlds beyond the everyday world – none of this has changed.

What do we experience when we recreate in modern form ancient rites and practices that sustained our ancestors for millennia? We are not they. We do not live as they lived. Our understanding of the world, and of the worlds beyond this world, is very different from theirs, but these ancient rites and practices appeal to us on many levels, because they open us to an enhanced state of consciousness. This does not necessarily mean leaving the body or seeing visions; it can be a heightened awareness in which we see, hear and experience the world around us differently. I know from my own experience that when we participate in such rites, the boundaries between 'I' and others, and between 'I' and the natural world, dissolve and shift for a time. This is hard to put into words, but imagine a state in which your thoughts come into my consciousness and vice versa; or a state in which a group of us all see the same vision. Perhaps you can imagine a state of consciousness where it seems as though the whole universe around you comprises cells of consciousness, all interconnected, all communicating with one another and becoming part of a greater whole.

We used to have to rely on words to explain such experiences to others. Now science can help us understand them in another way. Magnetic resonance imaging (MRI) and electroencephalography (EEG) can demonstrate exactly what happens in our brains and which centres are activated and integrated when we enter a shamanic or similar altered state of consciousness.[2] Does understanding the science of altered states of consciousness help us to experience these states for ourselves? Perhaps not, but it might make us think that they are worth exploring; for in our educated and scientific era, we are less able to take for granted the practices that for our ancestors were an unremarkable part of everyday life. Scientific research can help us better understand humankind's core spiritual experiences, the experiences we share that transcend differences between cultures and creeds. When we perceive commonality and connection with other human beings, regardless of skin colour, language, age, gender or sexual orientation, then our ideas of how we should behave towards one another change. Intense rituals, shamanic journeying, meditation and other practices take us into states of consciousness that can lead to deep feelings of love and connection. What may be surprising to you is just how similar these states are across traditions and cultures. They are an innate part of our biology. We dress them up in the language and cultural symbols of our time and place, but the feelings that the experiences evoke are shared by all human beings.

In our multicultural societies, the world's traditions whirl around in our consciousnesses and in our ever-mixing gene pools. To return to a simple magical spirituality is to reconnect with something that we can all share, but this is not to become stuck in the past. We are the people of tomorrow, not the people of yesteryear. We cannot put ourselves back into the mindset of our forebears, but we can take ancestral wisdom and combine it with the knowledge that science has brought us to create a new spirituality. By returning to the shared roots of humankind's spiritual beginnings, we can evolve new forms to meet the future. We can learn to understand the powers of the mind in order to shape reality within us and around us. We can embark on new adventures in culture and consciousness, so that the diverse cultural streams in which we now swim can merge into great rivers to feed the collective sea of human consciousness so that we can make the world anew.

Our gathering in a forest clearing in Germany comes to an end. With first light, we pack up our drums and follow the path out of the trees. It is as though the stars have fallen to the dewy grass, for our way is lit by glow-worms, and my heart is glad. For a few hours, we have reconnected with our deepest biological wild selves. Meditative techniques can help us to transform our inner being, but alone they do not bring us to the sacred flame within – the source of our being where our wilder self still dances beneath moon and star and drums for our gods. Stillness must meet ecstasy, equanimity must meet passion, if we are to be fully whole. Our destiny is winged; it is meant to soar the heights. Our dreams caress the stars but we must be rooted too in the natural world of earth, so that in the hall of the heart a flame may burn pure and warming, a vision of our life and world that takes us through the dark times and back into the light of the sun.

During our rite, my friend Stein allowed himself to step back from himself for a time, so that an archetype deep within his psyche could emerge. He became for a time the archetypal figure, the Horned God that appears in myths, rock paintings, dreams and visions all over the world. He provided a gateway through which we were able to share and experience a vision, an idea, of how such a god might be.

In such rites, we touch on the original religion of humankind, the shamanic practices that unite us with the world of nature, the realm of the stars above us, the deep caverns of the unconscious below us. Today, in our world of internet and smartphones, of fashions that change in a few weeks, of fragile climate and even more fragile governments, we sense a deep need for reconnection to the wilder self.

For me, the wilder self came back, and it takes me on a journey. The journey begins in Ireland.

14

Awakening to Land and Memory

The south of Ireland is beautiful this early November. Autumn is late. The trees are still covered with red and gold leaves, and bathed in sunshine with only the occasional showers that one of my aunts calls 'God watering the flowers'. Chris and I are on holiday and thinking of buying a house. Living in London is wonderful. Our jobs are well-paid. The city is one of the world's major cultural and intellectual hubs. It is also a magical and mystical hub. There are endless fascinating people, organisations and events for those pursuing a magical path. It is an exciting crucible of people and ideas, but now we have danced for the Horned God in a German forest.

Our experiences have reawakened my childhood connection with nature. We long for more contact with earth, sky and wind, to see sunrise and sunset not blocked out by buildings, to breathe clean air. Celebrating nature in ceremonies inside a building is no longer enough, but we cannot leave the city just yet. It is where we earn our livings, and as a wise magician once said to me, 'It's very difficult to do the Great Work on Social Security.' Head must be balanced with heart, but now the world is changing. We are not yet in the era of digital nomads, but we are early adopters of remote working. Much of the research and writing that we do does not have to be done in a city.

We have enough money saved to look for an additional base outside London, a place for magic and meditation. Ireland appeals but we have reservations. The outsiders' romantic view of Ireland is far from the reality of early 1990s rural life still dominated by the Catholic Church. My relatives' devout Catholicism, coupled in some cases with deep Republican anti-Englishness, means that as a Wiccan vegetarian with an English husband, they might prefer me as a visitor rather than as a neighbour.

We take a walk along Cork Harbour, still deciding what to do, when we see a ship setting sail. On its side is painted 'Brittany Ferries'. It is heading for the French coast and the Breton port of Roscoff. Simultaneously, we feel an impulse: 'Let's go there.' We know nothing about Brittany other than its part in the Arthurian cycle and the legends of Merlin and the Lady of the Lake, but it draws us.

We go. We walk through the magical forest of Brocéliande, where the magician Merlin is forever imprisoned by the fairy-witch Viviane. We visit the Château de Comper, birthplace of Lancelot. We discover that, for the Bretons, it is Brittany (Less Britain) not the island of Great Britain that is the final resting place of the Holy Grail. We visit Carnac's Neolithic stone alignments and a nearby 7,000-year-old burial chamber. We take part in the strange ceremonies of pardons, day-long festivals to celebrate local saints, many of them never officially recognised by the Catholic Church. There are saints to heal every ailment under the sun, and saints whose origins as Pagan deities are hidden only a little below the surface. We discover signs of folklore, traditional witchcraft and healing everywhere. The terrors of the witch persecutions never reached here, because as one seventeenth-century commentator explained, 'It is impossible to prosecute witches in Brittany because everyone is a witch.'[1] We feel a deep connection with this mystical land.

In February 1992, we complete our house purchase and move into our new home, an early-eighteenth-century farmhouse with a nineteenth-century addition, extended to accommodate a multigenerational farming family. It is surrounded by a one-acre wilderness of brambles, nettles, broom, gorse and neglect. It feels like a return to the rural world of my childhood. Brittany's people have lived as my father's family did for generations, in deep connection with the land that they farm. There is another source of familiarity. It may be a different country, but the vegetation is much the same as the south of Ireland. There is an overlap, too, in cultures. Brittany prides itself on being one of seven Celtic nations, along with Ireland, Scotland, Wales, Cornwall, the Isle of Man and Galicia. The local language of Breton is similar to Welsh spoken with a French accent. The *fest noz* or 'night feast' is much like a ceilidh, and Brittany's folklore reveals that same thin veil between the natural and supernatural as that of other Celtic cultures.

We begin to make the house habitable and to create a garden. Gardening involves machetes. Each day we spend some hours outside. We see the season's cycle, each day something new, something happening, the gradual shifts. We notice the day the swallows come each year to nest in the barn. We move the washing line from early April until September, when it is under their feeding flight path. We use wood for heating from trees on our own land. Working the land and connecting with soil, stone and wood are deeply satisfying. This is the real world. The artificial world of offices, lecture rooms and computer screens is not.

As incomers, we want to feel rooted in our new land, to connect to the energies and spirits of the place. Perhaps it is the Irish attitude to death that makes me feel that the natural place to do this is a grave. Where our ancestors are buried, our shared DNA is part of the soil; it is part of what makes the grass and trees grow. Here in France we have no parents' or grandparents' graves to visit, so we visit a Neolithic tomb. Long before Ireland's Newgrange or England's Stonehenge, the Neolithic inhabitants of Brittany began to erect standing stones and burial chambers for the growing population attracted by the farming, fishing and trading opportunities of what became a major Neolithic trade route from the western Atlantic coast into continental Europe.

We adopt the nearest passage grave as our own go-to place for meditation. We sit near the entrance, looking out over the landscape. Neolithic people of the region had very definite ideas about the positioning of tombs. They built them in high places and oriented their doorways towards the rising sun. Those working the fields could look up to see their ancestors watching over them. Traders and other strangers would see the tombs guarding the land. Our predecessors lived in close connection to their dead, who were not shut away in a distant heaven, but were part of the living community. They could ask the dead for assistance, wisdom and guidance. This did not involve séances. They could simply go to the tomb and a shaman would make contact with the dead to speak with them. We do not wish to speak to these ancient dead, but we want to sense their blessings, their friendliness towards us newcomers to their land.

The acid soil of Brittany means that the bones of those buried in the tombs have dissolved into the soil around them, but their spiritual presence can still be felt at the tomb site and, to connect with them, Chris and I make offerings. Human instinct when we visit the spirits of a sacred place, or the shrine of a deity or a saint, is to make an offering. We want to leave something of ourselves in the holy place to connect us with its energy, and to remind the supernatural allies of our existence. We might not label it as such, but it is a small act of magic. In churches, people light candles. In some traditions we make cairns and stones at the graves of holy men and women. At sacred healing wells all over Europe, people tie small pieces of cloth torn from clothing to the surrounding bushes or trees. At Neolithic sites in Britain, people leave all manner of crystals and candles that to them are deeply meaningful, but to a lover of natural places or to an archaeologist look like New Age tat.

We do not want to spoil or litter the tomb, which is looked after by local people, and the dead of all cultures prefer offerings of food and drink. We find a locally brewed beer that might not be so different from the beer that they drank. We pour a small libation on the ground near the entrance to the tomb. 'Unknown ancestors, bless us,' I ask. 'We do not know your names or gods but we ask you to accept this offering, which we pour on the land to honour you. Help us in our new life here to connect with the energies of the land and to honour its gods.' Then we drink and libate again. 'As we drink, we honour you.' These simple acts and ceremonies are the basis of religion, ways of honouring time and place and the beings around us.

The spring sunshine bathes our backs as we face the entrance to the tomb. High up in the sky, larks are singing. There are houses either side of the small field which has been left for the tomb, so the current inhabitants live in neighbourly companionship with those who are long gone. Chris and I both feel at home here, at peace, as though some connection has been made deep in our psyches that binds us to this land. We sense that the ancestors are aware of us. The offerings are acceptable.

There is something about the land here that opens the gates of perception. We live in a house with three hundred years of history, on a site occupied by humans since goodness knows when. Much of the stonework of the house and barns is recycled. We have a stone fireplace torn from a manor house during the French Revolution. We have a cornerstone that might once have been a standing stone. We soon find we do not need to go to a burial chamber to encounter the dead. We become more familiar with the house and discover we are not alone. The nineteenth-century part of the house is inhabitable. The eighteenth-century part is fine on the outside and all but derelict inside. We find ourselves sharing it with mice, beetles, woodworm, wasps, spiders and the undead. Doors open, footsteps clump up the stairs – older people in the village still wear wooden clogs – and sometimes out of the corner of the eye we see a faint presence of someone. Then there are the subtle dislocations in time. We are sitting in the dining room and the scene shifts, the furniture changes, curtains appear and a large 1930s radio plays music.

My psychic mother taught me as a child that good manners should be shown in all circumstances, so we say '*Noz vat*' to wish the dead goodnight. Their language would have been Breton, not French. When the Ankou, the Celtic death spirit, walks up the stairs one night and knocks on the door of a visiting friend, we recommend that if he returns she should say, 'Good evening, Disincarnate Entity, may I be of assistance?' The Breton translation is beyond us and we doubt that the Ankou speaks modern French. Responding to anyone with fear and loathing is guaranteed not to get a relationship off to a good start, and the Ankou, while a worrying portent, is a polite entity. He makes his presence known eight days before a death, so there is plenty of time to sort out a will and to get one's affairs in order. He is seen as a skeleton in a hat and long cloak, and the creaking of his wheels as his horse cart draws to a halt outside a house is a sign that someone's time is up. We are a bit worried about which of us will die, but it turns out to be an elderly aunt, so in a way we are quite relieved that the portent signals nothing completely out of the blue.

I try my 'Good evening, Disincarnate Entity' routine on other manifestations that turn up at the house. In the winter, our house and grounds are like a clear island in the mist. At the top of the drive, the mist is sometimes impenetrable, and occasionally a single tall wraith breaks off, descends down the drive and hovers outside the front door.

I do not know what the wraiths want, but we show friendly appreciation of the performance.

We experience other visitations, less welcome flashbacks, time slips. In the late afternoon, an armed car sometimes passes down our tiny lane. It moves silently, not something in our everyday world, a memory from World War Two. This seems unlikely, as our lane is so obscure, but then I discover that during the Occupation the château on the hill above us was the German officers' quarters. Our local area was torn apart in World War Two – not by bombs, but by conflicting loyalties. Breton nationalists collaborated with Nazis who promised them independence. Rival resistance groups betrayed one another in the power struggle being fought between Gaullists and Communists for control of France after the war. This is a world I know, a world of multilayered allegiances, and terrible memories. It was the world of my family during the Irish War of Independence and the Civil War that followed, a world that seeped into my childhood memories through the songs and the quiet, soft voices of the men playing cards, while we children sat under the table and played our own games.

We discover the wounds still run deep in our Breton village. There are divisions invisible to outsiders. We must be careful about these sensitivities when we hire workmen, we are told. If we have the Catholic roofer, the communist plumber will not come.

When I see the ghost of an armoured car driving by, I feel a woman's fear as she watches, and the relief when it passes by without stopping. When I look down the wooded valley behind the house, my eyes are drawn to a spot among the trees. The idea comes to me that there are arms buried in the woods. If I was a metal detector enthusiast, I might explore it, but I am not. In 2014, with the seventieth anniversary of D-Day, the parish magazine publishes an article by a resistance veteran. He describes the parachuting in of British officers to lead the resistance, the parachuting in of arms, the burying of the arms in the woods behind our house that I saw twenty years before in my vision.

I experience a flow between past and present, a toing and a froing triggered by the energy of the place, the land. Do stones and earth hold memory? It seems that in some places they do. And how much are we affected day-to-day, I wonder, by the emotions that permeate the buildings and the land where we live and work? Perhaps, in time, science will provide the answer, but for now this remains part of the mystery, something we humans have yet to understand.

As we tackle the garden, we discover that, as well as old memories, a few undead, the brambles and gorse, and a plantation of trees we did not know were ours, we have bought an enormous heap of stones – great rocks of white, orange and rose-red quartz, and blocks of semi-dressed granite that glisten with tiny white crystals. What does one do with a heap of stones in a land of standing stones? Some magically minded friends visit and, with levers and hard work, we use some of the stones to create a stone circle, a ritual space with a firepit in the centre. A block of rectangular white quartz becomes our altar. A circle of white stones in the New Forest was the first ritual space that I saw as a child. Now I have one of my own.

Together, we create an inaugural rite in the stone circle. We purify the space with incense and consecrated water, and we turn to face the four directions and say an invocation to the element associated in the magical tradition with each one – air in the east, fire in the south, water in the west and earth in the north. The focus is now on the centre and whatever takes place there.

To create ritual, we draw on ancient rites and myths. The way we respond to them – viscerally, emotionally, intellectually – is deeply personal. There is however a non-verbal language that we all share, whatever our culture or creed. It is a language of images and symbols that inspires the imagination, moves the heart and stimulates the psyche. These simple symbols have resonance across cultures. They appear in art from the earliest cave drawings and carvings on sacred stones, to contemporary art. They feel familiar, as though our brains are hardwired for them.

There are names Chris and I have used for two decades for the goddess and god of the seasonal cycle, but here outside on our land they seem artificial and wrong. They do not speak to us in this land of rich earth, granite and quartz; of salt-tinged breezes and soft misty rains; of bright sun, and clear night skies laced with shooting stars. Not knowing the right names, we call upon the divine energies simply as goddesses and gods of this land, and by flickering firelight and hissing and crackling wood, we sit in the circle and meditate to see what comes. Above us are glittering stars and a waxing crescent moon. We listen to the wind in the trees, to the hoots of the owls. We listen intently, with focused awareness. Then, into my mind, comes a sound, a word: 'Ah-n' or 'Ah-nah'. I sit for a while waiting for other people to come out of their meditation. One by one, our eyes begin to meet one another's across the fire, until everyone is ready to communicate. We compare notes. We have all heard 'Ah-n', 'Ah-nah'.

Intuition has found a name and thinking now takes over. We buy books on the Celtic history of Brittany. We discover the works of the historian of religion Françoise Le Roux and her husband, the philologist and linguist Christian-Joseph Guyonvarc'h, a professor of Celtic Studies at our regional university in Rennes, as well as the researches of Breton historian Gwenc'hlan Le Scouëzec.[2] What we heard was right. We learn that the goddess is 'Ahn-ah'. In Brittany, Ana is the Earth Mother, a mother goddess, goddess of the land and of the underworld – the same goddess who in Ireland is known as D'Ana, Dana or Danu. We have found our first deity.

Brittany's magic survived the sixteenth-century Protestants and the seventeenth-century Catholic Counter-Reformation better than many regions of Western Europe because Brittany had an advantage. The people spoke Breton, while the nobles and Church hierarchy spoke French. The language barrier meant that old customs continued and the local clergy kept sensibly to doing what their predecessors did, which was to allow the old to blend with the new. The result is that Brittany has a Catholicism of healing wells and ceremonies with sacred bonfires, of churches carved with horned animals and fantastic griffins, and sometimes so many female statues that there is hardly any male imagery at all. We learn to look closely at the statues. What at first looks like a conventional Catholic statue of the Virgin Mary and the child Jesus is often Jesus's grandmother St Anne with her daughter Mary.

When missionaries came to Brittany with the new Christian religion, it was not a straightforward sell. They needed to package the new faith in a way that was acceptable to the people. The main deity was the goddess Ana, who had a powerful hold on her people, so someone had a clever idea. In the apocryphal Gospel of James are the names of Mary's parents. Her mother is Anne. So the missionaries created new narratives. Ana was really Anne. Anne was a Breton widow, the Bretons were told. She was captured by pirates and taken to Palestine, where she was sold as a slave. Such kidnappings were part of everyday life on the western seaboard of Europe, so the story was plausible. In Palestine, Anne was bought and then became the wife of a new Jewish husband, Joachim. They had a daughter, the Virgin Mary. Jesus was now a quarter Breton, or maybe even half. In another version, Anne is a noble Breton woman who is already pregnant with Mary when she is cast out by her abusive husband and is guided by an angel to a boat that takes her to Judea. Anne eventually returns to Brittany, where the people greet her with joy because she has the power to control the weather and to heal. Like a good Jewish-Breton boy, Jesus comes to visit his grandmother in Brittany before he begins his ministry, so the mythological connection with Brittany is made even stronger.[3]

Whatever the variations in the myth, the message is clear. Your goddess Ana has an honoured place in our religion. She is the grandmother of Jesus and he is one of you. The new religion grafts itself onto the old. The goddess evolves, survives and retains her place in the hearts of her worshippers.

Now Ana returns without the Christian overlay. She becomes our local goddess, the one whose name we invoke for help, for protection, to take care of us in our new life.

★

We begin to celebrate the seasonal cycle in rites within the stone circle – rituals that mark the passage of the seasons and acknowledge our dependence on nature and all that she provides. Chris and I have celebrated these cycles since we began to work magically together, not long after we met. When we bought our first house in London, we set aside a room as a magical space, a temple. Soon others came to join us for seasonal rites.

The rituals are beautiful and symbolic honourings of the natural cycle. Winter Solstice, the shortest day in the northern hemisphere, honours the joyful rebirth of the sun. Its pre-Christian festivities became part of Christmas celebrations. The early-spring festival of Imbolc, or Candlemas, celebrates light in the darkness of winter and new hope as nature begins to wake with the first snowdrops and the birth of lambs. Spring Equinox brings a time of seed-sowing and a celebration of new creative activity. May Day honours nature in all its blossoming beauty, a celebration of the joy of life in the body. Midsummer celebrates the sun at its height. Its imagery is of leadership; the message is of taking responsibility. The outcomes of the summer's work are celebrated at the grain harvest of August Eve and the fruit harvest of Autumn Equinox. As nights grow longer and days shorter, the emphasis of the cycle shifts to thoughtfulness and contemplation, a turning inwards that leads to the celebration of Samhain or Hallowe'en, the festival of death and the dead, heralding a time of darkness until the cycle begins again at Winter Solstice and the days lengthen once more.

The rites are expressions of gratitude for the ever-renewing life force, for nature which provides us with the means to live, for being alive and for the joy of human existence. They celebrate what is *here*, *now*, in *this* body, in *this* time, in *this* place, with *this* particular group of people. They are a reminder that each thread in the fabric of our existence has its time and place and purpose. There are highs and lows, darkness and light, but the rites teach us to stand in the centre, in the place of equilibrium, and to accept the impermanence and change that is around us.

When we take time to be aware of the seasonal cycles of nature, it attunes us to enjoying the ongoing process of life all around us – birds building nests, moles burrowing, foxes calling, the flowing ocean waves and the blossoming trees. We align ourselves with the manifesting life force that stretches beyond our single individual existences, and gives us a sense of the changing but ever-renewing cycles of life. There is a solidity and a continuity in these celebrations. They take place around the same time each year, but every year is different. They are a cycle, but also a spiral.

We come to each year's celebration with another year of life experiences. Each year has its own rhythm, its own heroic quest of ups and downs, highs and lows, but seen in the context of an overall message, darkness turns to light and despair to hope. The cycle of the seasons reminds us of what is abiding and what endures. This is not fashion, worldly success or physical beauty. It is not our mistakes, our pain, our inadequacies. It is what lies beyond those poles of positive and negative emotions. It is deep joy in being alive and a deep sense of peace in the face of eternity.

As we perform the rites on our land, our knowledge of the deities of Brittany evolves. Ana is an earthy goddess, a goddess of the dark rich soil; the grandmother who nourishes and gives wisdom to the generations. We find her energy most strongly in autumn and winter; but what of the spring and summer in this land? Brittany is a peninsula. The sea brings with it mists, rain, wind and sun, but in summer Brittany is a land of long, golden afternoons and evenings. It is this yellow sunlight that in the nineteenth century brought artists here like Paul Gauguin, who painted *The Yellow Christ* and *Haystacks in Brittany.* We discover that it is Belisama who is the goddess of the summer half of the year that begins with May Eve and the Celtic festival of Beltane.

Friends visit for our first Beltane in our new home. As the sun sets, we light a new fire in the stone circle, for this is a fire festival – the fire representing the power of the growing summer sun. The flames crackle up and around us, as the quartz crystals in the granite of our farmhouse and barns sparkle in the last rays of the sun's golden light. I stand by the warming fire and invoke for the first time Belisama, bringer of summer. We sense her presence in the circle and around it.

'Gentle summer breeze, light in the sparkling drops of dew on the grass of May morning, hawthorn blossom, first pale-pink wild rose of summer, Belisama of the singing birds, who waters the fields with rains and greens the land, goddess of Beltane, goddess of this land, we welcome you.'

We meditate on Belisama and she comes like the Star card of the tarot, a beautiful naked woman kneeling by a flowing stream. We see her walking by the riverbanks of reeds and yellow irises. We feel her as energy and light, joyful and creative. There is love and laughter there, and also strength.

At our Midsummer festival, we invoke her again. In the northern hemisphere, the sun in its fullest strength enters the astrological water sign of Cancer. Midsummer has the energies of both water and fire – the water of gentle summer rains, as well as the warmth of summer sun. We try a traditional practice of the Scottish Highlands and tilt a cauldron of water to catch the rays of the sun. We shake the cauldron and the sun dances on the water, making it a rippling gold. We sense Belisama as a goddess of dance and movement, a bringer of blessings, enlightenment and healing.

We honour Belisama as goddess of summer and Ana as goddess of winter, and our relationship with them grows. We know little of how people centuries ago understood and experienced them, but for us Belisama is like the sunlight – she changes day by day. Ana is the stability of the earth. We honour them as they choose to manifest to us, new images and emotions overlaying old, in a reawakening of ancient tradition. The long-dormant seed sprouts in new spiritual creativity, and in the two goddesses we see and know and remember nature's beauteous summer and winter faces.

Friends and students visit from all over Europe and beyond. Our home becomes a place of healing and retreat; our stone circle a magical portal. We carry out seasonal rites, initiations into the Wiccan tradition, and handfasting ceremonies to celebrate marriage. Each ritual has its own resonance and beauty, as year by year the energy of the place builds. Some rituals are profound – rites of Wiccan initiation, healing rites, a Lughnasa celebration with shooting stars above us. Another year, summer storms come and lightning flashes as we invoke the harvest goddess. Some rites are celebratory and bring laughter – a handfasting where we invite special forces veterans to decorate the circle for the bridal couple. The bridegroom comes back bemused with a progress report: 'It looks like an explosion in a launderette.' I add to my list of magically useful things to remember: *Special forces veterans don't do drapes.*

There is love and laughter in the circle, and magical healings, as we bond to the land and awaken to its power. But when I need healing, I am not on my land.

15

When Magic Really Matters

There is a major difference between a monotheistic God, with a capital 'G', and the magical view of goddesses and gods. Terry Pratchett captured it perfectly in his Discworld novels. Magical gods are powerful but quirky. They are not the anthropocentric creation of monotheistic male prophets, gods whose sole focus is humankind. They have their own agendas and cosmic purposes that include all of this planet and beyond. If you experiment in magic, you may also come to a realisation: the gods have a sense of humour, it is just that humans do not always find it funny.

This is what comes to mind as I lie on the back seat of a car, groaning as we bump along on a dirt road that is taking Chris and me from a sheep farm in southern Australia to the nearest hospital. The first aid officer who is driving is doing his best to get us there as fast as possible, while also keeping the journey bearable.

In the first edition of my book *Wicca*, I wrote that self-initiation into the Wiccan tradition was a last resort, 'a bit like removing one's own appendix'. It might be necessary if stranded alone in the Australian outback hundreds of miles from the nearest doctor, but it is somewhat fraught with complications.[1] When it came to editing the second edition and I read the sentence again, I felt uneasy. Intuition told me to cut it. I took the sentence out.

Now, our friend Julia is on this year's organising committee for an Australian gathering of witches and Pagans. Would we like to come and be headline speakers? The Witches of Oz sound fun, but travel has not been good for us recently. The previous September – around nine in the morning on 11 September 2001, to be precise – we were walking in downtown Manhattan, heading towards the World Trade Center's Twin Towers, en route to a meeting with Penguin Books about the book I was then writing, *The Natural Magician*.[2] We never made the meeting and the rest, as they say, is history. Chris thought that, after this, Australia sounded like a nice, safe destination. We forgot that the last time we were there we ended up swimming with sharks.

The event is at the wonderfully named Kangaroobie, a cattle ranch and educational holiday centre. I start to feel a bit ill shortly after the flight to Melbourne, but think nothing of it. The jet lag for Australia is enormous. Chris and I get through the first few days of our trip, convincing ourselves that I have a stomach upset. We get to the event and meet the wonderful Australian magical and Pagan community. They are acutely aware of the sensitivities of the spirit of place and invite representatives of the Winda-Mara Aboriginal Corporation to open the event. They send a team of young men to perform a welcoming dance.

The warmth and enthusiasm of the audience is way beyond what they are used to. We understand the principles of honouring the people and spirits of the land, and this creates a connection between their practices and ours. The dancers extend their visit to spend more time with us.

We deliver our first and second workshops, but by the afternoon of the second day it is obvious something is seriously wrong. I have a stabbing pain in the lower right quadrant of my abdomen. I am pretty certain that I have appendicitis. Mel, the onsite nurse, confirms it. We are a long way from a hospital and the flying doctor cannot help. There is a major incident elsewhere and no helicopters are available. So now we are driving and I am moaning – occasionally screaming when the bump is too bad. It is a relief when we reach the smoothness of tarmacked road. We arrive at a small hospital, where they are expecting us. They rush me into a wheelchair and then to an examination room. I lie back, grateful for a stable bed. We wait. The examining doctor comes back. There are no surgeons on duty and no one is available to come in. We will have to drive to the next town, Warrnambool, where there is a larger emergency unit. He gives me a painkilling injection and we head off into the darkness.

'How much further is it?'

Another fifty kilometres. It is a long fifty kilometres.

At Warrnambool, a glamorous young doctor arrives in a white coat. 'Hi, I'm Julian.' Even in agony I can see that he is so ridiculously drop-dead gorgeous that he should be a rock star or in a Hollywood movie. The painkiller is wearing off and I am getting delirious – I want to giggle and scream at the same time. He tells me that a surgeon is being dragged away from his television to drive in. He has been watching an important home game for his Australian football team. Julian leans over me. 'You're in luck. His team won. He's in a good mood.' I fail to appreciate this male form of reassurance. He tries again. 'It's all very straightforward, simple keyhole surgery. There won't even be a scar. It will take half an hour. You'll be out of here in two or three days.'

Eventually, I am wheeled along a corridor into a small pre-theatre room. It is after midnight. Someone injects me. I slide into welcome oblivion as Chris bursts into tears.

Chris sits in a corridor, growing frantic. One hour passes, then a second. A nurse comes to see him. There are complications. The appendix has ruptured, I have peritonitis. My intestines are infected and must be pulled out and washed in saline solution, some part removed.

I wake up screaming. At least, I am vaguely aware of a piercing scream. I think it is coming from me. It seems the logical thing to do, but nurses rush in and stand over me looking shocked. Apparently, my scream has echoed from one end of the hospital to the other. They ask me to rate my pain level on a scale from one to ten. 'What's ten?' I wonder. Presumably I would not be coherent enough to ask myself this question if I were a ten. I try 'six'. They give me morphine. It blots out the pain and I take in where I am.

Chris is there. He refused to leave and has slept the night on a bed outside my door. Tentatively, I pat my stomach. It is held together by great metal staples. The pain subsides into the background of my consciousness, but large creatures like something out of *Alien* are crawling up the walls. My brain is fighting against the morphine. I sleep. I wake again in terrible pain. I realise that saying 'six' was a mistake. I learn the language of pain. I am an eight, I explain to the next nurse. She injects me with more morphine. It is woefully inadequate to see me through the night hours. The night staff will not give me morphine, and the three hours between when I wake up and the doctor coming each day are agony.

I am in a room of my own, which is great, but not a good sign in a public hospital. There are little hints though that all will be well. Bizarrely, the walls of the corridor outside my room are lined with familiar images. They are stunning photographs of the lighthouses of Brittany, the kind sold in the art galleries of our tourist towns. Quite how they ended up in a hospital in a small town in southern Australia I have no idea, but the images are comforting. In fact, the whole set-up seems like a small god's synchronistic jokes. Chris and I have used the name 'Aurora' for many of our magical groups. The plaque on my bedhead reads, 'Bed donated by the students of Aurora House.' The hospital phone number ends in 666. I find comfort in these little jokes from the universe.

All the techniques I have learned are now crucial. I adapt to the morphine. I see the hallucinations, but I can distance myself from them. The long years of meditation practice help. One part of my brain sees them; the other watches me watching them. I focus on my breath and ignore them, leaving them to crawl up and down the wall at will. After a couple of days they go away, leaving only the pain. I need a mantra, words to breathe with to manage the pain. I search my mental repertoire of magical texts, but nothing seems right. Those words are designed for intense, focused energy, for spells and rituals. I need something repetitive to occupy my brain.

The Buddhist words for taking refuge come to me, those I have chanted in temples and meditation halls:

Buddham saranam gacchami.
Dhammam saranam gacchami.
Sangham saranam gacchami.

I take my refuge in the Buddha.
I take my refuge in the Dharma.
I take my refuge in the Sangha.

But my Sangha is the magical community, not the Buddhist community. I change the words: 'I take my refuge in the Goddess. I take my refuge in her teaching. I take my refuge in her community.' It flows less well, but by repeating the three phrases in my mind when the pain is at its worst, I can regulate my breathing to an even rhythm. I resist my mind's attempts to fight the pain, instead allowing it to be what it is.

As my mind quietens, I find I can move the pain to one side of my brain, freeing up the other. I park it in the right hemisphere and move my focus of awareness to the left. I stay with the breath, the eternal breath of life, floating on it as though on a great cosmic sea. A presence draws close to me. It is a feeling, not a thought – an awareness, an empathy, a love – as if the love of the universe is floating on the mind-sea beside me. An image comes into my mind. It is of the Finnish story of creation, in which Ilmater Water Mother lays the egg of the universe in the great cosmic sea.

Then an image comes of Guan Yin, Bodhisattva and goddess of compassion, who carries a phial of healing. I meditate on Guan Yin allowing her pure energy to fill me, flowing down through my chakras and over my wounds. These goddess images lessen the fire of the pain.

The people of Warrnambool show us great kindness. The local B&B offers to wash Chris's clothes. One of the nurses asks her husband to take Chris out in the afternoons, so he can get away from the hospital for an hour or two. He takes Chris whale-watching at Logans Beach, a renowned nursery for the southern right whale. Chris's description of their calves playing in the waves entrances me. It gives me an objective. I am determined to get well enough to see the whales.

At first, the antibiotics seem to be working. I am getting better. Then they cease to work. Infection is spreading and I am going down. I try visualising and praying to Sekhmet, the lioness-headed healing goddess of Egypt. I have a statue of her at home and for many magical women she is a feminist icon, a goddess of battles against both enemies and disease, but I find her energy too fiery for my pain. The cat-headed goddess Bast is gentler, and visualising her helps. Her energy is more like the warmth of the sun. Her presence brings comfort, but the colours my mind needs most are blue, white and violet, the colours of the card of the High Priestess in the tarot. Her image and that of Guan Yin overlap. The High Priestess holds the Book of Knowledge, not the phial of healing. Yet the two converge for me, different images from different traditions overlapping in what they represent.

We are into week two and I have not been able to eat. I am becoming worse and getting thin, very thin, and cold, so cold. The freezing southern wind blows up from the Antarctic here, up through the open doors of the hospital, along the corridors, up the stairwell, into my room, into my veins. My arm is a bruised mess of drip feeds – saline, antibiotics. My buttock bones protrude so much they are painful to sit on. The room has no private bathroom so I force myself to make trips to the toilets, wheeling my drip along with me like a crutch. I look at myself in the mirror. I am yellow, skeletal and look like a seventy-year-old. As my body declines, I start to journey into the Otherworld. The pathworkings into death that I visualised with my cancer patients I now visualise for myself. I practise leaving my body and travelling the route. I want to be able to do it easily if my body suddenly fails me, for things are taking a darker turn.

One night I find myself being pushed on a trolley down a dark tunnel. At the end is a blinding light. Dead friends and relatives are waiting to greet me. I move through the light. I feel euphoric. I float out of my body and look down on myself. I look peaceful in the bed, and the feeling of lightness of being is sensational. It is a long time since I have had an out-of-the-body experience. Now I am free from pain and there is a sense of another world awaiting. There is a sound, a beautiful sound. I long to go forward into the sound, into the embrace of the people who are standing in the white-gold light.

What comes to me in the darkness of the night, when I feel near to death? I remember those things I have done with and for others – my marriage with Chris, friendships, building magical communities, teaching, writing, and experiences of transcendence in nature and in ritual. What seem important are living my truth; moments of pure joy, not material possessions; the magical books I have written, not my research reports. The things we ultimately value are those that express our core values and engage the whole of our being – the authentic self. Our experiences are our inner possessions, what we carry inside us. External possessions are merely luggage that we must discard before the journey. Dying is a no-baggage-only flight.

And when death approaches, there comes a point where it is OK for things to end. Life runs its course and, while we do not want to cause grief for our relatives and friends by going, we have completed our task and their lives are their responsibility now. There is a beauty in that closure, a peace, and the nearer it approaches, the less we have any desire to cling on. Nor is there any concern about the future, or desperation for continuation. Like a good book or film, it is time to finish the story and to await any sequel that may or may not come.

I hover on the edge of temptation. It feels as though I can let down the burden of the body and go forward. I want to go forward, *but Chris?* I wake up into a dual awareness. There is the light and the tempting vision, but I know I cannot leave Chris and I have work still to do here. I descend back into my body and unbearable pain. I come to in the half-light of dials and gauges that is a hospital room. Now I am frightened, really frightened. I am not ready to die yet. I fall asleep thinking, *Something has to be done – soon.*

Chris has been spending all day by my bedside, going back each night to the bed and breakfast found for him by the hospital. I wake up as he comes into the room. It is morning. 'We must get magical help,' I tell him, 'and a do-it-yourself will pack.' It occurs to me that dying intestate in Australia could lead to endless complications.

Chris goes to an internet café and starts contacting magical friends all over the world, asking them to visualise at a specific time me getting out of bed strong and well. Hundreds of people respond. I am awed by the outpouring of love, empathy and connection. Chris works out the best time for the healing, given the complications of time zones, so bathed in sunshine I lie on the bed while Chris holds my hand. I feel strange, vulnerable. Usually I am a healer, the strong one who does magic for others. Now I am the one to be healed.

We open our psyches. I have no expectations; I empty myself and wait. Then it comes – a tingling golden light, like energy flowing into my body. I drink it in through every cell, every pore, absorbing and absorbing until I can absorb no more. I lose consciousness and fall asleep.

I wake up in the afternoon. Chris is there. I am relaxed, but I have a desperate craving for carrot juice. I do not particularly like carrot juice, but the craving becomes intense. 'Could you find me carrot juice?' I ask Chris. 'Freshly juiced?' He looks doubtful but sets off to scour Warrnambool for a juice bar – amazingly, he finds one. I drink the juice down, every drop, at last something I can eat. There is something in it my body needs – Vitamin A? I do not know. Chris goes back for more.

We sit quietly into the evening. There is a softness in the room, a stillness, a golden energy, peace. I manage to sit up. The nurses leave the door of my room open so they can pop in and out. An emaciated man in street clothes comes to the doorway. I have never seen him before. He is close to tears, saying how terrible it is that this should happen to us on our holiday, but we sense that this is not what his distress is about. He is being drawn to the healing energy still in the room. I invite him to come in, to sit down. 'How about you?' I ask. He has Hodgkin's lymphoma. He has just had a second course of treatment and today they discovered a new lump. He has already lost three stone in weight and is very frightened. We talk to him, giving him time and space. A nurse comes and it breaks the moment. He goes. I hope he has benefited.

I wake up the next morning. For the first time, I have slept through the night. Chris has yet to come from the B&B. Without thinking about it, I get out of bed and unclip the drip. I go to the bathroom. I look at myself in the mirror; I am less yellow. I shower and put on clothes. I put on jewellery – amber earrings and an amber necklace. When I was most ill, the colour would have seemed overwhelming, but now the golden resin is smooth, warm and comforting. It brings a solar healing energy. I sit down in the armchair where Chris has spent every day since it all began. The consultant comes in on his morning rounds and looks at the empty bed.

'Where is the patient?' he asks.

'That's me.'

He stares at me. 'I didn't recognise you.'

Would I have died without the magical healing? Who knows? But the impact was immediate. One day I felt near to death. The next morning I got up from my bed and lived. I am on the road back to health.

After a few days, Chris drives me to see the whales. The calves leap, cavort and stand on their tails, graceful water acrobats. They seem entranced by the joy of doing whale stuff, just being a whale alive in the sparkling waves and under the warming sun. To watch them is healing.

When I am well enough to read email, I discover that rumours have flown around the internet. I find hundreds of well-wishers and a polite enquiry from a friend in the United States: 'It's a slightly odd question – but are you dead? Someone is posting that he attended your funeral and said a funeral oration.' I reassure him that I am indeed alive and ponder the benefits of lying low for a while. If I am dead, I do not need to answer all these emails. Maybe I need a T-shirt, I muse – 'Vivianne Crowley, not dead yet'.

Sometimes our belief in magical intervention fades. Sometimes the magic does not work, our vision fails us, and our powers weaken. I think there is a cycle of age with magic. As time goes on, the teenwitchery of early years gives way to a more meditative practice. But then there are occasions when the chips are down. When we need our gods and our powers, when we need our magical allies. When we can no longer struggle alone. Then we turn to what we know, we turn to the reservoirs of power and knowledge that are always there, if we know how to ask. We make ourselves vulnerable. We seek the help of others. We open ourselves to what we cannot imagine. We open ourselves to the power.

And if the love is strong enough, if the intent is true, then like an arrow the healing comes, the power of transmutation of one thing to another, an opening in the fabric of the universe through which change may flow.

Chris and I opened ourselves. We became a vessel, a grail, the cup of the heart waiting to be filled – and the power of healing filled that void and made me whole.

16

Journeying to the Otherworld

Journeying close to death in Australia reminds me of an insight from my childhood – our lives, though they seem long to us, they are but a grain of time. Time is short, life is fragile and the unexpected can and does happen. What have I not done that I want to do? I know I would like to write a book about spirituality and magical transformation, but not yet. I need first to attend to the things of this world.

Chris and I get back to England, our flight touching down in Bangkok on the way to pick up traumatised survivors of the Bali bombing. I collapse on the flight, and at Heathrow an ambulance delivers me back to our London home. I take a long time to recover. There are complications following the operation, and somewhere along the course of my treatment I have acquired liver damage. I suffer from extraordinary fatigue. I fall asleep without warning, sometimes when sitting up holding full cups of tea – not a good idea. Our life of freelance consulting, research, writing, teaching and extensive travel is no longer practical.

Chris takes a job in the City once more. When spring comes, I have just enough energy to do a nine-to-five job, but no more. I need a job in walking distance – one with health insurance, sickness pay for the ongoing complications, and a pension. I think about it for a while and then, when the time feels right, I read job advertisements. The gods kindly provide. I apply for the first role that looks right and get it. It is a senior research post in the public sector. It is difficult. Some days even the ten-minute walk home is too much and I need a taxi, but gradually, and after a final stint in hospital, my body repairs itself. I recover.

We step back from public teaching and step into the role of spiritual grandparents, our focus on supporting those who teach others. Now we have time to study, experiment and evolve our personal practice. We explore new avenues and new techniques. And now we are in Norway. It is our summer vacation, and we are taking the opportunity to go on a shamanic journey.

Chris drives us round the outskirts of Lillehammer, perhaps best known as the site of Norway's 1994 Winter Olympics and the eponymous Netflix series starring Steven Van Zandt homaging his role as Silvio Dante in *The Sopranos*. We head north to the Peer Gynt Vegen, the Peer Gynt Way, a dirt road open only from June, once the winter snows have gone. I find the kroner to pay the toll and we go through the barrier. The road climbs upwards. Against the skyline appear the mountains of the national park of Jotunheimen, meaning 'Giant-Home', Norway's highest peaks, where the snow never melts. We are glad now that we took the upgrade to a higher-powered car at Oslo airport.

We are in troll country. Ahead is Vinstra, home to the Peer Gynt Festival where Henrik Ibsen's play is performed outdoors to the music of Edvard Grieg's Peer Gynt suite. Ibsen's *Peer Gynt* is a magical journey into the human imagination in which the hero encounters the trolls. They like to eat humans, which makes for an image problem that takes more than a reputation management lawyer to fix. They also like to destroy homes and villages by bombarding them with rocks. Fortunately, like vampires, they can only come out at night. Trolls turn to stone in daylight, so they are creatures of the winter in Norway. We are in high summer, where daylight turns to twilight and then back to daylight again. No trolls for us today.

We are one thousand metres above sea level now, and as the road climbs above the treeline, the landscape opens out into high mound-like hills covered with scraggy grass and rocks. Some of the wooden houses have grass roofs. The scenery looks more like hobbit country than Troll-Ville, but the peaks in the distance remind me that these foothills lead to the high places beyond. It is easy to understand why the mountains ahead were thought to be the home of giants. The tourist brochures are full of images of hiking and cycling to experience Europe's wildest nature, but awe-inspiring though the scenery is, we are not here for tourism. We are to meet with a Norwegian practitioner of shamanism for a different kind of journey.

Shamanism is humankind's core religious and magical practice. It may even have existed before the first migrations out of Africa, some 70,000 years ago. At the heart of the shaman's practice is the ability to go into trance – to leave the physical body, journey into the Otherworld and return with new knowledge. The word 'shaman' is derived from a Siberian word and means 'one who knows'. Shamans are keepers of knowledge – of the herbs and words that heal; of the ways to foretell the future; of the ceremonies that smooth birth, marriage and death, and of those that mark the changing seasons. In an oral culture, they would be the memory of their people, a repository of myth, tradition, magic and song.

Our ancestors thought of the Otherworld as a geographical place. It was up there in the starry heavens, and down there in the deepest caverns of the earth. It was the home of otherworldly beings – some friendly, some unfriendly like trolls. Today, we might think of the Otherworld not as a place, but as a state. When we enter the Otherworld, our brains make a shift, our state of consciousness changes. The language of this world is visual and symbolic. It takes training and practice to understand what we see. Shamans are those trained to journey into the Otherworld and to help others to do so too.

We may think of shamanism as belonging solely to indigenous communities living a traditional lifestyle in remote places – but it is everywhere, once we know where to look. Any large city will have practising shamans. Some will be people trained in contemporary shamanic practices drawn from across indigenous traditions. Others will be shamans whose lineages go back centuries, if not longer. Some will be male, some female and some neither. In South Korea, nearly all shamans are female. In some societies, it is transgender and intersex people who are considered particularly well-suited to travelling between the worlds.

We can consult shamans on all manner of issues – health, fertility, marital and family problems, business decisions – all the everyday concerns of people everywhere. Shamans' businesses flourish because their clients usually come away satisfied. Academic researchers have endeavoured to understand how such archaic practices have survived, but the answer is simple – shamanism persists because it works.

All around the world, there has been a resurgence of shamanism, fuelled by our desire to reconnect with ancient spiritual practices. Some of the revival has been helped by anthropologists seeking to understand threatened and disappearing cultures. In 1951, the historian of religion Mircea Eliade brought out his famous book *Shamanism: Archaic Techniques of Ecstasy.*[1] Many have challenged his theories since, but the book inspired a new generation of academic researchers and spiritual seekers, and some who were both.

One of the most influential was an anthropology student at the University of California, the Peruvian-American Carlos Castaneda, who claimed to have learned shamanism from a Yaqui shaman, Don Juan Matus.[2] Carlos Castaneda's accounts of his experiences evolved into a series of twelve books that sold over 28 million copies and became the springboard for a whole international movement of shamanic revival, but many doubt that Don Juan ever existed. He may have been a composite figure based on shamans Carlos Castaneda had met, or a figure that appeared to him in his psychedelic voyages on peyote. But whatever Don Juan's origins, he became his inner guru; someone he could talk to, just as though there was a physical person sitting beside him. In creating such a figure, he was following a well-worn magical path trodden previously, not surprisingly, by the magician Aleister Crowley and his guardian angel Aiwass, but also by psychologist Carl Jung and his inner guru Philemon.

Carlos Castaneda's experiences struck a chord with a generation of spiritual seekers already familiar with Eastern gurus and psychedelic voyaging. Now there was a new source of inspiration to feed a spiritual hunger no longer satisfied by the materialistic West. Castaneda's books advocated a new way of seeing the world around us, a way of entering 'non-ordinary reality' – in other words, the magical world, the Otherworld.

One route into this world is through ingesting consciousness-altering plants such as the peyote cactus, ayahuasca vine, Datura and the psilocybin 'magic' mushroom, but these are largely illegal in Western countries. A solution for the adventurous is 'ayahuasca tourism' in Central and South America, but commercialised shamanic experiences can be physically and psychologically hazardous; for all consciousness-altering plants can have dangerous side effects when taken by the inexperienced. Methods such as drumming and guided inner journeying are less problematic and have become major ways of sharing shamanism with the world.

If we want to go on a trance journey, we can download drumming tracks from the internet, or we can drum for ourselves. Research has shown that most people can enter a trance by listening to a drumbeat in a rhythm of 4–4.5 beats per second for at least fifteen minutes.[3] Some people go into trance more quickly, and the more practised we are, the quicker it becomes. I can do it using my own bodhrán, but in Norway I go for my first journey facilitated by a skilled shamanic practitioner.

The first thing I noticed the night before was the way he moved. He was walking down from the green rounded hills, across the moss- and lichen-covered ground towards the cabins that have been hired for our week-long event. His movements were very slow, methodical, each step placed as though it mattered. When, a few years later, I go with him to a magical gathering in winter, north of the Arctic Circle, I will understand why. It is how people move when they are accustomed to wearing snowshoes.

Twenty of us sit on the grass in the sunshine outside a wooden cabin. We talk, exchanging experiences while we wait to go on the shamanic journey. We are from different countries and backgrounds, but we find common ground. We are all willing to go beyond the threshold of everyday awareness into those other states of being in which we experience the intense joy of existence in all its complexity, beauty and depth. Some talk of loneliness, of being a spiritual explorer when family and friends do not share their aspirations and values. In moments such as these, when we gather in retreats, seminars, workshops, informal groups, or even online, we can connect with those who share our ideas and beliefs. These are memories that can sustain us when the demands of everyday life seem overwhelming. They give us a store of experiences that remind us that we are not alone in our seeking. They are times of friendship and sharing that can give us the courage and inner strength to pursue our course, our personal journey into the wild places of the spirit.

We enter the cabin and draw the curtains to dim the light. Quietly, we place blankets and cushions on the floor and lie down. I am lucky and find a place on a sofa. Our journey leader does not speak. As I get to know him, I find that he rarely speaks. Later I realise it is a characteristic of the far north. In extreme climates, excess talking is a waste of energy, as is excess movement. People north of Tromsø do neither.

For a while, we lie in silence. I sit up to check what is happening, but he is simply sitting, waiting for the right time to start. I lie down again and relax. I am not in charge of this process. We have all day – a long, Norwegian summer day. There is no need to hurry. And then he begins to drum. The drum is a frame drum similar to a Native American drum or a bodhrán. Its skin is thicker than my Irish drum, the tone is deeper, and the beat is fast. I close my eyes and listen. I guess he is drumming at four beats per second, but it seems faster, louder and more insistent than when I play my own drum. Our combined body heat is raising the temperature and my head is struggling against the sound reverberating in my skull. I hover on the verge of a headache. Something in me wants to resist going down into the journey. I feel stifled, constricted. I take a deep breath as though I am diving underwater. I know that I must let go. The words of Star Trek's Borg Collective flit through my brain: *Resistance is futile.* I feel a nervous giggle, but suppress it. Then someone starts snoring in my right ear. Some of us got a bit too enthusiastic during last night's welcoming drum-in. When daylight hours are so long that it could just as well be three in the afternoon as three o'clock at night, it can be hard to remember to go to bed.

I let this thought go, and focus on my body. The itch on my right foot, the pine smell of the cabin's planks, the snore reverberating in my ear, now growing softer. I am floating away from thoughts. Floating, floating out and down, out of my body and down through the floor of the cabin, down to the space beneath where wooden struts support the floor, down to the dust and debris beneath, then down, down into the earth itself. I feel myself moving through rocks and soil. Have I become a mole? I let go of the thought, let go of my brain trying to analyse and label. I feel myself in the soil, but not in the rocks. I am soft, not hard. I flow around the rocks and out, out into the soil of the hills surrounding the cabin.

Then I sense something or someone else. Something old, another consciousness, is aware of me. I want to run away, an instinctive fear reaction, but I pause. I hover on the brink of fear, aware of the possibility but not going there. I am sensing something alien, another species of being entirely. Then I understand. The human footprint on this land is light. The soil beneath and around the cabins has been inhabited by humankind, but as I flow outward into the hills I can sense something older and deeper is alive here, another type of consciousness. Here, in the north, it can survive. This is not Brittany, or Ireland, or England, with thousands of years of human habitation. Here plough has not torn into the earth. Human beings have established few permanent settlements and have wandered over the surface much as the elk do, coming and going with the seasons, aeons passing with little change. Is the presence I sense that of the entities that Norwegian folklore tells us inhabit hills and mountains, caves and caverns? Is this what Henrik Ibsen was thinking of when he took his flawed Everyman hero Peer Gynt to meet the trolls in the Hall of the Mountain King? If so, I think the folk tales are wrong. I do not perceive these beings as opposed to humankind, but their priorities differ from ours. For those who live in soil and rock, time passes slowly. Our human lives are like a butterfly's. We will disappear. They will endure.

There is a hollow whistling sound in my ear. I become aware of the changing beating of the drum, the echoing wooden beater on the skin. It is drawing me back, but I don't want to go back. I am free somehow in my place within the earth, where the worms and insects make their home, where the sky and clouds change above me. Then I hear it, a *dum, dum, dum, dum, dum*, a fast beat that makes my heart race. My mind screams, *I don't want to come back*. Then the smell of the pine floor, the movement of the bodies around me. A smell of sweat – some of us are camping and showering is difficult. I am back. The curtains are drawn and the sunlight streams in. We blink at the brightness of the light. I have no idea how long the journey took – twenty minutes, one hour, two? It was not short, because I am very hungry.

Afterwards we talk, those of us who went on the journey. Some of us saw power animals, others ancestors from the distant past. Some flew like birds; others like me burrowed deep into the earth. Some received messages, asked questions and heard answers. For others, the journey was about seeing the world differently, from other perspectives.

Some of us have questions to ask our journey leader. Others feel the need to sit in silence. Each person's journey was different, but we share the sense that our consciousness separated from our human physical body and went to another place. For me, the journey brought a sense that other beings inhabit the earth, the spirits of soil and rock, of mountain and valley. These were the spirits that our ancestors worshipped long before we invented the gods that live in books.

For most of us nowadays, nature is beautiful but impersonal. This has not always been so. Our ancestors were animists, for whom nature and all the major features of the landscape around them were living sentient beings with personalities and consciousness. As children, we may still have an acute sense of the 'aliveness' of the world around us. A conventional education may partly suppress it, but our natural instinct is to treat other living beings and significant objects as personalities with purposes of their own. At work, we may suppress this instinct, but in our personal lives we talk to our cats, dogs, cars and computers as people.

Even if this animistic worldview seems just wishful thinking, it is a mindset that makes ecological sense. Research shows us that if we think of what is around us as having personality and purpose, it changes our interaction with it and increases conservation behaviours.[4] What happens if we think of a car or a bicycle as a living being? We think about its needs. We think about keeping it clean and caring for it. We think about its safety. This is likely to increase its lifespan, and we have less need to buy a new one. In other words, a form of animism helps us take what is around us seriously and to treat it well. This attitude can lead us to responsible behaviours that promote sustainability.

If we embrace an animist worldview, we have a different sense of the world – one in which the planet is not here to serve our purposes. It is not an inert rock to be exploited, but a living being, populated by other living beings, all of whom are just as important as us. We understand that we humans are not the pinnacle of creation, but an integral part of it, one of the many species that form the biosphere. By living, breathing and interacting, we feed one another; and together we create the atmosphere of our planet that protects us from the rays of the sun and enables biological life to flourish.

Science is revealing more and more about the interdependency of different species. One of the many systems within the wider system of the biosphere is what has been called in science journalism 'tree-net' or the 'wood-wide web'. Trees are connected to one another beneath the soil through a complex system of other organisms such as fungi. These diverse species support one another, forming a system that benefits all those who take part in it. It is a bit like a small tribe, in which individuals have different tasks and roles, all cooperating to one end – survival. Plants provide fungi with food; fungi help plants suck up water and provide nutrients such as phosphorus and nitrogen. Larger trees help smaller ones to grow by donating food to them via the fungal network, but they are not randomly altruistic. They prioritise their own offspring seedlings before other young trees, just as humans prioritise their children over those of strangers. These 'mother' trees are incredibly important. If humans kill a mother tree, then a whole system collapses.[5]

The wood-wide web is only one of the many ways in which nature creates interdependent systems that support life through a continual balancing of energies, a giving and taking, between all the living organisms in our biosphere. Indigenous and magical thinking takes us a step further, as does cognitive science. Beyond our biological connections, we are deeply interconnected on psychological and spiritual levels too. To be truly happy in the world, we need to honour our connections with all the human and non-human others around us. In this worldview, the continual exchange of energies involves not only plants and animals, but also non-physical beings and features of the landscape such as rocks, mountains and rivers. Instead of looking across a landscape and seeing solid immovable objects, we might see an interlaced mesh of cells, atoms and organisms, all giving and receiving as part of a greater whole.

If we treat other species and inorganic forms as objects to be used and disposed of as we will, we will use, consume and discard them with no sense of obligation towards them. If, conversely, we think of our lives as being in networked relationship to everything else, we will treat nature with respect, even gratitude, for its existence. A term that is often used for this relationship is 'sacred reciprocity', a translation of *ayni,* a word from the Quechua language of some of the peoples of the Andes. Sacred reciprocity is more than a description of the exchange of energies. It implies an ethical relationship between the parts and the whole that involves responsibilities towards all of our planet's creation.

The drum journey in Norway leaves me with a sense of profound gratitude. The aliveness I sense in soil and rock is an experience that fills me with hope for the Earth – our planet and home. Perhaps what humankind is destroying can be replenished. Perhaps we can learn to live differently; and, if not, there are older consciousnesses than ours with their own purposes, and they can survive and outlive our new upstart species.

These thoughts give me hope, but also a deep sense of peace. In centuries to come, perhaps humankind's conflict with nature can be resolved, or perhaps not. But whatever the outcome, I sense that the Earth and its biosphere can endure. I hope this will include human beings. And if we are to endure, we must find our way back into our relationship with nature, back to a rewilding of the spirit.

17

Supernatural Allies

It is best in life to travel light. I zoom through international airports with hand baggage only, while others stand frustrated as the luggage carousel revolves with no sign of their suitcase. The same is true of beliefs. We must travel light and trust in our own experience. Do not accumulate doctrines. Trust in the process, letting go of outdated content. Look at the spiritual and magical teachings that the world has to offer. Take their frameworks as symbol systems and working hypotheses that we can use to guide our lives. Select with discernment those that represent our highest values, those that inspire and give us new creative energy, those that teach us love not hate.

Some of us believe in the concrete reality of deities, but more and more in the West we live in a newly lonely world. Our inner and outer worlds have been desanctified, despiritualised and depopulated. Our ancestors lived in touching distance of non-material reality; surrounded by a supernatural realm of ancestors, fairies, elves, leprechauns, kelpies, wights, trolls, totem animals, and gods small and large, to whom they could turn in times of need. For some of us, this is still true; even if how we think of otherworldly beings is quite different from the views of the generations of yester-year. There may be gods, angels or spirits with whom we feel a special connection as the gods or spirits of our people or of our land. We may venerate a single deity, or we may speak with different beings that can cover all the myriad issues of life. We may feel a deep connection with parents or grandparents whose love and wisdom reaches out to us from behind the veil. These are our supernatural allies, and we can find them in the most unlikely places.

When the first edition of my book *Wicca* is published in 1989, it hits the zeitgeist. Each of us who writes about the magical tradition sees it through the lens of our own per-sonality and life experiences. My book is a vision of Wicca as a personal transformatory path, a way to reconnect to the deeper self.

Witches make good copy, and newspapers have always loved stories of the shock, horror and 'aren't these people weird' variety, but my book speaks more widely to the spiritual needs of the time. In an era of rising feminism, environmentalism and the spiritual void of post-Christian-ity, there is a hunger for new alternatives. The *Guardian* is the first to ask me for a major interview. The *Telegraph*, the *Spectator*, *Time Out* and women's magazines, of course, fol-low. The publishers advise me against putting a contact address at the back of the book, but I want to open avenues for readers seeking contact with the magical community. Thousands of letters flood in from all around the world. I take on the role of international co-ordinator of the Pagan

Federation. I set up an international network of contacts for those seeking Wicca and other magical and Pagan groups. Eventually it becomes a stand-alone organisation – Pagan Federation International.

Most letters are easy to deal with – people wanting information. Some are entertaining. Boy magicians write in asking if I would like to take them on in magical battle. Priests say they have asked their congregations to pray for me. A vicar's wife writes to ask if I think it is OK for their parish to continue having a five-pointed star on their church tower at Christmas. Why she thinks I am the right person to ask is deeply puzzling, but I reply that it is only a pentagram if they think it is – intention is all. Five points have always been fine for them. Why change?

Other letters give me real pause for thought. An elderly Irish man writes to say that he has seen my photograph in the *Guardian* and something drew him to it. He has cut out the photograph, put it in a frame and he now prays to me instead of praying to the Virgin Mary, and with better results. This is an ethical dilemma I was not anticipating. I am not answering his prayers, so do I tell him to stop? But if he finds it comforting, and he does sound rather lonely, who am I to deprive him? Something that my mother told me years before comes to mind: 'Everyone lives in their own reality, dear, and they're much happier that way.'

I try to think what is true for me about what he is saying, and I write:

Dear Matthew,

It was lovely to get your letter. I am glad that you find your prayers are being answered. All our sincere

> prayers ultimately go to the Divine source of all things and there are many pathways to the Divine …

He continues to write from time to time, then his letters stop. I sense that he has passed in peace through the veil to whatever lies beyond. I am glad that I could have been a source of comfort to him, even if answering prayers is rather beyond my remit. I prefer to leave it to the dead.

Chris and I are connoisseurs of all manner of places of pilgrimage – Christian, Pagan, Hindu, Jewish, Muslim. Many of the most powerful have existed for thousands of years. A place that is evocative draws human worshippers for generation after generation. The branding may change, standing stones may give way to chapels or mosques, but the sense of devotion that the place evokes does not. Other shrines, though, are not ancient. They become places of pilgrimage almost overnight.

One of the most moving places we see is in Chile. We are invited to run workshops there for people who are interested in exploring Western magical traditions. In between workshops and ceremonies, our hosts Madelaine and Felipe take us to a shrine, the Sanctuary of the Wind, at the entrance of an abandoned railway tunnel in Cajón del Maipo, a canyon in the Andes south-east of the Chilean capital, Santiago. Here, in July 1998, eighteen-year-old Guillermo Antonio Rojas Reyes – known as Willy – came to commit suicide. In a farewell note, he asked his family to visit him in this lonely place in the mountains. His family honoured his wish and built a small memorial shrine at the tunnel mouth. Each month when they visited, they left a child's windmill at the shrine. Soon, other visitors began to add to the memorial. Teddy bears, toys, flowers, poems, rosaries, coins – all manner of objects were left, initially with the intention of honouring Willy's memory. But then the shrine morphed. Somewhere along the chain of devotional actions, the emphasis switched.

People now pray to Willy, or Willito, 'Little Willy', as he is affectionately known, and he answers their prayers. Toy windmills and small weather vanes propel the prayers down the tunnel for Willito to hear. He was a football fan, so football scarves and shirts adorn the shrine from those seeking his assistance with sporting fixtures. Visitors leave letters with requests and votive plaques in thanks for Willito's help. Like the tragic deaths of many young people, no one knows exactly why this much-loved, talented and football-loving student took his own life; but by an imaginative transformation, each year made more powerful by the thousands of visitors to the shrine, Willy has transitioned from victim to quasi-saint.

I had never felt the need to accumulate a backup team of supernatural intermediaries. Contemporary magic relies much more on the human mind, but as the decades pass I find my worldview shifting. It becomes more animist, influenced by powerful experiences of ghosts and the spirits of place. If places have presence and personality, if the dead still linger and wander, if trees, animals, even rocks have awareness, perhaps I should explore how to make more non-human friends?

Chris and I have always venerated deities, but these are big gods, not ones to be troubled by trivial human matters. All throughout the history of human spiritual yearnings, we have filled our imaginations with intermediary layers of fairies, angels, demons and other beings. I feel no great emotional connection with any of these, but then I discover the Olympic Spirits. Now my go-to supernatural allies for mundane matters are these almost-forgotten gods that have survived in obscure books of ritual magic. The Olympic Spirits become for me what the Orishas are to a Voudou practitioner. They are friends and allies that I can turn to when in need.

One of Terry Pratchett's Discworld series is a wonderful novel called *Small Gods*. The underlying premise was well-known to our ancestors and makes perfect magical sense. Gods need our energies in order to stay 'alive'. The more we believe in them, the more powerful they become. 'There are billions of gods in the world', writes Terry. 'Most of them are too small to see.' They are not worshipped because 'what they lack is *belief*.'[1] I could echo Terry Pratchett and call the Olympic Spirits small gods, except that they never appear small – just the opposite, in fact. When I first start tentatively connecting with them, it is like waking a sleeping giant; long dormant because not many people go knocking at their door.

For our ancestors, the heavens were a mysterious place, and the movements of the planets and stars were interpreted by astrology and myth to explain the world around us. Astrology is based on a human-centric view of the cosmos, in which humankind is the summit of creation, the Earth is the centre of the universe and the seven 'planets' rotate around us. Nowadays, we know of course that some of these are not planets at all, but the Sun, Moon, Mercury, Venus, Mars, Jupiter and Saturn are still known as planets for the purposes of astrology and magic. These seven heavenly bodies were some of the brightest objects that could be seen in the sky in pre-telescope days, so our ancestors felt they must have special significance. They became goddesses and gods in many ancient religions.

One of the oldest ideas in the Western magical tradition is that particular energies are associated with particular planets. Whole magical systems were devised to create talismans to attract planetary energies. In the dualistic thinking of the monotheistic era, the energy of the planets was divided into good and bad. Rather than a harmonious universe, in which the aim is to achieve a balance of energies, the focus was now on accentuating the good and expelling the bad. Contacting the 'good' aspect of the planetary energy was angelic and permissible, but contacting the 'bad' was demonic; except, of course, that this is not how it works. If we think of the planetary energies as psychological characteristics that we might want to enhance in our lives, what might happen if we decide to identify with the energy of Mars, god of athletics and war? Initially, we become more energetic, more assertive, more active, more achieving. If we continue to accentuate the Mars energy beyond this point, the cauldron tips and we scald ourselves. We have an excess of Mars energy – assertive becomes aggressive, energetic becomes frenetic – and the cauldron spills and pours forth anger and pain. The energy of Mars is not in itself good or bad, but the amount of it can be. Too little and we are wimpish and ineffectual; too much and we are aggressive and violent. This is how planetary energy works.

Not many people know about the Olympic Spirits. You have to be the kind of geeky person who enjoys poring over grimoires. Johnny Depp's obsessive character Dean Corso in Roman Polanski's film *The Ninth Gate* is only marginally hyped from reality, but nowadays most of those obscure manuscripts that magicians lust after no longer have to be prised from the grasping fingers of mad book-hoarders who would kill for the sight of a long-lost grimoire. The magical manuscripts of the British Library, the Wellcome Library, Edinburgh University's alchemical collection, the Warburg Institute's Magic and Science collection, the Bibliothèque Nationale in Paris, Amsterdam's Bibliotheca Philosophica Hermetica aka the Ritman Library (courtesy of a donation from *The Da Vinci Code*[2] author Dan Brown), and dozens of others can be accessed online. Even the Vatican Library is letting some of its hoarded manuscripts digitally loose.

The Olympic Spirits make their first appearance in the *Arbatel of Magick*, a small book incorporated into the astrologer and physician Robert Turner's 1655 English translation of the *Fourth Book of Occult Philosophy*, attributed to the famous German lawyer and magician Cornelius Agrippa.[3] The authorship of the *Arbatel* is unknown, and Agrippa's authorship of the *Fourth Book* itself was not claimed until a couple of decades after his death. In the spiritual and magical worlds, it is perfectly usual to find long-dead people writing books. Dead Tibetan lamas do it all the time. Or, failing dead people, books are dictated by gods or angels, preferably on mountaintops. A sacred book is much more revered under the name of a renowned authority or a supernatural source, and there is another advantage beyond celebrity endorsement. In some times and cultures, it is much safer for the author of magical books to be conveniently dead.

The *Arbatel* gives the names of the seven Olympic Spirits and their attributes.[4] Phul is known as Lord of the Powers of the Moon and Supreme Lord of the Waters. Phaleg is the War-Lord and his planet is Mars. Ophiel transmits the energy of Mercury, planet of transactions and travel, and is described as appearing in a multiplicity of forms including a king riding a bear, a fair young man, a dog, a magpie, and clothes of changeable colours. Bethor's energy is that of Jupiter, and he can transport precious stones through the air. Hagith brings the energy of Venus and transmutes copper into gold. Aratron's powers are those associated with the planet Saturn and confer the power of invisibility. He manifests exotically guised as a bearded king riding a dragon, and more mundanely as an owl. Och is associated with the Sun and, apparently, has the power to extend human life to six hundred years while keeping the lucky person in perfect health. This sounds particularly unlikely, but he does have the more mundane attributes of bestowing health, healing and charisma – all the traditional solar attributes in astrology. I notice that they are all male. This is definitely a boys' club. Their descriptions are archaic and alien, their attributes unconvincing. Yet there is something about them that I like. I decide to make friends.

If I backtrack through the strange symbolic language of magic to analyse the attributes of the Olympic Spirits, I can make sense of them, but this is a symbolic language of half a millennium or more ago. It is not mine. Instead, I meditate upon the sigils or symbolic call signs of the seven

Olympic Spirits, to see what happens. For the meditations, I light a candle of a colour that is associated with the planetary energy of the spirit, and I allow a space to form in my psyche. It is like a sphere in my consciousness, an empty vacuum that contains no thought. In this state of no-thought, I wait and listen. I will give it as long as it takes for a sound, image or other sensation to form. I start with Ophiel.

After a time, I sense a movement in my psyche – a fragrance, a waft of a scent like blossom. I wait, then a sound like a clear ringing bell, silvery, high. Then a movement and colour, like the flapping of iridescent wings, a breeze on the face from moving air. A form starts to appear, enormously tall, shimmering with rainbow light, like sunlight reflecting off glass or clear water. The form moves upwards, taking off, flying, as though the walls and ceiling of the room have dissolved. Now we are outside, somewhere high above the cloud layer, laughing, playing and flying in shimmering sunlight and rainbow iridescence. There is something light, pure and marvellous about this vision, a strange clarity that I had not expected. I come back down to earth in my room. The walls become solid again. I am intrigued, surprised that meditating on these obscure spirits should be so intense.

Planet by planet, I work my way through meditative encounters with the Olympic Spirits. The images that come to me bear no resemblance to those of the archaic grimoire. No bearded kings ride in on dragons – on second thoughts, that is not quite true. Sometimes the traditional image does turn up, but almost as a joke. It dissolves and the energy behind it creates a form that speaks to me, a woman of my era and culture. The images remain male – mostly. The image of the Venusian spirit Hagith manifests as a queen in a green robe and copper jewellery with the occasional emerald. An intense smell of incense and roses precedes her. She is a spirit of erotic sensuality. Ophiel hovers somewhere in between, not really any one gender. Aratron, the Olympic Spirit of Saturn, appears as an older male figure, but occasionally as an older woman too. Whatever the gender, the Saturnian images convey wisdom, depth, a connection with earthly matters.

When we allow visual images to associate themselves with a concept, then that concept becomes more real for us. When we meditate over time on the image, it becomes more solid, three-dimensional. It is like pressing a button in the psyche and a hologram appears, a hologram that can speak and interact with us.

I adopt the Olympic Spirits and, over time, our relationship deepens. Their forms become more stable and manifest more quickly. Despite their size, there is something homely about them. When I meditate on them, it is like taking up a conversation where I left off before. It feels as though they are pleased to be woken, pleased that humans are taking an interest. It feels OK to chat to them about everyday concerns and to ask for their aid. Hardly anyone has spoken to them for centuries. Now someone is, they are enjoying themselves. I find them life-enhancing, even entertaining. Phaleg, the Olympic Spirit of Mars, lumbers around the house barely able to bring his form down to a size that will fit ceiling height. It is like having an enormous dog bashing about the furniture. I sit hyper-alert on the edge of my seat, in case he knocks something over.

After a few months, I make my first request. Sometimes we feel we need a magical boost to begin a new activity, or to let go and end something. Other times, we sense that we have reached the critical point when a magical intervention will give us the impetus to take something to a new level. Often, magic is simply a matter of putting ourselves in the right mindset to pay attention to detail and to focus on what we are doing. It is like oiling the wheels of everyday life. Sometimes we just need some magic to smooth the path.

After our experience in New York on 9/11, the ruptured appendix in Australia, a near miss with an IRA bomb, the mountain road we were travelling on in India during the monsoon season disappearing in front of us into an abyss under a bombardment of falling mud and boulders, and various other hazards, I still love travel but I am beginning to wonder how many of my nine lives I have used up. Chris wonders too, especially as I will be travelling to the States again – this time alone. We have annual travel insurance for mundane matters, but some additional astral insurance is good too. I am in need of a travel talisman. Who do we call? Ophiel!

Magic has always been a matter of timing. There are traditionally particular days, moon phases and times of day when it is appropriate to contact each planetary energy. If we do our magical acts at these appointed times, it gives them greater impetus and we will have more confidence they will work. If we are more confident, we are more likely to believe it. If we believe in it, we will open ourselves to the experiences that can make it happen.

On a Wednesday, the day of Mercury, Chris makes an eight-sided orange talisman with the symbol of Mercury on one side and Ophiel's sigil on the other. We light eight orange candles – eight and orange being the number and colour of Mercury in the magical tradition. We burn an incense containing ingredients associated with Mercury, and in the warm scent and orange glow of the candles we ask Ophiel for his protection. My journey passes smoothly and safely.

This kind of magic is transactional. Supernatural friends like gifts, offerings of appreciation – who doesn't? But what to buy or make for an iridescent airborne spirit? An image comes to me. It is Giambologna's beautiful 1580 statue of winged Mercury. He is naked but for a winged helmet and sandals. In one hand, he holds his caduceus wand; with the other, he points to the sky. Forever ready for take-off, he is poised on one foot in an arabesque borne up on a column of air blown from the mouth of the wind god Zephyrus. Once Giambologna's Mercury graced the gardens of the Villa Medici in Rome, but now he lives in the Museo Nazionale del Bargello in Florence in the divine company of Michelangelo's Bacchus and Apollo. The priceless original is 1.8 metres tall. Maybe a smaller copy would be acceptable, but where can I get a copy of a Giambologna? The answer pops into my head, perhaps courtesy of Ophiel. *Amazon.* I check. I had not thought of Amazon as a god-deliverer, but sure enough, Amazon can get us one, not from Italy but from Spain.

Chris and I track its three-day progress over the Pyrenees, and then north and west through France via various logistics hubs to rural Brittany. The copy is perfect and one-sixth of the size. We offer it to Ophiel with incense and thanks and display it. Ophiel now feels a presence in our lives. He brings to us a certain quality of lightness and laughter, of fluidity and shape-shifting, a feeling of joy.

All the different deities and supernatural beings that human imagination has created over the aeons live within the collective unconscious of humankind. The ancient gods sleep within us, and will awaken if we turn to them. They represent realities that go beyond the boundaries of the present knowledge or imagination of humankind; companions on our voyages on the sea of consciousness, our flights into the realms of psyche and of spirit. Facebook is replete with magical groups where people exchange their opinions about magic and, like all e-groups, the same debates appear over and over again. 'Are the gods real?' is a perennial favourite, one that misses the point entirely. To think of gods and spirits as energies in the psyche leaves our options open. We can enjoy their presence in our lives, while maintaining a cheerful agnosticism about their ultimate metaphysical reality. And the more important question is not whether gods are real, but: 'Do your interactions with your gods, supernatural allies, or God or Goddess if you prefer only one, enhance the quality of your life and make your heart sing?' If not, maybe forget about it, or change your supernatural allies.

18

Flying with the Phoenix

It takes a very persuasive Polish witch friend to convince Chris and me to take an evening flight from London Stansted in August at the height of the English school holidays. Our flight is jam-packed with Polish families heading home to see grandparents, plus fold-up pushchairs, screaming babies, fretful children and copious amounts of luggage. It is not the best start to a magical conference. 'Magic' and 'conference' are not words that many people put together. It is certainly a long way from how I began my magical life. We were more likely to be dancing naked in the woods by moonlight than sitting in chairs in conference halls.

Chris and I are heading for Kraków, once capital of the Kingdom of Poland. Legend says it was built above the cave of a fire-breathing dragon, and it has long been a magnet for magical practitioners. Kabbalists, alchemists and astrologers have all found their way to Kraków, but not on Ryanair. Agni and her organising team have convinced us, however, that a summer gathering with international experts is just what Poland's young enthusiasts for all things magical and witchy most need.

Most of the speakers are flying in from England, for Britain is the hub of the European magical revival. Through accidents of geography and a seventeenth-century Civil War that turned people off religious extremism, in England magic has flourished. But like all currents of thought, there are ebbs and flows. After our experiences in Australia and a need to attend to worldly priorities, Chris and I have been exploring and evolving our personal practice, working with friends privately and no longer publicly teaching. But now there is a shift, a change in the current. Something is stirring in the collective psyche. Magic is becoming mainstream. Treadwell's Bookshop in Bloomsbury, central London, has become an esoteric magnet, a hub presided over lovingly by former academic Dr Christina Oakley Harrington. New generations of teenwitches are discovering black clothing, tattoos and piercings, tarot and spells, but magic is appealing to others too. In our postmodern multicultural world, old rational certainties dissolve. There is an openness to alternative views of reality that is not confined to the esoteric few. Treadwell's is a meeting point between contemporary magical practitioners and academics who research the history of magic – the twenty-first-century equivalent of a nineteenth-century literary and occult salon. Doers and thinkers gather for an ever-expanding menu of talks, workshops and gatherings. The aesthetic is #darkacademic, the ambiance enhanced by a comfy sofa and a chaise longue. The downstairs reading area is redolent of magicians past, with a fireplace rescued from Parc Garland, the Cornish home of artist Pamela (Pixie) Colman Smith, illustrator of the iconic Waite-Smith tarot and a member of the nineteenth-century magical group the Hermetic Order of the Golden Dawn.

The flame of the magical current is burning strong, and the witchy, the occult, the academic, they all have their teachers and students. But Chris and I feel something else is needed – times of quiet reflection, contemplation and meditation. We begin to offer meditation evenings at Treadwell's, an eclectic mix of techniques – magical visualisation and journeying, concentrative and mindfulness meditation in the context of a magical and Pagan worldview. It opens a whole new strand in our magical work. We find ourselves being drawn back into public magical teaching. Juggling our commitments becomes more and more difficult. Our finances are more stable now. We have paid off mortgages and saved some money. We decide to give up the day jobs.

I do not let go completely of the world of analytical thought. My need to balance intuition and intellect is still strong. I return part-time to academia and find myself attending conferences at universities from Stockholm to Cambridge, from Cork to Los Angeles. The academic world has gone through a sea change. I am astonished at the amount of academic research into magical and Pagan spirituality. The study of magic is no longer the obscure interest of a few dusty professors in libraries of leather-bound books. There is a new willingness to engage with the realm where creativity and spiritual imagination meet.

Most academics are coy. They position their interest in magic as purely intellectual. 'Of course, we don't *do* magic' – except that some of us do. The gap between theory and practice is narrowing. In 2014, I attend the Visions of Enchantment: Occultism, Spirituality and Visual Culture conference, a collaboration between the University of Cambridge and the Arts University Bournemouth. It draws an international audience that I would never have thought to see assembled in the precincts of a Cambridge college. There are professors from leading universities, historians of art from famous museums, magicians, witches, artists, film-makers, and many who are two or more of these. Important scholars, such as Antoine Faivre of the Sorbonne, Emilie Savage-Smith of the University of Oxford, M. E. Warlick of the University of Denver and Marco Pasi of the University of Amsterdam, discuss art, alchemy, esotericism, witchcraft, ritual magic and Paganism. Lunchtime is enlivened by elderly professors wandering about the quadrangles of Aleister Crowley's alma mater with Marco Pasi's *Aleister Crowley and the Temptation of Politics* tucked under their arms. Nearly seventy years after his death, the 'Great Beast 666' is rehabilitated and intellectually respectable. Would he have been surprised? Maybe not. As musicians and artists will know, the culturally outrageous can become the respectable norm in less than the blink of an eye.

Over time, our meditation sessions at Treadwell's evolve in their demographic. Wicca and magic are spreading out from the English-speaking world into new countries. With the advent of cheap flights and the European Union's open borders policy, millions of Europeans from former Soviet satellite states arrive in England to work and to study. At one meditation session, we have twenty-five nationalities. Most of our attendees have come to England primarily for work, but some have come specifically to study magic.

One young Polish woman shows me her copy of my book *Wicca*, and tells me that she learned English so she could read it.

The traffic is not just one-way. The upsurge of interest in Wicca and other magical traditions leads to invitations to teach in Central and Eastern Europe and, for the first time, we are in Poland. Once we walk around Kraków's cobbled streets and the walled citadel of its medieval castle, we can see why. Poland's ancient royal capital is the perfect romantic setting for a magical event. So too is our conference hotel, with its decaying *fin de siècle* aura, art nouveau decor, high ceilings, tarnished gilt mirrors, chandeliers and haunted corridors.

In the United States and England, magic has been out of the closet for a couple of decades, and magical gatherings in hotels have become part of the normal witchy calendar. I am not quite sure how this will play out in Catholic Poland. The conference title is 'Spiritual Alchemy' but the hotel staff are catching on that this is not a typical conference. There are the usual trappings of projector, screen and neat rows of incredibly uncomfortable function chairs, but the witches, magicians and interested enthusiasts who turn up on Saturday morning look more like a rock concert audience than academic researchers. There is that same edgy excitement, for what our organisers are offering is much more than a programme of lectures. Later, Chris and I will lead them into an experience that many have never had before – a full-scale magical rite. This is the very first gathering of its kind in Poland. It feels like a new era is about to begin.

This is what our audience gathered in Kraków are hoping for – a positive alchemical change. Like young people all around the world, their future is uncertain and potentially dark. In Poland, the heady freedom of the post-Communist era has given way to a current of right-wing politics, anti-Semitism, homophobia and attempts to suppress women's rights. Bizarrely, given Poland's history, some young people are even labelling themselves Nazis; but the young radicals attracted to our conference have a different vision. Idealistic magicians throughout history have found themselves in trouble with kings, dictators, Nazis, Communists and fundamentalists of all kinds. In our current era, the magical vision of wanting a cleaner, greener and more sustainable future is less a utopian ideal than an urgent necessity. In turning to magic, Polish young people – like their counterparts across the planet – are developing a set of values and goals that goes beyond material aspirations, to a different vision of what they want their future to be. Chris and I want to support them. They are artists, writers, IT geeks, entrepreneurs, innovators, vegans, animal rights activists, feminists, LGBTQI+ and beyond, and we know that to resist the hostile currents around them, they will need to be resilient and to feel empowered to create change.

There is always a nerve-wracking moment before speaking to a new audience. Will they understand what I am talking about? I am not about to give them a talk about how to do spells or make potions, something quite straightforward in the witchy world, but rather a lecture on something that draws on Poland's magical history – spiritual alchemy. Kraków is steeped in alchemy. Our hotel is opposite the former royal residence of Wawel Castle where Kraków's very own sixteenth/seventeenth-century alchemist Michael

Sendivogius persuaded the Polish king Stephen Báthory to build an alchemical laboratory. Michael Sendivogius's generation of magicians thought of alchemy as a science, but one that would only work if the magician was in a particular state of spiritual consciousness. This involved meditative prayer and fasting. With the evolution of scientific knowledge, most alchemists gave up magical science for secular chemistry, but some continued with the spiritual practices. Alchemy evolved from the transmutation of one metal into another into something more subtle – the transformation of the alchemist.

For its practitioners, spiritual alchemy was powerful but dangerous. Its worldview took them way beyond the confines of Christian orthodoxy into the heresies that could lead to torture and death. To communicate their practice, alchemists produced books of beautiful symbolic images that only those taught by another alchemist could understand. Over the centuries, their meaning was lost, but the symbols still linger deep in the human collective unconscious.

It was Carl Jung who in the early twentieth century rediscovered the key to the alchemical images through a series of dreams. He dreamt that next to his house was another wing or annex. There, he found a wonderful library with sixteenth- and seventeenth-century books full of curious engravings and illustrations with strange symbols.[1] Later, he identified them as alchemical symbols and he discovered that many of his patients dreamt of similar symbols. He then had an insight. The stages of the alchemical process – the breaking down of base matter into its component parts, cleansing it and reconstituting it into precious gold – reflected the process of inner transformation in the human psyche to become who and what we truly are; in other words, the process of individuation that leads to the authentic self.

Magicians work with archetypal images because they stimulate the psyche. They are concepts of great emotional resonance that take their shape and form from the culture in which they manifest. In medieval and Renaissance alchemy, different birds symbolised the stages of the alchemical transformation process from base matter into gold. One of the most important of all the alchemical birds is the phoenix.

I have been inspired by the symbolism of the phoenix ever since I read the children's book *The Phoenix and the Carpet*,[2] in which a magic carpet takes the child protagonists into other dimensions. As a child, I did not believe in magic carpets, but the book stuck in my mind. This book and others like it hinted at those breakthroughs in consciousness that take us through the veil into other realms. There seemed to be much more to the story than met the eye. Given that author Edith Nesbit was a member of the Hermetic Order of the Golden Dawn, the clues about magic were most likely intentional.

In spiritual alchemy, the phoenix represents the culmination of the purpose of the Great Work, which is the transformation of the consciousness and personality of the magician, and the birth of the authentic self. The phoenix can also symbolise the transformation of societies and of groups. This was why I called my book about the twentieth-century Pagan revival *Phoenix from the Flame*.[3]

The phoenix and similar magical birds are found in many different cultures. For us, birds may seem commonplace, ordinary, but for our ancestors the migrations of birds to unknown places and back again, their ability to fly upwards towards the realms of the gods, and their heavenly songs made them creatures of myth and mystery. The phoenix myths vary according to their origins, but all agree that the phoenix is a rare, wondrous and powerful portent. To the ancient Greeks, the phoenix was a bird with beautiful fiery plumage whose coming foretells great events. It lives in Arabia and every morning, as dawn breaks and the sun rises, it bathes in the cool clear water of a well, then sings such a sweet and delightful song that the Sun God stops to listen. The phoenix lives for five hundred years, and when it senses its life is coming to an end, it builds a nest of aromatic, highly flammable cinnamon bark. This self-ignites into flowing, wing-like flames. The fire consumes the phoenix to ashes, but from the ashes a new phoenix rises. The newly reincarnated phoenix wraps the ashes of its old body in an egg of myrrh, and flies with it to the city of Heliopolis in Egypt, the City of the Sun. Here the phoenix lays the egg of ashes on the altar of the Sun God Ra, and the ever-renewing cycle begins once again.

The story of the phoenix is a magical myth, a collective imagining that expresses important truths and messages that can be understood on many levels. For young children who hear their elders retelling the ancient myths of their people, they are exciting bedtime stories. As we get older, we understand that there are messages in the myths, about our culture's worldview and relationship with its gods. We may also discover yet another layer of meaning – that myths convey eternal truths about psychological growth and change. The phoenix is a symbol of creative power. It re-creates itself from fire and is born anew. The message is one of spiritual maturity. No teacher, guru, priestess or priest can effect this transformation for us. It is one that we can and must do for ourselves. But this transformation is not gained without being willing to let go of the old self – releasing the old to make way for the new.

Our audience in Kraków has coped well with the uncomfortable chairs and the strain of listening to me talk phrase by phrase in English followed by a Polish translation. It is time for a change of energy, movement in body and mind; a time to internalise the ideas to create something new. We spread out coloured pens and paints on a table. Then we unroll an outline image of a phoenix that Chris has drawn on poster-sized art paper. This is to be the focus of our afternoon ritual. Together, we and our audience will create a rite to provide spiritual inspiration for their work in reviving the magical traditions of Poland. Each of them will have their own vision of what that might mean, but the phoenix image is to weave those visions together.

We ask everyone to take time in the day to contribute to the colouring of the phoenix. While we colour we will focus on our magical intention – what we want for the Polish magical and spiritual community. We ask people to incorporate personal symbols, runes, magical intentions in esoteric scripts – whatever they feel moved to do in order to feel a sense of ownership of the image. The phoenix will represent the combining of all the disparate ideas into something new, a group vision that is more than the sum of the individual parts. This is where the creative and the magical converge. We dig deep down within us to the source of our creativity, and harness it to archetypal images that speak to depths and layers of the psyche that go beyond everyday consciousness. We speak to the realm of dream and vision, the shamanic world of symbol and image. We speak to a deeper archaic self, to the DNA that we carry within us that still holds the imprint of the first cave drawing, the first petroglyph and the first crude map drawn with a stick in the ground.

We lay the phoenix down on the table and invite people to come and work on it meditatively. What would they really like to see grow within the new spirituality of Poland? The audience is quiet. I am not sure if they get the idea. Is the translation conveying what we mean? Then some of the more arty-looking go to the image. Others are shyer, more dubious – surely this is a little bit like primary school? Some are hungry and head straight for lunch. Some start to work intently on the image. Others who have left come back and wait their turn. There is quiet concentration, an ebbing and flowing around the image, a toing and froing in the room, some leaving, others arriving. Little by little, the black-and-white image is coming to life. Some begin to create a background. Flames now surround the phoenix, and symbols and scripts. I add some colour. Chris adds more flames. Organisers and other speakers contribute. Slowly something of beauty is born.

In the afternoon, we clear away the chairs and conference paraphernalia. Outside, the sky has turned rainy and is dark with clouds. Creating a magical atmosphere in hotel rooms is not easy. Smoke alarms preclude the use of incense and a gathering of strangers is not the usual basis for a transformative rite. Colour helps us create the right energy. Chris and I have changed into red robes and many of the participants have brought something red, orange or gold to wear for the rite, creating flaming colour in the darkening room.

We stand in a circle with the image of the fiery phoenix in pride of place on a gold-draped easel. In the centre of its breast is a white eagle on a red field, the coat of arms of Poland. Gold candles flicker on a red-draped altar in the middle of the room, their flames reflecting as sparkling light on the chandeliers and the mirrors on the walls. I teach the words of a chant we will sing in the rite. The repetitive chanting is to take us deeper into ourselves, to sense what we most need to transform in our own lives and to identify with the transformative power of the phoenix. Then, in an energised state of consciousness in this most magical of cities, we will empower the collective phoenix symbol.

There is a shift in energy and atmosphere. The experienced ritualists among us are calm, but for some there is an excited expectation about their first experience of a large communal ritual. The rite is beginning to take a shape and form that will create its own dynamic. Nothing needs to be forced. It will come from the collective energies of us all. A thought comes into my mind: *Trust in the process.* When we do magic, there is an old idea that there must be no 'lust for result'. We do the magical work and then stand back. Events have now passed out of our hands and we wait, neither hoping nor fearing the result. This is the opposite of how people often think of magic, which is as a means of imposing our will on external events. This magic is different. It is a creative act. It is about being willing to voyage into the unknown, without quite knowing how the rite will be for any one individual present, but trusting that the participants will find in it their own personal meaning.

Chris always travels with a temple gong, the perfect instrument for silencing a crowd and for dramatic moments in ritual. As the gong reverberates, voices die away, replaced by an expectant hush. I walk to the centre of the circle of people and stand by the altar. I do not know what I am going to say. I never do at this point. It is not something that can be pre-planned. It has to emerge out of the unconscious, from the sum total of the images, thoughts, emotions, desires, aspirations and longings of those of us assembled for the rite.

An image comes into my mind of a sphere of golden light. I visualise it, describing it forming around us so we are inside it. Then it begins to change shape. The sphere is now more like an egg, a symbol of creation in many spiritual traditions. The protective egg image creates a psychological barrier between us and the world, but also a sacred space, a shared field of consciousness in which a new thought-feeling-vision-idea can be born. The golden egg of light creates a space that feels private and contained, but we do not forget the practical. We have stationed someone at the door. This would not be the best time for the hotel staff to decide to refill the water cooler.

I invoke the energy of the fire-breathing dragon of Kraków and invite all in our rite to journey down, down, far down through building, down through the foundations, through layers of civilisation to soil and rock; descending not as I did in Norway to become at one with earth, but deeper. We go down into the fiery heart of the Earth, the core, the hub. We visualise fire rising up into us, through feet and spine into the solar plexus chakra, into the heart, into the brain. We are enflamed, at one with Earth-fire.

I go back to my place in the circle. Chris takes over, leading us in a visualisation. We are standing on a high rock plateau overlooking a desert landscape. Hawks are soaring on the thermals from the desert floor. The sun is low and red in the sky. Its rays are dazzling. They shine through a bush on the edge of the plateau and it seems as though the bush is on fire. We sense a presence manifesting in the flickering flames. There is a fluttering of fiery wings; then, in the centre of the fire, a beak and head appear. The phoenix emerges hovering above the fire, resplendent in the dazzling rays of the sun.

We commune with the spirit of the phoenix power, contemplating what we might need to change in our lives and in the world around us. What is it most important to change *now*? Each of us focuses on what our answer to this question might be. Then we are walking, running, flying, drawn irresistibly upwards until we are soaring with the phoenix. We soar higher and higher into the sky, towards the orb of the sun. The orb begins to fill our vision. We are flying into the flames of the sun, our bodies consumed by fire. We are burning but there is no pain; for now we are the phoenix, burning but ever-renewing, with the power of transformation within us.

Outside, the clouds suddenly clear. Intense late-afternoon sun floods through the windows, bathing us in golden light, and we begin to sing a chant to identify with the phoenix.

> I am the phoenix, the living flame, I arise from the ashes of the past . . .

These are words I have adapted from *The Egyptian Book of the Dead*, but now reborn to a tune created for the chant by Austrian and Czech musicians Chris and I have worked with.[4] Flowing and joyous, the chant builds in intensity. We begin to move to its rhythm. The movement becomes a trance-dance in honour of the phoenix. Our awareness synchronises. The chanting culminates then simultaneously we stop. There is a profound silence and the sense that something momentous has happened, a shift in consciousness. The phoenix has flown into the world. I am flooded with feelings of joy and gratitude for having taken part.

Something beautiful has occurred that is hard to put into words. We wander around the room talking quietly to one another and going to gaze once more at the phoenix, reluctant to leave the sanctified space of the ritual to re-engage with the outside world. This moment is special, holy, a time when we step outside of the realm of the ordinary into a realm where something happens that we cannot fully describe, but we know deep within us that it is life-transforming. Rites such as these are a creative fusion, fed by ancient symbols and archetypes and myths. They open a place in the human psyche where magic and creativity meet to enrich the spirit and inspire the heart. Such rites give us a sense of the eternal, the realm beyond the boundaries of the self. They give birth to new hope, new vision.

On Sunday afternoon the conference closes. Speakers, international experts, guests and organisers, we come together for a final ritual, then our job is done. The guests depart and we workers emerge into the cobbled pedestrianised streets of Kraków. The streets have their own magic.

Beautiful carriages drawn by matching pairs of immaculately groomed horses clip-clop through the Renaissance architecture past pavement restaurants, liquor stores displaying bottles of every exotic hue, and jewellery stores glinting with amber. We see why tourists come to this UNESCO World Heritage site in their droves, but it is not yet time for tourism. First, we have one more magical adventure before we leave Kraków.

Before the *enfant terrible* of the magical world Aleister Crowley burst onto the scene, Britain's most famous magician was Dr John Dee – mathematician, cryptographer, navigator, court astrologer and alchemist to Queen Elizabeth I, and the model for Shakespeare's Prospero in *The Tempest* and Christopher Marlowe's *Doctor Faustus*. His adventurous life has made him the subject of endless biographies, novels and museum exhibitions.

The popular image of the alchemist attempting to make gold is only part of the story. Alchemists also aspired to make other substances highly desired by wealthy clients, such as the *elixir vitae*, the elixir of youth, health, longevity and even immortality. Around 1582, Dr Dee claimed to have found the famous elixir in the mystical location of Glastonbury. The Polish count Albert Laski convinced the learned doctor that, with his elixir, he would be warmly welcomed in the courts of Central and Eastern Europe.

On 21 September 1583, John Dee boarded a creaking wooden ship to set off on a journey that would lead him to Kraków. The full purpose of the trip has been a matter of speculation for centuries, but he took to signing his private letters to Queen Elizabeth '007'. The zeroes represented eyes, and seven was a lucky number that offered protection.

He was telling her that he was her protective watcher. Almost certainly, Elizabeth's spymaster, Sir Francis Walsingham, had commissioned him to send back intelligence from the courts of Europe, but as far as he was concerned this was just a sideline to subsidise his magical travels.

John Dee had enough letters of introduction, well-connected friends such as Michael Sendivogius, fluent Latin and encyclopaedic knowledge to impress the kings and nobles he planned to encounter on his journey. Unfortunately, he also had an unstoppable urge to confront despotic rulers with unwelcome truths. All was going well on a visit to Prague, capital of the wealthy kingdom of Bohemia, until he offended King Rudolf II by telling him that the spiritual realms wanted him to reform his decadent life. He beat a hasty retreat back to Kraków, a city that a helpful spirit had already identified as favourable for his magical work. Like that other English mystical eccentric William Blake, John Dee's speciality was angels. Communicating with entities with neither bodies nor voices is tricky, so he adopted the same solution as did other magicians over the centuries. He employed a medium, a rather shifty former forger called Edward Kelley.

Why John Dee trusted Kelley to deliver accurate angelic messages is puzzling. Kelley must have been very persuasive. In any event, the magical partnership flourished long enough to become one of the most influential in the magical arts. Kraków's potential had been revealed to Dr Dee on 28 February 1584, when a female spirit called Madimi helpfully manifested and advised him to transfer his magical operations there. Once he had found a house suitable for himself, Edward Kelley, their wives, his magical library and other necessities of a travelling magus, magical activities began. On 12 April 1584, an angel called Nalvage began dictating a series of verses in a magical language they called Enochian and which became known as the Enochian Calls.[5] The Calls were so powerful that Nalvage insisted on dictating the sentences backwards, so as not to accidentally activate their energies.

Sadly, the original house rented by John Dee for his magical sojourn in Kraków is no longer with us, but the street is; so too is a similar fifteenth-century merchant's house just a few doors down from the magician's former lodgings. As well as close proximity to the original site, it has the added advantage that it is now the five-star Hotel Stary, which boasts luxury Gothic decor with precious metals, leather, exotic woods, oriental carpets, silk and marble – and a rooftop bar. It is a world beyond the decaying grandeur of our conference hotel, but a fitting environment for a magical adventure.

With a few judicious enquiries and the promise to buy copious amounts of champagne, funded generously by the Swedish magician among us and the staggeringly favourable kroner-zloty exchange rate, we secure the sole use of the rooftop bar for two hours. Our intention is to pay homage to our famous predecessor by replicating some of Dr Dee's magical practices. We lack the equipment to make gold or the *elixir vitae*, but we do have magicians among us who are skilled in something I have yet to experience: the intoning of the Enochian Calls. The Calls are designed to trigger consciousness change and to open gateways to a series of Aethyrs, or Otherworlds, envisaged as expanding in concentric circles from the everyday world.

In the beautifully warm August evening, a waiter serves glasses of champagne as golden sunlight lengthens and bathes the amber, ochre and pale terracotta-washed stonework of Kraków into a harmonious glow. The British Dee expert and his Swedish magician colleague begin to intone the Calls: '*Ol sonf vorsg, goho Iad balt, lansh calz vonpho: sobra z-ol ror i ta …*'

The social chit-chat dies away. It is not quite hair-on-the-back-of-the-neck-raising, but very close. I can see that we are all beginning to feel that frisson of energy through the body that comes when something is happening on some deep level of the psyche. The magicians' intoning is building, and becoming more and more intense. The waiter abandons his drinks tray and disappears downstairs, leaving us to serve ourselves. Then something unexpected happens – the sky changes. The beautiful summer evening remains, but a circle of dark clouds has appeared, surrounding the area of the city around the hotel and rolling steadily inwards towards us. The Calls stop, then the clouds stop, leaving a clear circle of sky above. I am looking at it as though in a movie, not quite believing what I see. It is as though the Calls are moving the clouds. I do not know what this means, but it is beautiful. The people, the light, the Calls, all fuse into a symphony of sound and colour – a perfect special effect. Steven Spielberg would love it.

Nearly always, I can rationalise magic. As a psychologist, I can talk about emotional contagion, the power of rhythmic chanting to shift brain patterns, the age-old power of ritual to capture the human imagination. We can explain much of magic through the theories of psychology, biology, physics, neuroscience and other 'isms 'and 'ologies', but sometimes there is no explanation. Just occasionally, very occasionally, the experience moves onto a different level. This does not mean that we will never be able to understand and explain what is happening, but it is an important reminder that we humans still know so very little about even this small part of the cosmos that we inhabit. We have a long way to go before we fully understand our synchronistic universe.

19

Beneath the Green Banner

The drumming has already started; whistles blow in a carnival atmosphere of excitement and anticipation. Chris and I and thousands of others emerge from London's Embankment underground station with our furled banners on the sunny Autumn Equinox morning of Sunday, 21 September 2014. Hundreds of thousands of people across 150 countries are turning out for the People's Climate March, the biggest-ever call for action on climate change. We are marching in London, New York, Rio, Bogotá, Santiago, Amsterdam, Paris, Madrid, Rome, Milan, Berlin, Warsaw, Delhi, Melbourne, and in great cities and small towns all around the world. The issue is so important that I find myself back on the streets marching, something I have not felt impelled to do for decades. We are marching for the planet.

Chris is once more president of the Pagan Federation. The last time was in the 1990s. Now he has been called upon to serve again. We head for the members' rendezvous point, and look for where to join the crowds waiting to set off. We find a spiritual groups section – Druids against Fracking alongside the Quakers and some Buddhists. We unfurl the Pagan Federation's banner and then our own personal green banner, painted with an image of a hare leaping over the face of a silver moon. It has attended many a magical event, but this is its first political protest.

The hare and moon symbol was created by jewellery designer Dawn Meadows in honour of Madge Worthington, the elderly English lady who in 1974 – together with Arthur Eaglen – initiated me into their Wiccan coven. It was she who suffered the vilification of an exposé instigated by the infamous Sunday tabloid the *News of the World*,[1] which in one of those strange magical spiral chains of causality resulted in the booklet *Witchcraft: A Warning* that helped show me my spiritual path. Madge was an amazing woman born into a British colonial family, who broke free of class and caste and became a radical thinker. She marched in the 1950s with the Campaign for Nuclear Disarmament, and supported the 1980s peace protest at RAF Greenham Common. She championed animal rights when few had heard of the concept. She warned about the dangers of radiation when it was routine to X-ray children's feet to check their shoe size. By the time of her death in 2005, she was recognised as a woman whose ideas were right all along.

Some of the last rituals that Chris and I did with Madge were for Earth Day, the global initiative begun in 1970 by Wisconsin senator and World War Two veteran Gaylord Nelson, to educate people about protecting the planet. The 1970 event was a resounding success – 20 million people participated. By December 1970, President Richard Nixon had created the Environmental Protection Agency. In those more politically enlightened days, environmental action was supported by both Republicans and Democrats.

In 1971, Greenpeace was founded. In 1972, with some hippie friends, I gathered in the garden of our shared house in south-east London to honour the Earth. My long-haired and bearded friend Bob, who at twenty-eight was the wise elder among us, spoke passionately about the rape of Mother Earth, the pollution of her atmosphere and the poisoning of her rivers. We were convinced. Most of our parents' generation thought us mad.

In 1990, for the twentieth Earth Day, Chris and I organise a Pagan Federation interfaith event on Horsenden Hill to the west of London, the site of a 2,500-year-old Iron Age settlement. Madge limps up the hill with her walking stick. We hand out biodegradable sacks and organise a litter clear-up, then stand in a circle holding hands. We say an invocation to honour the Earth, reaching across faith traditions to ask the Divine source of all life, 'Jehovah, the Goddess, Allah, by whatever name we call it,' to bring healing to our planet. We sing some simple chants created in the most part by the feminist, environmentalist Goddess community, the Reclaiming collective in California. Simple, rhythmic and accompanied by drumming, they are easy for newcomers to learn and join in.

We lead a visualisation, one that is being used at similar Pagan Federation events across the UK and beyond. We visualise a renewed Earth forming around us. In the east, tall industrial chimneys with their dense dark smoke and acrid smell fade away to a clear blue spring sky, clean white clouds and a fresh invigorating breeze. In the south, a vast desert with missiles flying overhead against a sound of gunfire fades into the silence of desert and oasis. In the west, a river flows into the sea, its surface besmirched with yellow foam and streaks of brown sewage, its banks strewn with dead fish. The image fades to a clear fast-flowing river with green water-plants and fish, leading to a clean blue-green sea where seabirds gather at the estuary. In the north, an enormous rubbish tip, plastic bags blown about by the wind, a stunted tree struggling for life, becomes a vision of green rolling tree-covered hills and grassy meadows, butterflies and bees flitting between the wild flowers.

At the end of the rite, we give out leaflets printed on recycled paper to the people who have gathered to watch and to those who have taken part. The leaflets describe what ordinary people can do to reduce pollution and conserve resources. The visualisation itself will not change the Earth. It is something for us to hold onto, an image to inspire us to action. We hope that we have won some hearts and minds.

In 1990, there were Earth Day events in over 140 countries. By 2000, 184 countries were involved. In 2009, at the urging of the President of Bolivia, Evo Morales, the personhood of the planet was recognised by the United Nations General Assembly – a triumph for an animist worldview.

Symbolic actions such as marches and community rituals can be powerful ways to inspire others. In 2014, Chris and I are not joining the People's Climate March because we expect our actions to have an immediate effect. Politicians are short-termist. They want to be the bearers of good news. Things are getting better, you are getting richer – these are the messages they think will win support. Hard messages about changing behaviour, consuming less and reducing our use of energy are not what they think will get them re-elected.

Our goal is to raise awareness until society reaches a tipping point. Only when demands for action swell from the people, the voters, from the majority and not the radical few … only then will our politicians act.

As we wait our turn to set off, news filters through. UN Secretary-General Ban Ki-moon is to join the march in New York, together with activist Jane Goodall and environmentalist and former US vice president Al Gore. Some politicians have got the message. In London, fashion designer Vivienne Westwood and musician Peter Gabriel join the throng. Actor Emma Thompson puts the message across to the media in direct terms: 'Unless we're carbon-free by 2030 the world is buggered.'[2] Each of us who wakes to the danger is a catalyst for those around us, but celebrity endorsement is not enough. We need to see that people close to us, people we identify with, see climate crisis as a problem that we must address.

Attitudes do not change incrementally. There are innovators who seize upon a new idea early on. They may be thought eccentric, even mad. In the early 1970s, all my hippie and magical friends were aghast at climate change and were radical advocates of behaving differently – of vegetarianism, organic farming, solar power, cycling – but few conventional people thought these issues important. Early adopters are a second, wider circle, who listen to the pioneers and believe them. They become catalysts who create bridges into mainstream thinking. Now, I can see that a third circle is building – ordinary everyday people worried about climate change.

The march sets off towards the Houses of Parliament; some people pushing baby carriages, others Zimmer frames. Our ages are eighties to eight months, everyone from elderly ladies who look like they might not survive the march to babes in arms. We are men, women, non-binary, white, black and Asian. The march has cut across class and creed. As we reach our destination, and our hare-and-moon banner flies proudly in Parliament Square, it feels like a transition to a new collective consciousness, another step in building momentum. Joining with those of like mind gives us strength and can create alliances across spiritual traditions, nationalities and ethnicities. These alliances can take us to the most unexpected destinations.

In 2015, one year after the climate change march, I fly into the Mormon capital of Salt Lake City as the Pagan Federation's delegate to the sixth Parliament of the World's Religions. The purpose of the Parliament is to address climate change. These are not frequent events. The first Parliament was held in 1893, to bring together those of faiths West and East. Now the umbrella has widened. The world's indigenous communities and their spiritualities are welcomed, and thanks to the work of pioneers such as Angie Buchanan, Andras Corban-Arthen and Deirdre Pulgram Arthen, Phyllis Curott, Olivia Durdin-Robertson and countless others, the magical and Pagan traditions are represented too. The irony of 10,000 people flying to discuss planetary disaster is enormous, and mitigated only by carbon offset, but the need for collective dialogue and action is great. The world religions have woken up. They too are campaigning to save our planet. Not all of their members, of course – the fundamentalist branches of all faiths are too busy fighting for their market share to notice that the world they are fighting over is about to disappear.

Visualise now the scene – a vast 679,000 square feet of indoor space, Salt Lake City's Salt Palace Convention Center. Outside, Native American elders light a sacred fire and sage smudge sticks, their smoke giving a fragrant and cleansing blessing to the space. They drum and offer prayers for the Earth.

The crowds stream into the Salt Palace. Its concrete walls and hideously psychedelic carpet disappear as the building fills with representatives from eighty countries and fifty spiritual traditions. Thai Buddhist monks in orange robes and canvas shoulder bags queue for coffee in front of a Native American chief in full war bonnet. Behind him is a female Christian minister in grey skirt and blue shirt with clerical collar, and to their right is a cluster of white-clad Sikh women, Native American elders with wheelchairs decorated to look like mobile thrones, representatives of peoples of the Amazon in brightly coloured woven shawls, Jewish men in skullcaps, a female African-American Zen priest in a brown robe, and nuns and imams. The air buzzes with conversation. Indigenous peoples from all parts of the planet, from the Maori of New Zealand to the Inuit of the Arctic, discuss common problems – rising sea levels for some, battles for control of diminishing water resources for others, the degradation of tribal homelands by mining corporations, and the battle for education, medical facilities and access to modern life through the internet while also retaining cultural identity and traditions. Lakota spiritual leader Chief Arvol Looking Horse of the Cheyenne River Reservation, 19th Generation Keeper of the Sacred White Buffalo Calf Pipe, speaks of how we must once again view Mother Earth as the source of life, not a resource. His language comes from the spirituality of the Lakota peoples, but it could just as well have been spoken by anyone in the magical traditions.

In 1989, Chris and I led an interfaith Earth-honouring ceremony in Canterbury, the seat of England's Christianity. This was not easy. Pagans were not really welcome. The gathering was in the cathedral precincts. I wrote as secretary of the Pagan Federation offering to perform a rite in honour of the Earth in the cathedral cloisters. We were granted instead a slot in a local park, safely away from the main body of the gathering. Despite this, the BBC thought it sufficiently important to bring round a camera team, so the Pagan presence was recorded. It was the first time an openly Pagan rite had been performed in Canterbury for over 1,300 years.

Now, much has changed. In the interfaith world at least, there is a recognition of what Pagan, Goddess and indigenous spirituality has to offer. Macha NightMare, Dr Candace Kant of Cherry Hill Seminary and I are to voice the goddesses in *Goddess Alive!*, a ritual theatre performance created by Macha and featuring stunningly beautiful goddess masks by artist Lauren Raine.[3] The production honours in mime and dance goddesses from the world's cultures, a recognition of the Divine Feminine and her power to unify across creed, colour and caste.

My friend Francesca Ciancimino Howell of Naropa University, America's only university with Buddhist roots – she is also the author of *Making Magic with Gaia*[4] – and I are to lead a multifaith meditative ceremony in honour of the Earth. Nearly thirty years ago, she represented the Goddess in our rite in Canterbury. Now we journey round the spiral to work together to honour the Earth again. We choose readings from the world's spiritual traditions, and invite their representatives to read a passage that leads us into meditation on what our congregations, temples, churches, circles, workplaces and places of education can do to address climate change. Our traditions may be different, but in our shared concern for our planet and for the future of humankind we can find common ground.

Looking down afterwards from the gallery at the crowds below me, I think, *If only it could always be like this*. If only differences could be set aside and humankind united by our love for our planet. I conclude that the Parliament is the most extraordinary event I have ever attended, a few days of paradise in a greedy and hostile world. It brings hope for humankind, for there is something crazy yet glorious about it, like some space station in a sci-fi movie where, in a far-flung corner of the universe, in peace and harmony all diverse beings converge.

There are new signs of hope. On Earth Day 2016, over 120 countries signed the landmark Paris Agreement. Greta Thunberg, another inspirational figure, has risen up to spread the message. Small decisions can have enormous consequences in that invisible chain of causality that takes us where we can never predict. Her journey began with a journey that she did not take. On 20 August 2018, the Swedish fifteen-year-old decided not to go to school, but to begin a school strike to raise awareness of climate change. She sat down outside the Swedish Parliament, demanding that the government take action to reduce carbon emissions. Slowly at first, then snowballing, social media coverage[5] led to major media coverage. The strike went global, and on Friday, 15 March 2019, 1.4 million young people in 128 countries took part. In April 2019, activists in 80 countries and cities took part in protests, marches and occupations of major landmarks. In response to the protests, governments in the United Kingdom, Ireland, Canada and France, and city authorities in Amsterdam, Milan, New York City, San Francisco and Sydney, declared climate emergencies and vowed to take action. A YouGov poll in September 2019 showed that the majority worldwide now believe that human actions are causing climate change that is resulting in serious damage to the planet and the global economy, and that their countries could be doing more to tackle the problem.[6]

The momentum for change is growing, but so too are the problems. Seas are higher, winds are wilder, droughts longer, wildfires fiercer, hurricanes more devastating. We live with an increasing sense of urgency that something must be done. The problem is enormous, but each of us in our own lives can contribute just a little. We can change minds and hearts, each of us creating a movement in the currents of the human psyche, a movement that can become a tide – a tide of change. For what we are working towards is a sea change in human consciousness. The degradation of our planet is a symptom, and it is our state of consciousness that is its underlying cause.

We can be driven to action by our insight into what is wrong with our planet, but our passion will grow stronger if we experience our true relationship with what is around us, a view of the self that is shared by indigenous and magical traditions. Over the last two millennia, we came to view human beings as the summit of biological creation, and other species as mere objects for our exploitation. If we realise our deep connectedness with all beings, this view becomes untenable. When our sense of self expands and what was previously 'other' and 'not-me' becomes a deeper part of 'me', this spiritual and philosophical realisation can have a profound impact on how we live. It makes sense to protect the planet when we experience *ourselves* as the planet.

If we can develop a sense of the ecological self, then sustainable behaviours become much easier. We do not have to convince one another intellectually. We can experience the need for change on a much deeper level. Such feelings can be the basis of environmental ethics. We can see a growth of empathy towards nature in the upsurge in vegetarianism and veganism. In part, this preoccupation is connected with health and our concerns about food quality, but it also reflects a deep unease about the ethics of our treatment of animals in mass factory farming.

The last decades have seen more and more people drawn to live in the convenience of cities, but even the most urbanised among us retains a strong affinity with the natural world. Something within us wants to make a connection of consciousness that the language and religions of Western society do not recognise or accommodate. The psychoanalyst Erich Fromm created a Greek-based word 'biophilia', from *bio*, meaning 'life', and *philia*, a form of love, to describe our passionate love of life and of all that is alive.[7] Biophilia gives us an innate drive to form loving connections with other living organisms. The internet is full of cute photographs and videos of interspecies friendships – cats with dogs, dogs with horses, horses with goats – because these friendships strike a deep chord within us. Biophilia helps our species to survive, and we see its manifestations all the time. We are programmed to ooh and aah over the small fluffy young of other animals, for example, because it makes sense to protect the next generation of species that are essential to our biosphere. Our natural wild selves lived in close proximity to the animals that we hunted and domesticated. We depended on trees for fuel, and the seasons for our crops. Now the relationships are more hidden. Most of the time, we never have to think about our dependence on nature; yet we are still drawn to plants, trees, birds and animals. We sense at an unconscious level our interconnectivity with other species, and we long to renew it.

Our ancestors knew instinctively that our biosphere was an interlinked and interlocking consciousness, but somehow as we developed science and technology we found it easier to pretend that the planet was insentient matter for us to use and exploit. These attitudes have given us a high standard of living, undreamt of by earlier generations, but at a terrible price. We have created a population explosion that now threatens to destroy the very resources that brought it into being.

In the official classification of the International Union of Geological Sciences, this current phase of the Earth's existence is the Holocene epoch that began 11,700 years ago, after the last major ice age. Atmospheric chemist and Nobel Laureate Paul Crutzen argues however that we are experiencing rapid and catastrophic environmental changes that are ushering in a new epoch.[8] This is the epoch of the Anthropocene, from the Greek *anthropos*, meaning 'human', and *cene*, derived from the Greek *kairos* meaning a pivotal time when the human collective psyche goes through an enormous upheaval. During such a time, the statues of the old gods are toppled and their places taken by new gods – or by no gods at all. Old barriers disappear, old prejudices are reassessed. Indigenous and magical knowledge that was once cast aside is found to contain solutions to the problems of tomorrow.

Human beings are one of the newest species on our planet, but our position has become so dominant that we are causing mass extinction of millions of other life forms. We are the new kids on the block, the new toddlers at the nursery who are just learning to tie our shoelaces. If we look at this positively, it means that all the mistakes that our species is making are just an inevitable part of growing up, and we can learn to do better. In the meantime, the toddlers are in charge of the planet and are causing chaos.

Intellectually human beings have advanced, but in terms of emotional intelligence and maturity, we really are like toddlers. The problem is that it is all about 'me' and 'mine'. We even have political slogans that glorify this dysfunctionality – 'America First', 'Britain First'. In other words, *I will privilege myself and those like me, and forget that I live on a planet.* This type of thinking is flawed on so many levels. We could explain the problem in economic or political terms. We could turn to social science. But there is another way of looking at it, which is to say that it is flawed on a much deeper level because it fails to understand the true nature of reality. The truth about biological life forms, humans included, is not separation, isolation and independence, but symbiosis, interconnectivity and mutual dependence. When our thinking becomes global, then we realise the obvious – nature takes no notice of national boundaries; nor do pandemics, tornados, droughts or pollution. The real problems of our planet can be solved only if humankind unites to work together to solve them.

Those of us who live in countries where public demonstration is permitted are in an enviable position. Many others cannot protest, cannot lobby, so we who can must act for the rest. But marching and ritualling for Gaia is not enough. The easiest way to heal the earth is to change human behaviour. The easiest place to start is ourselves. When problems are so great, we can feel overwhelmed. If we succumb to the size of the problem then we can react with denial or despair. We can even come to hate and despise our own species, and to forget that we have powers of creativity and ingenuity as well as those of destruction.

When problems seem overwhelming, there is a hexagram in the I Ching that always comes to mind – 9, *Hsiao Ch'u*, the Taming Power of the Small. 'Only through the small means of friendly persuasion', the text tells us, 'can we exert any influence.'[9] The hexagram often appears when we are in a position of weakness and we need to focus on small cumulative changes in order to achieve the goal we seek. When it comes to achieving sustainability for our planet, if many of us make small changes, they add up. Small actions become big actions when the actors are many. We might also say that when the journey is long, it can be hard to begin, so we begin with small steps – and just keep going.

20

Touching the Stone

The road less travelled always appeals to me, much more than the four-lane highway. It has taken me to magical rituals, shamanic journeys and meetings with remarkable women and men in many countries around the world. The hidden routes into the psyche and uncharted territory draw me much more than the well-trodden path. This is true on the mundane plane as well, where Chris and I specialise in driving along the kind of roads where one needs a four-wheel-drive Land Rover. Unfortunately, we do not own one. Given our love of going the 'pretty way', often over mountains, we really should. The western Pyrenees where the paving ran out high up on the French side of the border; that terrifying Alpine route, a death trap in darkness, where Hannibal took his elephants to attack Rome; various 'shortest' GPS routes that turned into dirt tracks and went straight through Welsh sheep farms and up and up and up – we have done them all.

This journey is not by choice, though, but necessity. We are going to a wedding.

The invitation sounds wonderful, the Midsummer marriage of two gay Italian witch friends in a country mansion converted to a hotel, up above the sparkling waters of Lake Maggiore. We check it out on TripAdvisor. The advice is clear – do not attempt to arrive after dark. We look at a map and see the contours and a writhing snake of a road. We get the message. We drive through the tunnel from France so we can start our ascent in the afternoon. Our GPS tells us it is 3.5 kilometres to the hotel. The drive is terrifying. Our long right-hand-drive British car cannot get round the steep sharp bends in one go, so we climb up the single-track road in a series of three-point turns that involve backing perilously close to the void, lots of low gears, and a few points when it seems the engine will cut out. After fifteen minutes and 3.5 kilometres, we discover we are at the bottom of the grounds. The hotel is another 2.5 kilometres up, and up. We pray to the local gods that no one decides to come down and then carry on, thanking them again when we reach the top without having had to find a way to pass another car.

Our journey to Italy is one of many. They begin with an invitation to speak at the annual magical extravaganza that is Witchfest in Fairfield Halls in Croydon, a prosaic south London setting for a seriously witchy event. Afterwards, we are approached by a group of Italians. They are running a similar, smaller event in Italy. Would we like to come? We go and present our take on the magical traditions. They ask us back. It becomes a regular programme of events, and the Italian Wiccan community builds. Like Catholic Poland, Italy's magical scene suddenly takes off, nurtured by the commitment of our friends Davide and Maurizia, and the energy and passion of those they draw round them.

The wedding is romantic, the food and music wonderful, and it is a reunion of long-term friends. The event and the beautiful views across Lake Maggiore soothe away the trauma of the journey, then two days later it is time to descend. This is slightly less scary, and at least this time we get the views. We reach the lake-shore road and turn left for Switzerland. The drive along the narrow road is less terrifyingly steep, but has the added hazard of speeding tourist buses. We are excited though. The wedding venue is near the Swiss border, so we have been able to arrange something that I have wanted to do for a very long time. It feels like a pilgrimage.

Certain places evoke feelings in our imagination, even if we have never been there. They are associated with people, events and ideas that are special to us. They have a magical resonance. For a Catholic it might be Rome, for a Muslim Mecca, for an American the lands of her ancestors, for an Irish exile O'Connell Street or the Cliffs of Moher, and for a modern-day Pagan – Stonehenge. When I started my quest for the Grail as a teenager, I did not know where it would lead me, but I knew that Carl Jung's writings were a trigger. They made me realise the connection between magical consciousness and finding the authentic self within. For him too, the Grail Quest was an interior journey, a symbol of the spiritual journey of individuation and reunification with the authentic self. As a lover of Jung's work, one of my would-be pilgrimage spots is Eranos.

I have long been fascinated by the community that built up around the Eranos gatherings held at the estate of the

Theosophist and spiritualist Olga Fröbe-Kapteyn, in the village of Moscia on the shores of Lake Maggiore – below Ascona, in Italian-speaking Switzerland. Ascona in the early part of the twentieth century was rather like Sedona in Arizona and Glastonbury in England are today. It was a New Age, hippie-style paradise where people moved into houses, enjoyed the beautiful climate, practised naturism and sexual liberation, tried out new art forms, created rituals and experimented with magic.

It was in this heady atmosphere that in 1928 Olga Fröbe-Kapteyn felt inspired to build a two-hundred-seat conference hall adjoining the villa on her estate. Someone once described her as 'one of those people who float through life an inch or two off the ground'.[1] She decided to follow her intuition and to begin building the hall, even though she had no idea why she was building it. A trip to Connecticut and a conversation with the esotericist Alice Bailey gave her the key. She would create a gathering of leading thinkers from the sciences and humanities. The guiding principle would be an *eranos*, a Greek word for a banquet where each guest contributes a dish of food – but here the contributions would be mind food.

Eranos became a famous annual event. The invitations went out and Carl Jung responded, as did Erich Neumann, Richard Wilhelm's son Hellmut (also a leading sinologist), Mircea Eliade, Joseph Campbell, Daisetz Teitaro Suzuki, Erwin Schrödinger, Marie-Louise von Franz, Emma Jung, Aniela Jaffé, Laurens van der Post, Kathleen Raine and Gershom Scholem – so many people whose work I have read and admired. The gathering became a *Who's Who* of scholarship in spiritually oriented thinking.

Now Chris and I are here. We park above the estate and take the winding path down through the exotic gardens to the buildings and lake below. The wonderful manager Gisela shows us into the Library, our apartment for our stay, and there we are, surrounded by volumes of the *Eranos Yearbooks* and photographs of the participants. We admire the painted furniture and the wood-burning stove. We examine the tiny statues of ancient gods. At night, we sleep beneath a romantic draped white mosquito net. In the day, we walk barefoot on the wooden floorboards. In the evening, we sit by a lakeside window, sipping white wine and gazing across to Italy, as the waters of the lake lap at the rocks below. We eat outside in the garden at the round stone table I have seen in black-and-white photographs of Carl Jung and the other Eranos participants eating and drinking into the long summer evenings after the day's intellectual feasting is done. We explore the garden paths that join the buildings of the estate. We walk where they walked, we swim where they swam, and dive off the jetty where they dived. The continuity with the past is strong. One day we bump into Olga Fröbe-Kapteyn's grandchildren on the private beach.

We trace with our fingers the inscription that Carl Jung chose for the stone altar in the garden. The Latin reads, 'To the Unknown Spirit of this Place'. We sense here the energy that is found in places where people have engaged over long years in a spiritual endeavour. It is the peaceful energy found in the gardens of monasteries and temples. The spirit of this place is 'Unknown' because we cannot give it any human name. It comes out of the elements, out of rock and lake, and sky and trees, and deep harmonious links between human and human, human and nature. For us, as for others who have stayed here, this feels like a sacred space, this place of peace above the waters of Lake Maggiore, consecrated to knowing achieved not through intellect alone, but through direct experience and contemplation.

One day Gisela shows us around the bedrooms where Carl and Emma Jung and Joseph Campbell and his wife, the dancer Jean Erdman, slept. When a biographer describes Jean Erdman diving into the waters of the lake,[2] I know now their coldness and the exhilaration of launching myself into the great stretch of water. We read and make notes in the library. I read Marie-Louise von Franz's book of lectures on spiritual alchemy in this place where the spirits of Carl Jung and all those who came here seem to permeate the very walls.[3]

Time speeds by. I would like to spend weeks here, just writing and contemplating, but the morning comes when must leave to drive home to Brittany. We have planned the route but, once we have taken our bags up the garden steps to the car above, a sudden thought comes into my mind. Could we make a detour, I ask Chris, to see the place where for Marie-Louise von Franz it all began – the Tower built by Carl Jung at Bollingen by Lake Zürich as his spiritual retreat. We know the Tower is a private holiday home of the Jung family. We will be able to see only what is visible from the lakeside track. Nevertheless, I feel an overwhelming urge to see this magical Tower, so much of which Carl Jung built himself, learning to lay stone upon stone, applying mortar with a plasterer's trowel. Bollingen was for him what Brittany is to us, a place to reconnect with nature and the physical world. Here he restored his inner energies before returning to his people-oriented life of patients, students and teaching. Alone, listening to birdsong and the lapping waters of the lake, he had time to incubate his ideas, ideas that have long been influential in my life.

Marie-Louise von Franz went there, overcoming her introversion. At the age of eighteen she received a surprise invitation from a student she barely knew, a nephew of Carl Jung's mistress Toni Wolff, to go with him and a group of young men to lunch with Jung at the Tower. The nephew invited her because he had noticed her in lectures. Although she was introverted, she had a driving intellectual curiosity. She was the one who asked their professors challenging questions. He thought she would be less boring for Carl Jung than his less intellectually confident friends.

Her instinct was to refuse the invitation. The idea of travelling with a group of rowdy young male students to have lunch with a famous person she had never met was daunting, but something drove her to accept. Her acceptance changed her life. The nephew was right – Carl Jung did not find her boring. She became his researcher, intellectual confidante and collaborator in developing his most important ideas on synchronicity and alchemy. It was a relationship that lasted until his death.

We examine the map. Switzerland is small. If we travel north before turning west to France, we could drive into German-speaking Switzerland and stop at Bollingen on the way. We set the GPS for Brittany via Bollingen, but it lets us down. We do not end up on another adventurous mountain road, but somehow it takes us straight past Bollingen. We are about to turn round and go back when it occurs to me that this is in essence a pilgrimage. The perfect way to arrive is, as most of Carl Jung's guests did, on foot from the village nearby.

We park in the village and walk along the lakeside track, my iPhone in hand. On the satnav map someone has placed a little dot to mark the site of the Tower, but we can see only trees. We carry on. A few hundred metres later, the Tower is nowhere to be seen. We must have missed it. We turn back and then I get it. From this new angle, we can just see the top of the Tower peering over the treetops. The lush greenery of mid-June, plus decades of growth, have all but hidden it from the track.

We cross to the wall around the Tower to take some photographs, although there is not much to see. We are about to leave when a four-by-four draws up, driven by a middle-aged man. An elderly lady climbs out. I am embarrassed to be photographing the outside of a family home, and in my rather defunct German I apologise for intruding on their privacy. I explain that I am a psychologist of religion and have taught Carl Jung's work as part of a master's degree at the University of London. The elderly lady glances meaningfully at the man and he gives a slight nod. 'I am Jung's granddaughter,' she says in English. 'Would you like to come in?'

Of course we would. She ushers us through the gateway and across the threshold. Inside the courtyard, she shows us the outdoor kitchen where her grandfather cooked. She offers us water to drink from the well, a later innovation. At first, Carl Jung used the water from the lake, but eventually he called in a water diviner to source a well. She shows us the tiny staircase to his bedroom and his paintings. We hear her tales of visiting him at the Tower and of family meals outside under the stars. Then she invites us to touch the cubic stone.

Visitors to the Jung family's upmarket main residence further along the shores of Lake Zürich were often startled to find him not in his library surrounded by erudite tomes, but below on the lake shore making mud pies. His skills soon advanced to masonry and then stone carving. Years later, a stonemason recalled how 'Old Jung' had a feeling for stone. He understood how to work with it, as few modern masons could.[4] For him it was creative play, a liberating antidote to his sedentary life as a therapist and writer.

As the Tower at Bollingen evolved, he began constructing a high wall around it. He ordered a triangular cornerstone, but the quarry made a mistake and sent a large cubic stone instead. He decided it was meant to be and kept it. It became a sacred stone, lovingly worked to bring out letters and shapes.

As our fingers trace the carvings, we hear metal on metal, the chisel, the hammering. We smell the dust and feel the small flecks of stone on the skin as they fly off the block. Sparks too fly and sometimes burn. On one side of the stone, Jung carved a Latin verse that the medieval alchemist Arnaldus Villanovanus wrote above the door to his house in Montpellier in southern France, together with the Ouroboros, a snake eating its tail, a symbol of the ever-renewing cycle of life, death and rebirth. A translation reads:

> This stone is had in small regard,
> With men of slender wit,
> But yet the wise and learned sort
> Make great account of it.[5]

The stone is the Philosopher's Stone, the magical substance that can turn lead into gold, or which in spiritual alchemy transforms our inner psyche from its unevolved state into enlightened consciousness. This is the alchemist's *magnum opus*, the Great Work that occupied Carl Jung's whole life and still occupies mine. A stone is a simple thing, a product of the natural world; we are surrounded by stones every day of our lives. The verse conveys the idea that the potential for enlightenment is all around us in our everyday experiences – if we have eyes to see.

On the side of the stone that faces the lake, Jung carved a Latin quotation about the Philosopher's Stone: 'I am found everywhere,' the Stone tells us, 'I have known neither father nor mother.'[6] In other words, the inner wisdom that brings transformation has always been there, just waiting for us to find it. We can find it in nature and in the depths of our own psyches, in our innermost being. On another side of the stone, he carved a Greek inscription with an image of the dwarf Telesphorus, son of Asclepius, the Greek father of medicine deified as a god of healing, whose temple on the island of Kos Chris and I visited years before. Telesphorus's name means 'accomplisher' or 'bringer of completion'. He symbolises recovery from illness, but also the accomplishment of the Great Work – the difficult task of spiritual transformation.

A translation of the inscription reads that Telesphorus 'glows like a star out of the depths. He points the way to the gates of the sun and to the land of dreams.'[7] He carries a lantern and his image is much like the Hermit card in the tarot. As I trace the outlines of the carving with my fingers, it feels like a message flowing through my fingers to my brain. To accomplish the inner magic, we need our times of retreat, of silence. The times when we feel alone in bearing light in the darkness. Yet we are not alone, for at a deeper level we share and bear with others the hope of inner light appearing in the darkness for all humankind.

We drive home to Brittany feeling deep gratitude to the Jung family for sharing with us their space. It is only when we reach Brittany and drive past the turning to the magical forest of Brocéliande, where in Breton legend the magician Merlin gives up all his secrets to Viviane, the Lady of the Lake, that I remember what Carl Jung had wanted to carve on the fourth side of his cubic stone, the side that remains blank still. It was '*Le cri de Merlin*', the cry of the magician Merlin imprisoned forever by Viviane. It is a cry that on misty autumnal nights still haunts the trees of enchanted Brocéliande.

At a certain point on the inner journey, we discover that it is no longer the everyday ego that is driving the chariot of our existence, but the deeper, wiser self. We can listen to the voice of the self, or we can reject it; but if we listen we can find the strength to swim out into the great ocean of the collective unconscious, braving the waves and whatever swims beneath, to see where the currents will take us. If we learn to trust our instincts and intuitions, then the magical connections can happen for us. Our meeting with Carl Jung's granddaughter and her invitation into the Tower was important for me. Yet, if we had not overshot the turn, if we had not turned the journey into a pilgrimage and walked to our destination, then we would have been and gone before the Jung family returned.

These synchronistic events are not always important for their externalities – to visit or not to visit Carl Jung's Tower was not a matter of life and death to me – but they are important on an inner level. The signal that some change is happening in our inner world and we need to take notice. Chris's and my visit to Naggar Castle thirty years before, to view the Himalayas as Nicholas Roerich painted them, marked a transition to our public magical teaching. The Himalayas in their mighty stone fastness are awe-inspiring, but they are not mountains that can be easily climbed. In Switzerland, surrounded by the Alps, we touched a cubic stone, something close to the earth, closer to everyday reality.

Back home in Brittany, I read in my black-bound note-book the notes that I made at Eranos about Marie-Louise von Franz's *Alchemy*. She wrote of the Ouroboros, the snake eating its tail, as a symbol of the reconciliation of opposites. Where the opposites meet 'a flow is born', of what alchemists call 'mystical or divine water'. Life then becomes 'a meaningful flow, a manifestation of the Self.'[8] It feels to me that what flowed at Eranos and Bollingen were the waters of a cosmic love, filling and overflowing the Grail of the open heart. All through our time in Italy and Switzerland, there was a sense of inner consolidation, a grounding; as though an Ouroboros had formed in my heart chakra, eating karma, a process of digestion and expelling. I intuit its meaning as a coming into myself, all my being now focused in one place of becoming.

21

Magical Womanpower

As I walk from South Kensington underground station past the Natural History Museum in London on a summer's day, it feels as though another new current is being born in the collective psyche of the arts magical.

I am heading in the June sunshine towards an event in another unlikely setting, Baden-Powell House. This former headquarters of the Scout Association, once at the heart of establishment Britain, was opened in 1961 by Queen Elizabeth II, her uncle Prince Henry, Duke of Gloucester, and an honour guard of 142 Queen's Scouts, in an occasion covered by a BBC broadcast. As I climb up the steps to the entrance, I wonder what Lieutenant General Baden-Powell, 1st Baron Baden-Powell, OM, GCMG, GCVO, KCB, KStJ, DL, veteran of the Boer War and World War One, founder of the Scout movement, and to some a controversial war criminal, would have thought about today. Baden-Powell House is to host the first Magickal Women Conference.

If the programme of our conference would have shocked Lord Baden-Powell, so too would the audience. The conference is inclusive and welcomes women, whether assigned female at birth or not. In fact, all are welcome. The contemporary magical community transcends gender. Those who are creative and environmentally aware find empowerment within it; so too do those who can feel marginalised by mainstream society – those who are queer, mixed race, on the margins. The magical current is an overthrowing of patriarchal religion and a return to the ethos of older societies, in which as shamans, priests, priestesses, magicians and witches, people of all genders found a role. To be betwixt and between, to be 'other', to be a third or fourth sex, can be a source of magical and spiritual power.

I thought I was arriving in good time, but already the exhibition area is packed. Tickets sold out weeks ago and people have come from all around Europe and beyond. Some of us would pass for one of South Kensington's museum visitors. Others, with their exotic hair, clothes, tattoos and piercings, look as though they do not often appear in daylight. Some of us are witchy; others lean towards dark academic. Some are in conference-mode business chic, while others pay homage to designer hippie revival. We are white, black and brown. We are young, old and all decades between. We are magical and witchy women and others of all generations, attracted by the event's title, the first of its kind. We are drawn by the vision of the co-organisers Sue Terry, tarot reader and doctoral candidate at the University of Surrey, and Erzebet Barthold – author, artist, bookbinder, managing director of Hadean Press, and a member of the magical group the Ordo Templi Orientis.

The event is new, different – a merging of the feminist, the magical and the artistic. Thirty years ago, I was one of the few women speakers at magical conferences. Now there are enough magical women to fill a conference programme. The presenters are magic-makers, witches, storytellers, dancers, singers, booksellers, writers, poets, artists, alchemists, scholars. The conference is a celebration of women and the occult; an exploration of involvement across time and cultures, from ancient Mesopotamia to the Caribbean to contemporary Korea, via Victorian magical London, *fin de siècle* Paris, early-twentieth-century nature mysticism, the Surrealists, and contemporary writers and artists. It is a heady brew. The air buzzes with anticipation. I can hear from our excited talk, see from the engagement in people's faces, feel in the vibrating atmosphere that there is a real hunger for this event. The organisers have their timing exactly right. As we approach the third decade of the twenty-first century, magical doorways are opening. Just as women artists are being rediscovered, so too are the women of the arts magical. It is definitely my kind of event.

The doors to the main lecture hall open and we flow into our seats to hear the opening talk by Dolores Ashcroft-Nowicki. She is a grande dame of the magical world – mother, grandmother and head of a magical teaching order, the Servants of the Light, one of the many that sprang from the original inspiration of the Hermetic Order of the Golden Dawn. Dolores is one of those amazing creative and energetic people who in her nineties is a prolific author and still inspiring those who seek to walk a magical path. She comes onto the stage and at once she engages us. Her speech is passionate and enthralling. Her message is about survival, the power of women to triumph over oppression and repression of their spiritual and magical lives.

Decades before, when magic was more underground, we ritualled together in a summer woodland under the moon and stars, she representing the Mother and I the Maiden aspect of the Triple Goddess of life, death and rebirth. Now magic has mainstreamed, no longer confined to the shadows and the margins, to the forests and secret curtain-drawn rooms. What was shunted into the sidelines as rejected knowledge has stepped out into the sunlight, but it has not lost its wild roots. The conference celebrates women's wild magic, a magic of the body, of sensing the ebb and flow of the inner tides, of the monthly blood flow and the urge to create, to dance, to sing, to glory in being alive. It is a spirituality that has no fear of the human body, no shame, no urge to flee human existence to some supernatural realm beyond. Instead, it seeks to open the gates of the psyche so that the realm of spirit is present everywhere in everyday reality; to open ourselves to the love of life that makes the heart sing.

Dolores's speech comes to an end with a standing ovation and we flow out of the hall. People peel off, up and down, right and left, into the workshop rooms, but for me it feels good to just walk the corridors and take in the atmosphere, to bump into old friends, to commune with the creative energy that is bursting through the event. All around is the work of talented women artists in all manner of media. The theme of humankind's relationship to nature is strong. I am drawn to award-winning photographer Sara Hannant's installation. Her photographs emanate the creative energy of the elements – of earth and air, fire and water, the cycles of nature transforming around us.[1]

Hers is a work of engagement, interaction and magic. She invites us to make a small piece of magic of our own, to take, tie and add to the installation a piece of organic cotton that she has consecrated by dipping it in Cornwall's sacred Sancreed Well. At Sancreed, visitors come to make offerings by tying to a tree 'clouties', strips of coloured cloth imbued with magical intentions. All over the world, we humans engage in this simplest of spells, tying strips of cloth, wool, cotton or string to a living tree. We tie our offering and send a wish into the beyond, with the hope that it may be granted. Our grasp of what lies beyond may be hazy, but it does not matter. This is instinctive lived religion, the folk traditions that bring reassurance and give us strength in the daily struggles of life, a sense of burdens shared, of someone or something being on our side. Here at the conference, there is no sacred well or tree, but with a spirit of reverence we can make the same gesture as did our ancestors before us. I think about what to ask and then I know. My magical request now becomes obvious. I ask for enhanced creativity – for where better to ask for such a gift than at so creative a gathering?

All around me is the creative magical output of women celebrating reconnection to nature – to earth, sky, star, tree, to our wild origins when human consciousness began. I am drawn then to the work of Victoria Musson.[2] She is closely connected to the land, her family tenant farmers. She works with the materials of nature – wheat, wild rushes, acorns, pheasant feathers, whatever comes to hand from the Derbyshire countryside around her. With a sickle, she cuts grain and shapes it into sculptural forms. Her beautiful Harvest Goddess image evokes the messages of the traditional early-August celebration of the grain harvest – Lughnasa in Ireland, Lammas in England. It is a festival at the height of summer's heat, but when summer is past its peak. Grasses and grains dry out, flowers reach their final blooming, and shortening days take us inexorably towards autumn. The festival is a reminder of death's presence in the cycle of life.

In one striking photograph, tarot card XIII, the Death card, is positioned against ripened corn. It brings to mind the ancient archetype of the Sacrificial God, the corn king sacrificed to renew the fertility of the land. I remember in my childhood the sight of blood upon ripened wheat ears, a reality when the threshing machine trapped the hares and rabbits; when the farmer shot the encircled fox, hiding in the last stalks in the centre of the field. Carl Jung's words come to me: 'I saw how we live toward death, how the swaying golden wheat sinks together under the scythe of the reaper, like a smooth wave on the sea-beach.'[3] I see in Victoria Musson's work the grown wheat that has died to create the bread that others may live. One day, I too will return to the earth, my spirit released and my body nourishing the soil from which new growth will come.

As I walk around the conference venue, engaging with the artwork, absorbing the energies, the conference seems to me a crucible. The atmosphere is electric with the creative power of hundreds of magical women gathered together in this space. In the period of my life when I worked on the psychology of innovation, I read Professor Lynda Gratton's book *Hot Spots*.[4] This comes to mind now.

Hot spots are crucibles – an alchemical mix of time, place and people coming together in cooperation with an igniting purpose, a willingness to work across disciplinary boundaries, and the time and resources to experiment and innovate. This conference is a hot spot. It has energy, vibrancy, ideas, joy and excitement. I am hearing presentations that remind me of my values and activate past knowledge and future avenues for new learning. It is the type of atmosphere in which other people's ideas and insights create synergies with our own.

With all the airy and fiery energies around, I need to earth myself once more in the known, the familiar. I find it in a presentation by screenwriter Scarlett Amaris on artist Una Woodruff. Like many lovers of all things magical, I collect witchy humour as well as erudite grimoires. One of my favourite illustrated books is Una Woodruff's *Catwitch*, a gentle, funny tale of a kitten who becomes the familiar of the witch Eva Eden.[5] After many a mishap, he helps her find the magical unicorn's horn, thus thwarting the efforts of the wicked male magician Alexander Wylie, who wants it for his own evil purposes. *Catwitch* is a story that can charm children and adults, a story of a woman triumphing over misused male power.

Una Woodruff's book *Witches*, with its text by occult novelist, writer and philosopher Colin Wilson, goes deeper to reveal a darker side of witchcraft.[6] When I look at the images again now, I see them with new eyes. They convey both the fear of witches and witches' fear of the forces of persecution. They remind me of how much women of power are feared and reviled by men. Why is it so threatening; why is the fear so deep-seated? We see it in the death threats sent out by enraged men to women politicians – the denigration, the efforts to make another human being less than human. We saw it when, during her 2016 presidential campaign, Hillary Clinton was labelled 'the wicked witch of the left' and a 'witch with a capital B'. One solution is to embrace the image of the witch, as did many of her female supporters, who fought back by proudly calling themselves 'Witches for Hillary'. They adopted the witch as a symbol of empowerment that subverted the rhetoric used against women who are perceived to threaten male privilege.[7]

Other presenters, too, evoke the fear that men have of the witch. My mid-teens' foraging in the second-hand book stalls of London's markets delivered many treasures, some of which were the early-twentieth-century novels of Mary Webb – *Gone to Earth*, *The Precious Bane* and *The Golden Arrow*.[8] For decades, I thought that everyone else had forgotten her, but now she is honoured here by novelist, witch and scholar Rebecca Beattie.[9] I discovered Mary Webb's writings when I had just moved into the concrete jungle of London. I identified with her rhapsodic yearning for a return to embeddedness in the land, its soil and its customs. Hers was a knowledge of the witchery of deep rural England, of cunning men who acted as the only doctors that people could afford, of sin-eaters who in Protestant Britain were folk magicians who eased the fear of death by taking away people's sins. Literary critics compare her writing to that of Thomas Hardy and, like him, she evokes the darker side of rural life for women, and how easy it can be for women who are different to be accused of witchcraft because of their neighbours' hatred and fear.

Yet all is not dark for women of magic. One chapter of Una Woodruff's *Witches* is about the organisation at the heart of the late nineteenth and early twentieth century magical revival, the Hermetic Order of the Golden Dawn. Its structured syllabus of magical teachings attempted to incorporate all the known knowledge and techniques of the Western magical tradition – astrology, divination, visualisation, meditation, and powerful rites to attain changes of consciousness that lead to spiritual growth. Early histories of the Golden Dawn focus on the three male Freemason co-founders, but in the twenty-first century we are rediscovering the contribution of its women. Unusually for the era, the Golden Dawn admitted women and men on equal terms to its membership and leadership roles, and women responded.[10]

The Golden Dawn became a crucible, a hot spot of talented people from the sciences, arts and spirituality. Most of the important magicians of the era belonged at some point to the Golden Dawn or one of its later offshoots.[11] Drs William Wynn Westcott and William Robert Woodman, Samuel Liddell MacGregor Mathers, Moina Bergson Mathers, Arthur Edward Waite, Florence Farr, Aleister Crowley and Dion Fortune all passed through some or all of its teaching system. Artist Pixie Colman Smith, novelists Arthur Machen, Algernon Blackwood, Arnold Bennett and Edith Nesbit, brought fantasy, magic and socialism to the general public. Allan Bennett, later a Buddhist monk, brought Buddhism to the West. Under his pen name of Fiona Macleod, the Scottish poet, novelist and Gaelic-speaker William Sharp breathed his Celtic mysticism into poetry and prose. Actor, writer, feminist, socialist, theatre producer and philanthropist Annie Horniman worked with Golden Dawn members William Butler Yeats and actor, feminist and revolutionary Maud Gonne in establishing Dublin's Abbey Theatre, later the National Theatre of Ireland, an important cultural platform for an independent Ireland.

Here at the conference, we celebrate the Golden Dawn women and their enormous contribution to the magical revival. Elaine Bailey presents the work of Dr Anna Bonus Kingsford, one of the first women doctors in England, a visionary social reformer, anti-vivisectionist, campaigner for vegetarianism, and trailblazing advocate for women's rights. She became President of the London Lodge of Madame Helena Blavatsky's Theosophical Society, but she broke away to find her spiritual inspiration in the West. Her Hermetic Society was the forerunner to the Golden Dawn, and brought to it Anna Kingsford's vision of the equality of women and men. Her work was inspired by an animist worldview that the cosmos around us is sentient, alive. In *Clothed with the Sun,* the book of her visions, she reverses the social order of her day. Womanhood reborn is about to give birth to a new aeon, one in which women will come into their power and re-vision the world.[12]

The women of the Golden Dawn pursued the work of human transformation not just through magic and ritual, but through art, literature, music and dramatic performance too. Florence Farr wrote plays to stimulate her audience's imagination and arouse their curiosity to know more. *The Mystery of Time*, performed at the Albert Hall Theatre in January 1905, was about an intense form of meditation practice. This went far beyond the health and healing aims of secular mindfulness today. Florence Farr invites us to fix the mind on that 'imperceptible point of Time called the Present', and rid ourselves of all wandering thoughts that take us into past or future. If we succeed, we will find ourselves 'melting into the state beyond Mind in which the Past and Future have no part.'[13] This is a state beyond ordinary words, conveyed only through evocative image and feeling: 'I stood naked in a bleak and dark eternity and filled it with my exultation.'[14] Her emphasis is on finding the Divine within – finding our own inner sources of authority and authenticity. 'Free yourselves from your environments,' she tells us. Believe nothing without weighing and considering it for ourselves; for something that is true for one person may not be true for another.[15]

Across the span of a century and more, Florence Farr's words ring true for all; but especially so for women, for those betwixt and between, for those who do not accept the status quo and want the world to be a better place. Her message is needed now. Women, men and non-binary, many of us live in societies where we have been able to choose our religion or belief, or not to believe at all. In many parts of the world, we still have the right to vote for politicians to represent us, the freedom to choose whether to study, what clothes to wear, how to conduct our sex lives, what to eat and whom to eat it with. These are all choices that contribute to making human life worth living. They are the choices that make it possible to be the person we are meant to be. But they are choices that can easily be taken away.

These thoughts bring me back to Clarissa Pinkola Estés's Wild Woman. We have need of her passion, of her refusal to be tamed, because there are dark forces in the world that must be opposed. In some countries, the scary images of Margaret Atwood's *The Handmaid's Tale* no longer seem so far removed from reality. There are tyrants who threaten our freedom; political dictators who dress their regimes in the veneer of legality. There are corporate empires where single individuals with more wealth than sovereign states can exercise a terrible power over our lives and that of our planet. There are amoeba-like networks of terrorists who seek to impose their deranged ideologies on others, come what may. There are those who intend to take all our freedoms away from us. And we must refuse.

We refuse to become like them. We will hold to our values that speak of the worth of all of humankind; the values that connect us to others and create unity not separation, that involve collective responsibility, not a giving over of our power to others. We will hold on to the values that inspire us to dance for our goddesses and gods and create spiritual practices and teachings of love and compassion, of joy and freedom. We choose not to hate or to acquiesce. We can choose to become heroes and sheroes. We can choose to resist.

The conference gives me new creative ideas, new visions, new strength. It reminds me that the women I admire in my spiritual and intellectual life are not women who live constrained by stereotypical female roles, but rather women who liberate themselves to live the whole of their being. The conference fills me with enormous respect for all these sheroes and heroes of the past who opened the hidden ways. Sue Terry and Erzebet Barthold, our conference organisers, aimed to 'pay homage to the women of the past who challenged the status quo by embracing mysticism, esotericism, and occult teachings'.[16] For me, they have succeeded. We have honoured the past and embraced it in order to shape the future. We have seen how the ideas and ideals that have inspired the magical women of the past – awakening the latent powers within us, reclaiming the right of all human beings to personhood and self-expression, reconnecting with nature, finding the wildness within, experiencing our magical powers, becoming witches and priestesses, reawakening the Goddess and the ancient gods – all these strands and currents that inspired me and women before and after me are now coming to fruition.

Magic is feeding the mainstream, and the currents that fifty years before took me on my magical path have come to the fore of human consciousness. Magic is changing, evolving. The journey into witchdom that I began in my teens has become a journey for personal transformation, but a journey that makes sense only if we return to our place of origin, if we bring back the treasure hard to find that others may share it. I sense a change is coming, my future reshaping. I am coming around on the spiral. As I walk away from the conference, I feel a new phase is about to begin.

22

Awakening to New Gods

With time, the dead cease to walk in our house in Brittany. The manifestations become less frequent once we concrete over the beaten earth floor in the eighteenth-century part of the house. Before we owned one, I thought a beaten earth floor was just loose earth, but after three hundred years of human footfall the surface is like polished black linoleum. It took months before we realised it was earth.

Over time, the mists dissipate too. We are not sure why – changes in farming methods perhaps, climate change, a modernisation of the psyche? The wraiths cease to visit, which makes me sad. It feels like the old mysteries of the land are going too. Dual carriageway comes to our part of Brittany, so all the countries of Europe can eat our meat and cheese. Trucks with number plates from Russia and Belarus head to the agri-processing factories. Corporate delegations from China fly in brandishing contracts for Breton milk to be exported as milk powder. The older generation take their wooden clogs off for the last time, and the funeral columns of the local newspaper outstrip more and more the births. With the passing of the elders, old memories and customs pass. That peculiar little chapel where, above the altar, instead of a crucifix there is a wooden pentagram hung with horseshoes – the hamlet starts taking it down during the summer visitor season, then after a few years it is not rehung. Tourist questions that no one wants to answer make people shyer of older customs. On St John's Day, the Midsummer bonfires are still lit and blessed by a priest so the Christian sanctifies the Pagan practice, but most people skip all aspects of the spiritual and turn up for the four-course meal, music and dancing that follow.

In 2019, we decide to sell our house in London. Brexit is looming, the UK economy is shaky and house prices are falling. We put the house on the market tentatively, not sure if anyone will buy, and we return to our home in Brittany where we have our spiritual connection to the land. We know the local culture and history. We have visited, meditated and sometimes performed rituals at special places connected to Brittany's Celtic and pre-Celtic past. We have put down our roots. Now we begin putting in the groundwork to leave England and to settle in Brittany full-time. We pay for some essential renovations. We kick-start all the bureaucracy necessary to make the transition. We find a bilingual accountant to extricate us from the British tax and social security system and transition us into the French equivalents. We log on at two minutes past midnight to get into the system to get the difficult-to-obtain interview for that essential French document, a *carte de séjour,* a resident's permit to enable us to live permanently in France.

Everything is in motion. The only additional thing I need to do is to pick up the phone and call the UK Social Security headquarters in Newcastle, for the piece of paper that we need to register with the French health system. I put off picking up the phone the first day and then the next, and then another day passes by. Living permanently in Brittany seems a really sensible idea, but something inside me is unconvinced. As we hover in indecision, we realise that this is a situation where we need to see the bigger picture.

I do I Ching readings from time to time, but my go-to divination system is the tarot. Today, there are hundreds, maybe even thousands, of different designs of tarot decks, from copies of fourteenth- and fifteenth-century Italian and French decks, to decks that represent all the different streams of esoteric and magical thought. They have become the inspiration of writers, artists and dancers. Even a James Bond movie featured a tarot. A special pack was designed for the film *Live and Let Die*, in which Roger Moore played James Bond. The plan was for Surrealist artist Salvador Dalí to be the designer, but sadly the film's financiers baulked at his fee. The commission went to a Scottish artist, Fergus Hall, who created the Tarot of the Witches.

My favourite tarot for readings remains my Waite-Colman Smith tarot, which is nearly fifty years old. I keep the cards in a wooden box, and they are in good condition still. All of us when we start on a magical path tend to read the tarot a lot. Now, even though I own ten different tarot decks and use the cards for meditation, I rarely read the tarot for divination. Foolishly, because it had not occurred to me that I might want to consult an oracle for this life-changing decision, my Waite-Colman Smith pack is in London.

Chris and I adopt the contemporary solution to our problem. We order a new Waite-Colman Smith pack from Amazon. Maybe having pristine new cards is not a bad idea when we feel that whatever decision we make will take us on a completely new course. The cards arrive the next day. Even in rural Brittany, Amazon delivers fast. We wait two days to do the reading and do it on Spring Equinox. The equinoxes are times in the physical life of our planet when tides and winds are high. There is an energy in the air, a sense of change as light and dark shift their balance. Spiritually and psychologically, it feels a good time to make decisions.

The tarot has been in Europe for over seven hundred years, and the four major suits – Wands, Pentacles, Swords and Cups – are largely unchanged. The major arcana were more variable, but have gradually whittled down to twenty-two cards with evocative names and images, such as the High Priestess, the Magus, the Hanged Man, Death, the Devil, the Moon, the Sun and the Star. The tarot can be a gateway to intuition, inspiration, even illumination. Whatever pack we use, the images are powerful. Their meaning is never obvious but they stimulate the psyche. They become like a question to which we almost know the answer, and in that creative interaction between known and unknown, the unconscious is stimulated to produce answers that we could not have reached by conscious thought.

We start laying out the reading about the implications of moving to Brittany. The Fool appears, the Devil, the Hanged Man, the Eight of Swords. We do not even need to get to the end, but we do. It gets no better. I can truly say it was the most negative tarot reading I have ever done. It looks like if we go down this path we will feel psychologically trapped and it will be bad for us financially. To check, we do a reading for being resident in England. There is joy there, friendship, financial security. Our course seems set. We decide to take our house off the market. Towards close of play on Friday, our estate agent rings with the weekly marketing update. We put the phone on speaker and are about to tell him apologetically that all his efforts have been in vain, but he gets in first. 'Congratulations, we have an offer at the full asking price. We have done due diligence on the buyer and it all stacks up. It's a cash sale and she wants to push ahead as soon as possible.' It turns out that a local jogger had popped into the estate agency on the off chance. She had often jogged down our quaint little lane and thought that she would love to live there, if ever a house came up for sale. He took her round to see our house and she made an offer immediately. We thank him and put the phone down in a state of shock. It has all fallen into place so neatly that we sense we really should move after all, but if not to Brittany, then where?

A guided visualisation during the next spiritual psychology workshop that Chris and I run in London provides the answer. It is a visualisation about the journey of life. Chris is leading it, so I decide to go on the journey myself. I find myself out of London with Chris travelling towards a small town, heading north-west into golden late-afternoon light. The town could be anywhere from the Chiltern Hills to Kinsale in County Cork, for another option is to become resident in Ireland. Afterwards, Chris and I talk about my visualisation and the tarot reading we did about staying in

England. Prominent in it was the theme of friendship. We complete our house sale and go house-hunting in the Cotswolds, where we have a lot of magically minded friends. After a few days' search, we buy a house.

At Samhain, Hallowe'en, we take possession of our new house. It is new for us in two senses. It is nearly three hundred years newer than our house in Brittany, and we know little about the area. We begin to explore the energy of this English landscape, walking the hiking routes, which pleases our dog mightily, and reading up on the history and archaeology. We knew that Gloucester and Cirencester were Roman cities, but I had not realised the extent to which Romans had settled here and embedded themselves in the local land and culture. The Romans conquered Brittany too, but there the Celtic tribes were fiercer and wilder. It was Asterix the Gaul territory, where Romans kept to the trade routes and fortresses and did not venture far into the thick forests that covered the inland fastness. In England, despite Boudicca's uprising, it was different.

When in England we think of Romans, we think of Italians – but as the Roman Empire grew it became multicultural. Joining the Roman legions served much the same function as does joining the US military for someone from a small American town today. It offered travel and an income; providing of course that you survived the fearsome locals. Many veterans of the Roman legions retired to Britain. All were Roman citizens, but they came from the British Isles, from elsewhere in Europe and sometimes from the North African legions. Having done their service, they settled to marry, raise children and farm. And they brought with them their gods.

The Romans were in England for only a few hundred years, but as we start to open ourselves to the energies of the land, much to our surprise the Romano-Celtic deities make themselves felt. They start to appear to me in my dreams, at first as hazy outlines, or faint voices, and then more clearly. The Roman overlay is there, but I sense the older deities that lie behind it. Tabloid newspapers seem to think that religious tolerance is some strange new late-twentieth-century fad, but two thousand years ago the Roman Empire was a multifaith empire. Christians aside, in the main it was religiously tolerant. Provided you were willing to acknowledge the secular powers by participating in the state cult and venerating the emperor, you were free to worship your local deities and to engage in creative fusion. In an expanding empire exposed to many different deities, it was natural to think that maybe your goddess of the harvest was not so different from my goddess of the harvest. My goddess of the harvest served my people well where we lived before, but the local goddess here might want worship too, so why not worship them both at once? In Aquae Sulis (modern Bath), the Celtic goddess Sulis, who presided over the sacred thermal healing spring, fused with the Roman goddess of wisdom to become Sulis Minerva. The many-skilled Celtic god Lugus or Lugh was fused with Mercury, the multitalented messenger god.

Our most popular local deities were the triple mother goddesses, the Matres. Their image is in the Roman museum in nearby Cirencester. They are goddesses of prosperity and abundance, and appear with bread, fish and other foods. They were worshipped as the Matres in many other European countries, but here they were also known as the Suleviae, a name that connects them to the goddess Sulis of Bath.

Our search for a male deity reveals the Romano-Celtic god Apollo Cunomaglos, Lord of the Hounds, whose image was dug up in 1875 on the Sudeley Castle estate. It is thought that his temple was in the woods nearby. To the Romans, Apollo was the beautiful god of music, dance, poetry, healing and archery. The local people worshipped Cunomaglos as a god of hunting who appeared with a stag and a hound. Quite why and how Apollo and Cunomaglos came to be fused is a mystery. It could be because Apollo is brother to the huntress-goddess Diana, whose statues often show her with hounds and stag. It could be that Apollo was also a patron of medicine, and that healing hounds were kept at his temples. Many cultures have discovered that dog saliva is antibacterial, and dogs can detect the changes in body odour associated with illnesses such as cancer. The research is so promising that there is now a charity in the UK that trains medical detection dogs.[1] We adopt Apollo Cunomaglos as one of our local deities; and, since we have adopted an abandoned Mediterranean hunting dog too, Apollo Cunomaglos's protection can extend to all the species of our family.

Winter Solstice approaches and we begin Yuletide preparations. We dig up an old Christmas tree left by our predecessors and bring it into the garden room. It is too tall for the main part of the house and the cooler air here will help it survive. The idea of bringing greenery into our homes at this time of year is ancient. Even if our celebrations are mainly indoors, we want to remind ourselves of our connection to the natural world outside. Unlike

Brittany, we have built no stone circle on the land, but for our first rite in our new house we want to use all of the space, both inside and outside – a sanctification of all of our home. We plan to go outside from the intermediate space of the garden room into the garden, where we have a fire dish to keep us warm. Here we live in the tamed landscape of England, not in Brittany's wilder spaces. No animals will come from the forest to watch our fire, but even so we can capture some time under the moon and stars before retreating inside to the warmth of the meditation room.

We invite friends to join us and to co-create a ritual. Some of us take charge of decorating the meditation room for the rite and others for writing invocations to deities of the place – Apollo Cunomaglos and the Suleviae, the Triple Mothers – and to a god not of the place but of the season. The Winter Solstice celebrations in the Roman calendar were a feast that honoured Saturn, god of time, ageing and agriculture. Saturn ruled over a past Golden Age of prosperity and innocence. His feast was a return to the Golden Age, a bit like a rosy vision of childhood. Like modern Christmas, Saturnalia grew. It started as a one-day festivity then expanded either side of the Solstice to 17–23 December – a week of feasting, gift-giving, games and merriment much like our Christmas customs today.

On Solstice day, we decorate the tree in silver and white. We decorate the meditation room with golden hangings to represent the rebirth of the sun. We set up an altar with golden candles and a goddess sculpture by Glastonbury artist Phillipa Bowers, to represent the mother goddess who gives birth to the sun child on Solstice night.[2] The altar creates a focal point for the rite, its candles a soft and welcoming light.

We make an incense for censing the sacred space. We choose ingredients associated in magical tradition with the energy of the sun. Frankincense is one of the most expensive tree resins, the one used for incense for kings. The name comes from Old French, *franc encens* – 'noble incense' – an appropriate resin for the festival that celebrates the rebirth of the sun, the solar child who shall become the summer king. With mortar and pestle, we pound the frankincense resin into small fragments and add drops of orange oil, its sweet citrus aroma a reminder of sunny days. We add crushed cinnamon with its rich, warm tones. A few more drops of oil, a little more resin. Making incense is like cooking, but we feed the sense of smell rather than that of taste. The external preparations mirror the preparation within. We take time to meditate, to create a clear circle within our own consciousness, to let go of whatever is preoccupying us and let ourselves just *be*.

As evening approaches, we gather around the tree holding lighted candles and copies of the most Pagan carols that we can find – wassail songs and Norman Iles's versions of the Pagan carols restored.[3] Carols were not originally church songs, but folk songs of the people sung to celebrate the changing seasons. They were sung not in church but outside it. We sing the Somerset and the Gloucestershire wassail songs that were sung door-to-door while the poorer collected money from the richer. The songs bless the household for the coming year – as long as the wassailers are given their ale and donations. We sing carols in honour of the Solstice and the returning sun, our voices reverberating through the stone-paved garden room. Reflecting in the glass roof above, the candles we hold make a circle of flickering light as we stand around the tree. A friend who runs a choir sings a solo, piercingly beautiful in the wintry night.

We process outside with our candles to light the fire dish. Chris has made a fire of dry seasoned birch wood. It blazes upward quickly, the flames illumining the darkness. We say a blessing with words adapted from the *Carmina Gadelica*, a collection of Scottish Gaelic prayers and charms collected and translated into English by folklorist Alexander Carmichael in the nineteenth century.[4] With the Christian veneer stripped away, the core remains a beautiful Celtic vision of empathy with the elements of sky, fire, sea, earth and wind.

We light the fire in the name of the Mighty Ones, our spiritual ancestors and guides, and ask for a blessing on the house, the gathering, on friends, neighbours, on those who have harmed us and on all those around us. We stand around the fire in silent meditation, watching the flames. We send out thoughts of peace, goodwill and love. The feelings are akin to what in Buddhism is called *metta* (loving-kindness) and *karuṇa* (compassion). Celebrating the seasonal cycle with others helps us to see ourselves as part of the greater whole of humankind, of the biosphere, of the universe and of that which lies beyond. We allow an inner movement of energy that reaches out to the universe with a flow of feeling. This open, loving, non-judgemental warmth embraces the world and gives us a sense of meaning that brings joy and hope in the darkest time; for love is closely akin to joy.

I sense it is time for this part of the rite to come to an end. One of us goes ahead to light the candles and incense in the meditation room. We process silently into the softly glowing space, where the candle flames reflect off the wall hangings in shimmering gold. The soft lighting and incense move us further out of everyday consciousness towards that hypnagogic state between sleeping and waking when the brain produces imagery. We cross a spiritual and psychological threshold into the *temenos*, a Greek word for a temple enclosure or sacred space. We make a shift in consciousness from *chronos*, conventional time, into *kairos*, the opportune and decisive moment for action. There is a shift that is at once both beyond and back – back to our mammalian selves that operate in the sensory realms; beyond to wider states of consciousness, where boundaries dissolve between individual and collective, the realms from which dreams and visions come.

As we sanctify the meditation room with the elements, with salted water and our incense, I take a hazel wand and draw a symbolic circle around the perimeter of the room. We stand now in a microcosm, a space between the worlds, a space where new ideas, images and energies can be born. The circle creates a space in the jungle of competing thoughts, emotions, sensations, intuitions and memories that clutter our brains; a place where we can free ourselves of everyday clamours and demands. It is the simplest of spiritual spaces, an archetypal symbol of wholeness that has been used for millennia as a sacred place of healing and a refuge. It does not have the implicit hierarchy of a rectangular church or temple. We stand about the circumference as equals; each one of us able to see all the rest.

One by one people step forward to say their invocations. Apollo Cunomaglos we invoke as the sunlight that warms and impregnates the earth in the coming spring. His energy seems both gentle and powerful. We invoke the Triple Goddess as the pregnant Mother who will give birth to the reborn sun, and the Maiden and Grandmother goddesses who are there to ease the birth. There is a shift in the quality of the energy in the room, a profound peace comes that at the same time feels like a new beginning. Sometimes it can be difficult to create a magical atmosphere in a new place, but here it feels as though the house has been waiting for its space to be filled with this energy of love and light. The Unknown Spirit of this place is welcoming what we bring.

In the morning, I manage to activate for the first time the water pump that moves the water between our garden ponds to keep it fresh. The sound of flowing water echoes what I feel – flowing energy and a clearing of mind and heart. Then I make a discovery. Through the overgrown bushes around the pond I see two pointed pieces of stone peeking up. I clamber into the shrubbery and push back the vegetation. It looks like the head of a dog, but as I pull back more dead leaves and bushes, I discover a reclining stone statue of a deer. After nearly two thousand years, it seems that Apollo Cunomaglos, hunter of deer and patron of the hunted, has awoken and descended from his ruined woodland shrine to claim this place for his own.

Our move to consolidate our base in England is just in time. Our on-the-road teaching existence around the world is again no longer viable, not because I am ill or solely due to climate change, but because the world is ill. Covid-19 comes, travel ceases. Now I have time to write the book I thought about in Australia eighteen years before. I have come around on the spiral of one phase of existence. Another can now begin.

23

Wild Once More

Many of us spend the whole of our existence living out a life that is not truly ours; one we would not have chosen. It is surprisingly easy to live according to the agendas of others. We may even prefer to do so. It can be much easier than taking responsibility for charting the course of our own destiny. Some of us may think it is impossible to live the life we want to live. We may feel that we have gone too far down a particular road in terms of career, relationships or responsibilities for partners, progeny, parents and pets. It is true that we cannot rewrite the past. We can determine the future, but first we need to wake up to embrace the present, the here and now, who we are and what is around us.

The Covid-19 pandemic gave us two gifts – a vision of how our planet might be green and clean again, and a reminder, timely but painful, of the fragility of human life. We humans are like butterflies in the grand scheme of things, our lives only a microsecond or two in cosmic time. When I was ten I was acutely aware of the passage of time.

I am not sure why. Perhaps it was an unconscious sense that childhood was ending. My body was beginning to change in the unalterable evolution of puberty. I wrote a poem I called 'Time Dreams'. It was not a brilliant poem, but I remember it still because I was trying to explain an insight that I felt was important. It came to me one summer night, when I was looking out to sea.

> Time, like a bird on the wing,
> flies on everlastingly.
> Time like silvery sea
> flows on for eternity.
> Our lives though long they seem to us,
> they are but a grain of time,
> and yet to me like a precious jewel,
> is that grain that life of mine.

When the threat of death is all around us, we become acutely aware of the value of life and the importance of living our lives as we want to live them right now. It is the ever-becoming *now* that we can change and time is always running out. Life is short and all too soon there will be no other *now*. The external circumstances of our lives are not always something we can change, but we can change how we relate to the universe around us. We can live each moment as though what is within us is important, because we are the cells within the body of a greater whole, that of the collective unconscious of all humankind, an interwoven web of imagination and memory.

We can find much wisdom in books and teachings, but the ultimate sources of truth are out there in the mysteries of the cosmos – and down and within, in the depths of our being. My own journey has been led by feeling and intuition. It was born of a feeling of connection to nature that did not seem to fit the worldview around me, but as the decades have passed those insights that I had as a child have emerged more and more to the fore of mainstream society. The journey was shaped, too, by a realisation that my consciousness, 'I', was not dependent on my body – a phenomenon now called nonlocal consciousness by those who are pioneering our understanding of the interface between neuroscience and physics. And there was another motivating drive too – the idea that each of us has a unique individual spiritual journey to make to come to our own personal realisation of the deeper self within that is linked to the Divine. This was my personal quest for the Holy Grail.

There is a saying in Wicca that if we cannot find what we seek within us, we will never find it outside of us. Joseph Campbell in his book *The Hero with a Thousand Faces* expresses this very beautifully. The 'perilous journey', our own spiritual quest, is, he writes, 'a labour not of attainment but of re-attainment, not discovery but rediscovery'. When we reach the end of the journey, we discover that the powers that we sought have been within us all the time, 'only waiting to be known and rendered into life'.[1]

The true Holy Grail of the spiritual quest is to achieve unification with the deeper self, the source of our authenticity. At first, the contact is fleeting. We have momentary experiences of it but perceive it as something external to us – perhaps as a god or goddess or angel; perhaps an inner guru, as did Carl Jung with Philemon, or Carlos Castaneda with Don Juan. Over time, the contact becomes more frequent and we experience fleeting times of unification with this inner voice of wisdom. Finally, we realise that this voice is part of us, our deeper wiser self, a self that stands outside time and endures perhaps through incarnations. Sometimes we lose contact with the deeper self, and the voice falls silent for a time. Perhaps we do not like what it is telling us and we rebel. But if we pursue our quest and spiritual path, we come to a point where we find that we become more and more aligned to this deeper part of our being. We find we can decentre ourselves from the everyday preoccupations of the ego to achieve a new perspective on life, one that is longer, wider, deeper.

Different spiritual traditions can speed our quest, but we do not need to follow a particular path if none draws us; for what is important in these traditions are values and simple processes that connect us to the deeper self. Meditation, dream work, ritual, time spent in nature; time when we allow our creativity to flow – in art, creative writing, song, music; times of oneness with the body, another type of flow that we find in running, yoga, sailing, swimming, dance or drumming – in whatever it is that works for us. These are the processes that allow us to let go of everyday preoccupations and orient us to what is important and to what gives us joy. These experiences give us new insight and energy to live our goals and dreams and see them through.

We can start our spiritual quest at any age, for it is lifelong. There is no final revelation, for at each stage of the journey we discover there is always so much more to experience and learn. As I come round on the spiral into the last phase of my adult life, it feels as though a new phase is beginning; but this book is a reflection of my spiritual quest so far. It has been a journey through consciousness, symbols and esoteric traditions, to finding that within our innermost being is a source of wisdom and knowledge, a deep well, from which we may drink. The quest has taught me tolerance, to accept and honour the shared wisdom and truth in all spiritual traditions, and a willingness to see myself and all others as flawed beings – but struggling, ever struggling, to open ourselves to love and wisdom, like buds seeking to flower. We humans, though flawed, are like myriad points of light, each one of us a star. Within each one is a flame of life and consciousness and there is great beauty in that. But when we come together to share with others, when we create community and bonds of love that link and join us, then the stars become constellations, and reveal shape and meaning that create a greater beauty.

The spiritual journey that we start, perhaps feeling alone, cast adrift in uncharted waters, brings us in time to be no longer alone, but in deep communion with the authentic self that is in a deeper connection still – to the whole collective psyche of humankind. Instead of perceiving ourselves as isolated, self-contained egos, we can experience ourselves as members of a whole human family, united with the families of all other species, together in the biosphere of Gaia. This deeper connection can bring joy but also pain, for the authentic self is an ecological self and the world we have created does not feed our deepest longings. Our cleverness has outstripped our wisdom. The technological advances we have created have taken a terrible toll, not just on human beings but on the whole planet.

All around us is the cosmos, vast in space and time, vast beyond our wildest imaginings, extraordinarily beautiful, complex and mysterious. Many ancient creation myths speak of the universe around us as a web that is woven into being by weaver-goddesses. Science too now speaks of the universe as a cosmic web, one comprising vast interconnecting filaments of clustered galaxies and gases separated by giant voids. The matter we know, the stars and galaxies that we can detect, account for only five per cent of its content. Ninety-five per cent is dark energy and dark matter, which is beyond what our human instrumentation can currently see or measure.[2] What science can tell us is that we know that there is so much out there that we do not know. Yet we can wonder, marvel, appreciate and rejoice that the cosmos exists around us and in us. It is us and we are part of it. Our Earth is only a tiny speck in the vastness, but to us it is of supreme importance. It is home, the only home we have right now, and we need it for future generations.

Allow your mind to play for a time with the idea that we are, as the old hippie song goes, made of stardust. It is true that the elements in our bodies came into being millions of years ago, in a galaxy far away.[3] Despite all our flaws and failings, we human beings are an extraordinary creation, a species of hopes, dreams and visions of insight and power, each one of us a unique representative of our kind. If we look around the world as viewed through newsfeeds, we might find it difficult to believe in the future of humankind. It is easy to despair when we see some of the terrible things that we do, but there is hope too. We have survived so far. We have adapted and bounced back in the face of nature's challenges of famine, flood, wildfire and storm. We continue to survive our self-created challenges of war and violence. How have we done so? The answer lies in our greatest gift: our human imagination, which gives us the power to see how we can make the world a better place. If we remind ourselves of human creativity, of our remarkable visions that we turn into painting, sculpture, music, song and dance, then we can have greater faith in the ability of our species to change. For it is our imagination that we will need if our species is to survive into the future – and our love.

Although I enjoy the intellectual world, I know that the intellect alone, unmediated by intelligence of heart and spirit, is a dangerous thing. That flawed magical genius Aleister Crowley taught that 'Love is the law, love under will'.[4] But if we turn, not to the male heroic archetype, but to the Wild Woman who leads us to the world of nature, what she teaches is not 'love under will' but 'will under love'. It is in our loving relationships with one another that we find strength of will, the motivation to go forward, the courage to change what must be changed.

The need for inner transformation is something we can feel in our own individual lives, but it is important on a much wider scale too. We need a radical transformation of human consciousness that cannot be achieved by this political ideology or that world religion. Nothing can change unless we change ourselves. This is now the time, the *kairos*, to effect a great change, for we stand at the beginning of a new aeon.

The precession of the equinoxes refers to the apparent rotation of the heavens around Earth first observed by the ancient Greek astronomer Hipparchus of Nicaea. This means that the zodiac sign on the spring horizon gradually changes. Our astrology is based on calculations four thousand years old, when Aries the Ram was the zodiac sign on the dawn horizon at Spring Equinox. Pisces, the Fishes, became the sign at the beginning of the Christian era. The sign on the horizon at the spring dawn is now Aquarius, the human figure of the Water-Bearer. In esoteric thinking, this is the archetypal energy that will dominate the human psyche for the next two thousand years. With the changing of an aeon, old forms of religion die away and something new is born. Just as monotheism was the child of the Age of Pisces, Aquarius will bring new forms of spirituality based not on patriarchal monotheism and external gods, but on finding the Divine within the depths of our own being.

In the twentieth century, the dawning of the Age of Aquarius was welcomed as a transition to all the positive qualities of Aquarius. We hoped for an aeon of humanism and humanitarianism, a time in which we would honour the uniqueness and autonomy of each of us, but also recognise our deep interconnection. We embraced Carl Jung's idea of the collective unconscious, the group psyche of humankind. We looked to a new dawning of a deeper and wider consciousness that would help us to overcome our individual isolation and to experience how each of us is a cell in a greater whole.

New births come with birth pangs. The beginning of a new era is a dangerous and volatile time. At these powerful times of transition, change becomes intense. Hopes, aspirations, expectations and fears become ingredients in a boiling cauldron of ideas and emotions. The flames leap up, the pot boils and overflows, and the past is swept away. It is a time of conflict. In any transition, there are forces impelling us forward into the future, and forces that are resisting with all their might that which is to come. The opposing forces will be present in our politics, in the environment and in the wider cosmos. By the process of synchronicity, the inner world and outer world mirror one another. These progressive and regressive forces will be present in our own psyches too; for however much we want change, we also fear it.

Each aeon has a shadow side, just as each of us as individuals has a shadow. At the beginning of a two-thousand-year cycle, we are experiencing not only the hopes of Aquarius, but its shadow too. The shadow of each of the zodiac signs comprises all the worse traits of its opposite sign in the zodiac. The age just passed was Pisces, which sought to teach universal love, but its shadow was the negative side of Virgo. The inspired ideals of spiritual teachers became codified texts and rules; conflict developed between spirit and matter, spirituality and sexuality. In Aquarius, we liberated ourselves from Virgo's shadow, but now we are experiencing the shadow of Aquarius. This is Leo, the proud and regal lion, whose other symbols are solar child and solar king. Leo's shadow is a crowned and conquering child, a childlike tyrant, who threatens to throw his toys out of the pram, or press his nuclear button, if his will is not obeyed. All over the world, we see people abandoning the democratic vision of freedom and our responsibility for ruling ourselves, to hand over autonomy and power to fear-creating dictators who seek to divide and rule.

Fortunately, many predict that the masculine Child-King archetype will soon give way to the true archetype of the aeon, that of the Goddess of Justice – in Ancient Egyptian religion, the goddess Ma'at. It is she who in Egyptian religion presides over the Weighing of the Heart in the Halls of Judgement as we enter the afterlife. Holding aloft her symbols of sword and scales, the statue of the Goddess of Justice outside law courts is a reminder of this ancient archetype. Ma'at's is a justice tempered by mercy, love and compassion. This is justice that is not so much impersonal as transpersonal, in service not to this faction or that, but to humankind and to the greater good.

There are signs that the archetype of transpersonal Justice is becoming more prominent in the human psyche. Gradually we have extended our concept of justice to laws that protect human rights – voting rights, equality rights, anti-discrimination rights, reproductive rights and the right to freedom of expression. The impetus to this type of justice is born of empathy – we empathise with other human beings and want them to be treated as we want to be treated ourselves. Now our sense of empathy is extending and we are advocating for animal rights and Earth's rights too. Despite all our human failings, we are evolving.

Mass movements and shifts of consciousness often seem to come out of nowhere, but that is not really so. They occur when enough of us have felt the ripples of those who are ahead of us on the curve. Changes happen in the unconscious long before they penetrate the membrane between our conscious and unconscious minds. We cannot do what we cannot imagine, which is why those at the cutting edge of art, sci-fi and magic are always ahead of where humankind is going. We imagined space travel centuries before it was physically possible. The dream gave birth to the urge to create the science and technology to make it a reality. Now we need a new dream, a dream of what we human beings can become.

A transformation of human consciousness is desperately needed and for this we will need a new spirituality, one that roots us in our deep connection to one another and to all of our planet's creation. This we can find if we turn inwards to the collective unconscious, the repository of the dreams and visions of the past, a treasure trove of images and ideas, of myths, thoughts and visions of our antecedents, of ways that sustained our species since our first evolution into consciousness and self-awareness.

Our world religions are but a couple of thousand years old and based on the words of male prophets born in a particular time and culture. There can be wisdom, love and power in these teachings, but there is also all the baggage of the societies and cultures from which they are born. There can also be misogyny and fear of difference, vested power interests, obsession with form over the original inspiration, and a blindness to the need for teachings to evolve to meet the planetary realities in which we live.

Now we are seeking new narratives, a new spirituality that is inclusive and honours the Earth. We are seeking reconnection with the narratives that gave us a sense of our relationship with nature and with the starry realms above.

Once, we watched what our elders did and copied their practices from generation to generation. Now we must find inspiration anew, turning inwards to our creative vision and outwards to those still alive to their ancestral traditions, to rebuild the practices of seasonal observance and honouring the life cycle. These are the simple ceremonies that honour the changing seasons of nature and the changing seasons of human life – birth, sexual maturity, mating, parenting, grandparenting and death. They teach a veneration for the gift of life, for the gift of consciousness, for the amazing privilege of being born into this wondrous universe of ours. They create a spirituality that can be found in field and forest, as well as in buildings made by human hands; a spirituality that can be shared across the diverse cultures of our planet.

For some of us, our feelings of reverence for what is beyond focus around a single source we call Goddess or God; for others, there is not one Divine but many. For many of us, and increasingly, such feelings transcend all human concept of deity. Nevertheless, we shall not be left orphaned of the gods. Their presence is still close to us. They live within the collective psyche and there they will endure; for their images are embedded deep. The Horned God and the Great Goddess awoke from sleep to reconnect us to nature, and to inspire us to give birth to a new spiritual vision. Now we can stand with them, and with Ma'at, archetype of transpersonal justice, to gaze out into the cosmos and allow its beauty to inspire us with hope and with the courage our species will need to face the challenges to come.

Wherever you are on your spiritual journey, I hope that my experiences will help you deepen your understanding of your own inner world, inspiring you to explore and enrich it further, and to reconnect ever more strongly with the source of wisdom and power within you – your authentic wilder self.

Notes

For full publication details, see Bibliography.

1 Throwing Off the Shackles

1. Vivianne Crowley, *Wicca: The Old Religion in the New Age*, 1989.
2. Charles Richard Foster Seymour, *The Forgotten Mage: The Magical Lectures of Colonel C. R. F. Seymour*, ed. Dolores Ashcroft-Nowicki, 1999, p. 24.
3. Joseph Campbell, *The Hero with a Thousand Faces*, 1972.
4. Clarissa Pinkola Estés, *Women Who Run with the Wolves*, 1992.

2 Entranced by Trees

1. William Henry Davies, *Songs of Joy and Others*, 1911, p. 15.

3 Discovering Witchery

1. Charles Williams, *War in Heaven*, 1930.
2. Aloysius Mullins, *Witchcraft: A Warning*, 1970.
3. Mullins, Witchcraft: A Warning, 1970, p. 11.
4. June Johns, *The King of the Witches*, 1969.
5. André Breton, *Manifestoes of Surrealism*, 1972, pp. 1–48.

6. Mao Tse-tung, *Quotations from Chairman Mao Tse-tung* [*The Little Red Book*], 1966, p. 71.
7. Sigmund Freud, *On the Sexual Theories of Children*, 2013, p. 14.
8. M. Esther Harding, *The Way of All Women*, 1971; Harding, *Women's Mysteries, Ancient and Modern*, 1971.
9. Charles Godfrey Leland, *Aradia, or The Gospel of the Witches*, 1974, p. 114.
10. Ibid., p. 6.

4 Dreaming of the Horned God

1. Margaret Alice Murray, *The Witch-Cult in Western Europe*, 1921; Murray, *The God of the Witches*, 1970, pp. 13–17.
2. Katherine Louise Oldmeadow, *Princess Charming*, 1923.
3. Philip Heselton, *In Search of the New Forest Coven*, 2020, pp. 197–208.
4. Thomas Moore, *A Religion of One's Own*, 2014.
5. Carl Gustav Jung, *Modern Man in Search of a Soul*, 1933.
6. Pausanias, *Description of Greece,* 1886, Book X, Chapter 26, p. 264.
7. Jung, 'The Philosophical Tree', in *The Collected Works of C. G. Jung, Vol. 13: Alchemical Studies*, 1967, para. 335.
8. Stefan G. Hoffman et al., 'Loving-kindness and compassion meditation: Potential for psychological interventions', 2011; Antonio Crego et al., 'The contribution of meaningfulness and mindfulness to psychological well-being and mental health: A structural equation model', 2019; José Ramón Yela et al., 'Self-compassion, meaning in life, and experiential avoidance explain the relationship between meditation and positive mental health outcomes', 2020.
9. Jung, 'The Relations between the Ego and the Unconscious', in *The Collected Works of C. G. Jung, Vol. 7: Two Essays in Analytical Psychology*, 173, para. 266.9.

5 Opening Ourselves to the Universe

1. Richard Wiseman, *The Luck Factor*, 2003.
2. Joseph Campbell with Bill Moyers, *The Power of Myth*, 1988, p. 120.

3. Erwin Schrödinger, *My View of the World*, 1964.
4. Wiseman, *The Luck Factor*, p. 86.

6 Healing Spirit

1. Ivy Northage, *Mechanics of Mediumship*, 1973; Northage, *Mediumship Made Simple*, 1986.
2. Hilary Mantel, *Beyond Black*, 2005.
3. Jung, 'Human Relationships in Relation to the Process of Individuation (Cornwall Seminar): Unauthorized Notes', 1923, p. 26.
4. Lewis Carroll, *Through the Looking-Glass*, 1871, p. 68.
5. Marjorie Aarons, *The Tapestry of Life*, 1979.
6. Jeanne Achterberg et al., 'Evidence for correlations between distant intentionality and brain function in recipients: A functional magnetic resonance imaging analysis', 2006.
7. Rita Pizzi et al., 'Non-local correlation between separated human neural networks', 2004; Chiara Marletto et al., 'Entanglement between living bacteria and quantized light witnessed by rabi splitting', 2018.
8. Dean Radin et al., 'Distant healing intention therapies: An overview of the scientific evidence', 2015.
9. Chris A. Roe et al., 'Two meta-analyses of noncontact healing studies', 2015.
10. Dalai Lama, 'Prayer is not enough', 2020.

7 Magic in Mind

1. Jamie Doward, 'Buddhist, teacher, predator: Dark secrets of the Triratna guru', 2019.
2. Wiseman, *The Luck Factor*, p. 86.
3. Roberto Assagioli, *Psychosynthesis*, 1975; Assagioli, *The Act of Will*, 1973.
4. Olivia Robertson, *Field of the Stranger*, 1948, p. 70.
5. Deborah Cracknell et al., 'Marine biota and psychological well-being: A preliminary examination of dose-response effects in an aquarium setting', 2015.
6. Ulrich et al., 'Effects of exposure to nature and abstract pictures on patients recovering from heart surgery', 1993.

8 Dialoguing with Oracles

1. *The I Ching, or Book of Changes*, trans. Richard Wilhelm and Cary F. Baynes, 1968, pp. 133–136.
2. Jung, 'Synchronicity: An Acausal Connecting Principle', in *The Collected Works of C. G. Jung, Vol. 8: The Structure and Dynamics of the Psyche*, 1969.
3. Marie-Louise von Franz, *On Divination and Synchronicity*, 1980.
4. Jung, 'Synchronicity', 1969, p. 519, para. 967.
5. *The I Ching*, 1968, pp. 608–609.
6. Ibid., pp. 20–21.
7. https://www.streetwisdom.org/about/.

9 Making Magic

1. Terry Pratchett, *Witches Abroad*, 1992, p. 7.

10 Magically Mindful

1. Sam J. Cooley et al., '"Into the Wild": A meta-synthesis of talking therapy in natural outdoor spaces', 2020.
2. Shunryū Suzuki, *Zen Mind, Beginner's Mind*, 1970, p. 21.
3. Glenn Albrecht, 'Creating a language for our psychoterratic emotions and feelings', 2011.
4. Gregory N. Bratman et al., 'Nature experience reduces rumination and subgenual prefrontal cortex activation', 2015.
5. MaryCarol Hunter, 'Urban nature experiences reduce stress in the context of daily life based on salivary biomarkers', 2019.
6. Rita Berto, 'The role of nature in coping with psycho-physiological stress: A literature review on restorativeness', 2014.
7. Gregory N. Bratman et al., 'The impacts of nature experience on human cognitive function and mental health', 2012.
8. Ruth Ann Atchley et al., 'Creativity in the wild: Improving creative reasoning through immersion in natural settings', 2012.
9. Roger S. Ulrich et al., 'Effects of exposure to nature and abstract pictures on patients recovering from heart surgery', 1993.

10. Kieran C. R. Fox et al., 'Is meditation associated with altered brain structure? A systematic review and meta-analysis of morphometric neuroimaging in meditation practitioners', 2014.

11 Reaching the Peaks

1. Helena Roerich, *Letters, Volume 2*, 1967, p. 255, Letter 24 August 1936; p. 473, Letter 5 April 1938.

12 Magical Healing

1. Ethan Basch et al., 'Boswellia: An evidence-based systematic review', 2004; Thomas Efferth and Franz Oesch, 'Anti-inflammatory and anti-cancer activities of frankincense: Targets, treatments and toxicities', 2020.
2. David L. Felten and Mary E. Maida, 'Psychoneuroimmunology', in Vilayanur Subramanian Ramachandran, ed., *Encyclopedia of the Human Brain*, 2002.
3. Stanley C. Krippner and Allan Combs, 'The neurophenomenology of shamanism: An essay review', 2002.
4. Helané Wahbeh et al., 'Shamanic healing for veterans with PTSD: A case series', 2017.
5. Elizabeth C. Roxburgh et al., 'Synchronicity in the therapeutic setting: A survey of practitioners', 2016.

13 Invoking by Moonlight

1. Ilanit Gordon et al., 'Physiological and behavioral synchrony predict group cohesion and performance', 2020; Alan R Harvey, 'Links between the neurobiology of oxytocin and human musicality', 2020 ; Martin Lang et al., 'Sync to link: Endorphin-mediated synchrony effects on cooperation', 2017.
2. Pierre Flor-Henry, 'Brain changes during a shamanic trance: Altered modes of consciousness, hemispheric laterality, and systemic psychobiology', 2017; Michael J. Hove et al., 'Brain network reconfiguration and perceptual decoupling during an absorptive state of consciousness', 2016.

14 Awakening to Land and Memory

1. Fanch Guillemin, *Sorciers de Bretagne*, 1998, p. 20.
2. Françoise Le Roux and Christian-Joseph Guyonvarc'h, *Les Druides*, 1986; Gwenc'hlan Le Scouëzec, *Bretagne Terre Sacrée*, 1996.
3. M. Gustave Geffroy, 'La Bretagne au Centre', *Le Tour du* monde, 1903, p. 507; Charles Chassé, 'Le culte Breton de Sainte-Anne et la vénération des Vierges noires', 1945.

15 When Magic Really Matters

1. Vivianne Crowley, *Wicca: The Old Religion in the New Age*, 1989, p. 52.
2. Crowley, *The Natural Magician: Practical Techniques for Empowerment*, 2003.

16 Journeying to the Otherworld

1. Mircea Eliade, *Shamanism*, 1989.
2. Carlos Castaneda, *The Teachings of Don Juan*, 1968.
3. Michael J. Hove et al., 'Brain network reconfiguration and perceptual decoupling during an absorptive state of consciousness', 2016.
4. Kim-Pong Tam et al., 'Saving Mr. Nature: Anthropomorphism enhances connectedness to and protectiveness toward nature', 2013.
5. Lacy Cooke, 'Mother trees recognize kin and send them "messages of wisdom"', 2016; Suzanne Simard, *Finding the Mother Tree*, 2021.

17 Supernatural Allies

1. Terry Pratchett, *Small Gods*, 1993, p. 15.
2. Dan Brown, *The Da Vinci Code*, 2003.
3. Heinrich Cornelius Agrippa von Nettesheim, *His Fourth Book of Occult Philosophy*, 1655.
4. Ibid., pp. 187–193.

18 Flying with the Phoenix

1. Jung, Memories, Dreams, Reflections, 1995, p. 228
2. Edith Nesbit, *The Phoenix and the Carpet*, 1904.
3. Vivianne Crowley, *Phoenix from the Flame*, 1994.

4. https://www.youtube.com/watch?v=WA1bjPOrgZw; available for download from: https://www.amazon.de/Phoenix-Pagan-Piper-Project/dp/B075LMDRXK/.
5. Rafał T. Prinke and Kamila Follprecht, 'John Dee and Edward Kelley in Cracow: Identifying the House of Enochian Revelations', 2015.

19 Beneath the Green Banner

1. 'The priest and the black mass', *News of the World*, 2 February 1969.
2. Melissa Davey et al., 'People's Climate March – as it happened', *Guardian*, 2014.
3. https://www.masksofthegoddess.com/.
4. Francesca Ciancimino Howell, *Making Magic with Gaia*, 2002.
5. Damian Carrington, 'School climate strikes: 1.4 million people took part, say campaigners', *Guardian*, 2019.
6. Matthew Smith, 'International Poll: Most expect to feel impact of climate change, many think it will make us extinct', 2019.
7. Erich Fromm, *The Anatomy of Human Destructiveness*, 1973, p. 365.
8. Will Steffen et al., 'The Anthropocene: Conceptual and historical perspectives', 2011.
9. *The I Ching*, 1968, pp. 46–47.

20 Touching the Stone

1. Ronald Hayman, *A Life of Jung*, 2002, p. 316.
2. Stephen and Robin Larsen, *Joseph Campbell, A Fire in the Mind*, 2002, pp. 359–362.
3. Marie-Louise von Franz, *Alchemy*, 1980.
4. von Franz, *C. G. Jung: His Myth in our Time*, 1998, p. 234, f.n. 65.
5. Arnaldus Villanovanus, 'Rosarium Philosophorum', 1550/ c.1750.
6. Jung, *Memories, Dreams, Reflections*, 1985, p. 254.
7. Ibid.
8. von Franz, *Alchemy*, p. 174.

21 Magical Womanpower

1. https://www.sarahannant.com/.
2. https://www.victoriamusson.com/victoriamusson.

3. Jung, *The Red Book*, 2009, p. 268.
4. Lynda Gratton, *Hot Spots*, 2007.
5. Una Woodruff and Lisa Tuttle, *Catwitch*, 1983.
6. Una Woodruff and Colin Wilson, *Witches*, 1981.
7. Chloe Berge, 'Why are women turning to witchcraft?', 2018.
8. Mary Webb, *Gone to Earth*, 1917; Webb, *The Golden Arrow*, 1916; Webb, *The Precious Bane*, 1924.
9. https://www.rebeccabeattie.co.uk
10. Henrik Bogdan, 'Women and the Hermetic Order of the Golden Dawn: Nineteenth Century Occultism Initiation from a Gender Perspective', in Alexandra Heidle and Joannes Augustinus Maria Snoek, eds, *Women's Agency and Rituals in Mixed and Female Masonic Orders*, 2008, p. 246.
11. Robert Andrew Gilbert, *The Golden Dawn: Twilight of the Magicians*, 1983.
12. Anna Bonus Kingsford, *Clothed with the Sun*, 1906, p. 7, Vision 2ii.
13. Florence Farr, 'The Mystery of Time: A Masque', 1905.
14. Ibid.
15. Farr, 'Flying Roll No. XIII: Secrecy and Hermetic Love, By S.S.D.D.', in Francis King, ed., *Astral Projection, Ritual Magic, and Alchemy*, 1987.
16. https://www.magickalwomenconference.com/

22 Awakening to New Gods

1. https://www.medicaldetectiondogs.org.uk/about-us/.
2. https://phillipabowers.co.uk/index.php.
3. Norman Iles, *Who Really Killed Cock Robin?*, 1986. Iles, *Restoration of Cock Robin*, 1989.
4. Alexander Carmichael, *Carmina Gadelica*, 1972.

23 Wild Once More

1. Campbell, *The Hero with a Thousand Faces*, 1972, p. 39.
2. 'Dark energy, dark matter', NASA Science, 2020.
3. Kerry Lotzof, 'Are we really made of stardust?', 2018.
4. Aleister Crowley, *Magick in Theory and Practice*, 1960, p. 346.

Bibliography

Aarons, Marjorie, *The Tapestry of Life: Through the Mediumship of Lillian Bailey*, London, Psychic Press, 1979.

Achterberg, Jeanne, Karin Cooke, Todd Richards, Leanna J. Standish, Leila Kozak and James H. Lake, 'Evidence for correlations between distant intentionality and brain function in recipients: A functional magnetic resonance imaging analysis', *The Journal of Alternative and Complementary Medicine*, vol. 11, no. 6, 2006, pp. 965–971.

Agrippa von Nettesheim, Heinrich Cornelius, *His Fourth Book of Occult Philosophy: Of Geomancy, Magical Elements of Peter de Abano, Astronomical Geomancy, the Nature of Spirits, Arbatel of Magick*, trans. Robert Turner, London, John Harrison, 1655.

Albrecht, Glenn, 'Creating a language for our psychoterratic emotions and feelings', Health Earth [blog], 8 September 2011, http://healthearth.blogspot.com/2011/09/creating-language-for-our.html (accessed 16 July 2016). .

Assagioli, Roberto, *Psychosynthesis: A Manual of Principles and Techniques*, Wellingborough, Turnstone Press, 1975.

——, *The Act of Will: A Guide to Self-Actualization and Self-Realization*, New York, Penguin Books, 1973.

Atchley, Ruth Ann, David L. Strayer and Paul Atchley, 'Creativity in the wild: Improving creative reasoning through immersion in natural settings', *PLoS ONE*, vol. 7, no. 12, 2012, e51474, https://doi.org/10.1371/journal.pone.0051474.

Basch, Ethan, Heather Boon, Theresa Davies-Heerema, Ivo Foppo, Sadaf Hashmi, Jens Hasskarl, David Sollars and Catherine Ulbricht, 'Boswellia: An evidence-based systematic review', *Journal of Herbal Pharmacotherapy*, vol. 4, no. 3, 2004, pp. 63–83, https://doi.org/10.1080/J157v04n03_06.

Berge, Chloe, 'Why are women turning to witchcraft?' *Fashion*, 29 August 2018, https://fashionmagazine.com/culture/witchcraft-2018/ (accessed 15 December 2019).

Berto, Rita, 'The role of nature in coping with psycho-physiological stress: A literature review on restorativeness', *Behavioral Sciences*, vol. 4, no. 4, 2014, pp. 394–409, https://doi.org/10.3390/bs4040394.

Bogdan, Henrik, 'Women and the Hermetic Order of the Golden Dawn: Nineteenth Century Occultism Initiation from a Gender Perspective', in Alexandra Heidle and Joannes Augustinus Maria Snoek, eds, *Women's Agency and Rituals in Mixed and Female Masonic Orders*, Boston, MA, Brill Academic Publishers, 2008, pp. 245–264.

Bratman, Gregory N., J. Paul Hamilton and Gretchen C. Daily, 'The impacts of nature experience on human cognitive function and mental health', *Annals of the New York Academy of Sciences*, vol. 1249, no. 1, 2012, pp. 118–136, https://doi.org/10.1111/j.1749–6632.2011.06400.x.

Bratman, Gregory N., Paul Hamilton, Kevin S. Hahn, Gretchen C. Daily, and James J. Gross, 'Nature experience reduces rumination and subgenual prefrontal cortex activation', *Proceedings of the National Academy of Sciences of the United States of America*, vol. 112, no. 28, 2015, pp. 8567–8572, https://doi.org/10.1073/pnas.1510459112.

Breton, André, *Manifestoes of Surrealism*, trans. Richard Seaver and Helen R. Lane, Ann Arbor, MI, Ann Arbor Paperbacks/University of Michigan Press, 1972.

Brown, Dan, *The Da Vinci Code*, New York, Doubleday, 2003.

Campbell, Joseph, *The Hero with a Thousand Faces*, Princeton, NJ, Bollingen Series XVII/Princeton University Press, 1972.

——, with Bill Moyers, *The Power of Myth*, ed. Betty Sue Flowers, New York, Doubleday, 1988.

Carmichael, Alexander, *Carmina Gadelica: Hymns and Incantations*, vol. I, Edinburgh, Scottish Academic Press, 1928.

Carrington, Damian, 'School climate strikes: 1.4 million people took part, say campaigners', *Guardian*, 19 March 2019, https://www.theguardian.com/environment/2019/mar/19/school-climate-strikes-more-than-1-million-took-part-say-campaigners-greta-thunberg (accessed 25 April 2020).

Carroll, Lewis, *Alice's Adventures in Wonderland; Through the Looking-Glass, and What Alice Found There*, illus. John Tenniel, London, Macmillan, 1871.

Castaneda, Carlos, *The Teachings of Don Juan: A Yaqui Way of Knowledge*, Berkeley, CA, University of California Press, 1968.

Chassé, Charles, 'Le culte Breton de Sainte-Anne et la vénération des Vierges noires', *Annales de Bretagne*, vol. 52, no. 1, 1945, pp. 60–67, https://doi.org/10.3406/abpo.1945.1833.

Ciancimino Howell, Francesca, *Making Magic with Gaia*, York Beach, ME, Red Wheel/Weiser, 2002.

Cooke, Lacy, 'Mother trees recognize kin and send them "messages of wisdom"', Inhabitat [website], 8 June 2016, https://inhabitat.com/mother-trees-recognize-kin-and-send-them-messages-of-wisdom (accessed 11 August 2016).

Cooley, Sam J., Ceri R. Jones, Arabella Kurtz and Noelle Robertson, '"Into the Wild": A meta-synthesis of talking therapy in natural outdoor spaces', *Clinical Psychology Review*, vol. 77, 2020, p. 101841, https://doi.org/10.1016/j.cpr.2020.101841.

Cracknell, Deborah, Mathew P. White, Sabine Pahl, Wallace J. Nichols and Michael H. Depledge, 'Marine biota and psychological well-being: A preliminary examination of dose-response effects in an aquarium setting', *Environment and Behavior*, vol. 48, no. 10, 2015, pp. 1242–1269, https://doi.org/10.1177/0013916515597512.

Crego, Antonio, José Ramón Yela, María Ángeles Gómez-Martínez and Ahmed A. Karim, 'The contribution of meaningfulness and mindfulness to psychological well-being and mental health: A structural equation model', *Journal of Happiness Studies*, vol. 21, 2019, pp. 2827–2850, https://doi.org/10.1007/s10902-019-00201-y.

Crowley, Aleister, *Magick in Theory and Practice*, New York, Castle Books, 1960.

Crowley, Vivianne, *Jung: A Journey of Transformation: Exploring His Life and Experiencing His Ideas*, Wheaton, IL, Quest Books, 2000.

——, *Phoenix from the Flame: Living as a Pagan in the 21st Century*, London, Thorsons, 1994.
——, *Principles of Jungian Spirituality*, London, Thorsons, 1998.
Crowley, Vivianne, *The Natural Magician: Practical Techniques for Empowerment,* London and New York, Michael Joseph/Penguin, 2003.
——, *Wicca: A Comprehensive Guide to the Old Religion in the Modern World*, 2nd edn, London, HarperCollins, 2003.
——, *Wicca: The Old Religion in the New Age*, Wellingborough, Aquarian Press, 1989.
——, *A Woman's Kabbalah*, London, Thorsons, 2000.
Dalai Lama, '"Prayer is not enough": The Dalai Lama on why we need to fight coronavirus with compassion', *Time*, 14 April 2020, https://time.com/5820613/dalai-lama-coronavirus-compassion/.
'Dark energy, dark matter', NASA Science [website], https://science.nasa.gov/astrophysics/focus-areas/what-is-dark-energy (accessed 22 May 2020).
Davey, Melissa, Adam Vaughan and Amanda Holpuch, 'People's Climate March: Thousands demand action around the world – as it happened', *Guardian*, 22 September 2014, https://www.theguardian.com/environment/live/2014/sep/21/peoples-climate-march-live.
Davies, William Henry, *Songs of Joy and Others*, London, A. C. Fifield, 1911.
Doward, Jamie, 'Buddhist, teacher, predator: Dark secrets of the Triratna guru', *Observer*, 21 July 2019, https://www.theguardian.com/world/2019/jul/21/sangharakshita-guru-triratna-buddhist-dark-secrets (accessed September 22, 2020).
Efferth, Thomas, and Franz Oesch, 'Anti-inflammatory and anti-cancer activities of frankincense: Targets, treatments and toxicities', *Seminars in Cancer Biology*, 2020, https://doi.org/10.1016/j.semcancer.2020.01.015.
Eliade, Mircea, *Shamanism: Archaic Techniques of Ecstasy*, trans. Willard R. Trask, London, Arkana, 1989.
Estés, Clarissa Pinkola, *Women Who Run with the Wolves: Myths and Stories of the Wild Woman Archetype*, New York, Ballantine Books, 1992.
Farr, Florence, 'Flying Roll No. XIII: Secrecy and Hermetic Love, By S.S.D.D.', in Francis King, ed., *Astral Projection, Ritual Magic,*

and Alchemy: Golden Dawn Material by S .L. Mathers and Others, Rochester, VT, Destiny Books, 1987, pp. 163–166.
——, 'The Mystery of Time: A Masque', *Theosophical Review*, vol. 36, no. 211, 1905, pp. 9–19.
Felten, David L., and Mary E. Maida, 'Psychoneuroimmunology', in Vilayanur Subramanian Ramachandran, ed., *Encyclopedia of the Human Brain*, San Diego, CA, Academic Press, 2002, pp. 103–127, https://doi.org/10.1016/B0-12-227210-2/00292-2.
Flor-Henry, Pierre, Yakov Shapiro and Corine Sombrun, 'Brain changes during a shamanic trance: Altered modes of consciousness, hemispheric laterality, and systemic psychobiology', *Cogent Psychology*, vol. 4, no. 1, 2017, pp. 1–34.
Fortune, Dion, 'The Rationale of Magic', *London Forum*, vol. 60, pp. 175-181, September 1934.
Fox, Kieran C. R., Savannah Nijeboer, Matthew L. Dixon, James L. Floman, Melissa Ellamil, Samuel P. Rumak, Peter Sedlmeier and Kalina Christoff, 'Is meditation associated with altered brain structure? A systematic review and meta-analysis of morphometric neuroimaging in meditation practitioners', *Neuroscience and Biobehavioral Reviews*, vol. 43, 2014, pp. 48–73.
Freud, Sigmund, *On the Sexual Theories of Children*, London, Read Books, 2013.
Fromm, Erich, *The Anatomy of Human Destructiveness*, New York, Holt, Rinehart and Winston, 1973.
Geffroy, M. Gustave, 'La Bretagne au Centre', *Le Tour du Monde: Nouveau Journal des Voyages*, vol. 11, no. 40, 1903, pp. 461–541.
Gilbert, Robert Andrew, *The Golden Dawn: Twilight of the Magicians: The Rise and Fall of a Magical Order*, Wellingborough, Aquarian Press, 1983.
Gordon, Ilanit, Avi Gilboa, Shai Cohen, Nir Milstein, Nir Haimovich, Shay Pinhasi, Shahar Siegman, 'Physiological and behavioral synchrony predict group cohesion and performance', *Scientific Reports*, vol. 10, no. 1, 2020, p. 8484, https://doi.org/10.1038/s41598-020-65670-1.
Gratton, Lynda, *Hot Spots: Why Some Companies Buzz with Energy and Innovation and Others Don't*, Harlow, Prentice-Hall, 2007.
Guillemin, Fanch, *Sorciers de Bretagne*, Morlaix, Skol Vreizh, 1998.

Harding, M. Esther, *The Way of All Women: A Psychological Interpretation*, London, Rider & Company, 1971.

——, *Women's Mysteries, Ancient and Modern: A Psychological Interpretation of the Feminine Principle as Portrayed in Myth, Story and Dreams*, London, Rider & Company, 1971.

Harvey, Alan R. 'Links between the neurobiology of oxytocin and human musicality', *Frontiers in Human Neuroscience*, vol. 14, 2020, p. 350, https://doi:10.3389/fnhum.2020.00350.

Hayman, Ronald, *A Life of Jung*, London, Bloomsbury, 2002.

Heselton, Philip, *In Search of the New Forest Coven,* Nottingham, Fenix Flames, 2020.

Hofmann, Stefan G., Paul Grossman and Devon E. Hinton, 'Loving-kindness and compassion meditation: Potential for psychological interventions', *Clinical Psychology Review*, vol. 31, no. 7, 2011, pp. 1126–1132, https://doi.org/10.1016/j.cpr.2011.07.003.

Hove, Michael J., Johannes Stelzer, Till Nierhaus, Sabrina D. Thiel, Christopher Gundlach, Daniel S. Margulies, Koene R. A. Van Dijk, Robert Turner, Peter E. Keller and Björn Merker, 'Brain network reconfiguration and perceptual decoupling during an absorptive state of consciousness', *Cerebral Cortex*, vol. 26, no. 7, 2016, pp. 3116–3124, https://doi.org/10.1093/cercor/bhv137.

Hunter, MaryCarol R., Brenda W. Gillespie and Sophie Yu-Pu Chen, 'Urban nature experiences reduce stress in the context of daily life based on salivary biomarkers', *Frontiers in Psychology*, vol. 10, 2019, https://doi.org/10.3389/fpsyg.2019.00722.

The I Ching, or Book of Changes, trans. Richard Wilhelm and Cary F. Baynes, London, Routledge & Kegan Paul, 1968.

Iles, Norman, *Restoration of Cock Robin: Nursery Rhymes and Carols Restored to Their Original Meanings*, London, Robert Hale, 1989.

——, *Who Really Killed Cock Robin?: Nursery Rhymes and Carols Restored*, London, Robert Hale, 1986.

Johns, June, *The King of the Witches: The World of Alex Sanders*, London, Peter Davies, 1969.

Jung, Carl Gustav, *Dream Analysis 1: Notes of the Seminar Given in 1928–30*, ed. William McGuire, London, Routledge/Bollingen Series XCIX, 1984.

——, 'Human Relationships in Relation to the Process of Individuation (Cornwall Seminar): Unauthorized Notes', ed. M. Esther

Harding, notes by M. Esther Harding and Kristine Mann, July 1923, https://brbl-dl.library.yale.edu/vufind/Record/3684132 (accessed 27 May 2020).

——, *Memories, Dreams, Reflections*, ed. Aniela Jaffé, trans. Richard Winston and Clara Winston, London, Fontana, 1995.

——, *Modern Man in Search of a Soul*, London, Routledge & Kegan Paul, 1933.

——, 'On the Nature of the Psyche', in Carl Gustav Jung, *The Collected Works of C. G. Jung, Vol. 8: The Structure and Dynamics of the Psyche*, trans. R. F. C. Hull, Princeton, NJ, Princeton University Press/Bollingen Series XX, 1970, pp. 161–66.

——, 'The Philosophical Tree', in Carl Gustav Jung, *The Collected Works of C. G. Jung, Vol. 13: Alchemical Studies*, trans. R. F. C. Hull, London, Routledge & Kegan Paul, 1967.

——, *The Red Book: Liber Novus*, ed. Sonu Shamdasani, trans. Mark Kyburz, John Peck and Sonu Shamdasani, New York and London, W. W. Norton & Company/Philemon Series, 2009.

——, 'The Relations between the Ego and the Unconscious', in Carl Gustav Jung, *The Collected Works of C. G. Jung, Vol. 7: Two Essays in Analytical Psychology*, trans. R. F. C. Hull, London, Routledge & Kegan Paul, 1967, pp. 122–241.

——, 'Synchronicity: An Acausal Connecting Principle', in Carl Gustav Jung, *The Collected Works of C. G. Jung, Vol. 8: The Structure and Dynamics of the Psyche*, trans. R. F. C. Hull, London, Routledge & Kegan Paul, 1969, pp. 421–458.

Kingsford, Anna Bonus, *Clothed with the Sun: Being the Book of Illuminations of Anna (Bonus) Kingsford*, eds Edward Maitland and Samuel Hopgood Hart, London, John M. Watkins, 1906.

Krippner, Stanley C., and Allan Combs, 'The neurophenomenology of shamanism: An essay review', *Journal of Consciousness Studies*, vol. 9, no. 3, 2002, pp. 77–82.

Lang, Martin, Vladimir Bahna, John H. Shaver, Paul Reddish and Dimitris Xygalatas, 'Sync to link: Endorphin-mediated synchrony effects on cooperation', *Biological Psychology*, vol. 127, 2017, pp. 191–197, https://doi.org/10.1016/j.biopsycho.2017.06.001.

Larsen, Stephen, and Robin Larsen, *Joseph Campbell, A Fire in the Mind: The Authorized Biography*, Rochester, VT, Inner Traditions, 2002.

Le Roux, Françoise, and Christian-Joseph Guyonvarc'h, *Les Druides*, Rennes, Éditions Ouest-France, 1986.

Le Scouëzec, Gwenc'hlan, *Bretagne Terre Sacrée: Un Ésoterérisme Celtique*, Spézet, Coop Breizh, 1996.

Leland, Charles Godfrey, *Aradia: The Gospel of the Witches*, London, C. W. Daniel Company, 1974.

Lotzof, Kerry 'Are we really made of stardust?', Natural History Museum [website], 2018, https://www.nhm.ac.uk/discover/are-we-really-made-of-stardust.html (accessed 20 October 2020).

Mantel, Hilary, *Beyond Black*, London, 4th Estate, 2005.

Mao Tse-tung, *Quotations from Chairman Mao Tse-tung* [*The Little Red Book*], Peking, Foreign Languages Press, 1966.

Marletto, Chiara, David M. Coles, Tristran Farrow and Viarko Vedral, 'Entanglement between living bacteria and quantized light witnessed by rabi splitting', *Journal of Physics Communications*, vol. 2, no. 10, 2018, p. 101001, https://doi.org/10.1088/2399-6528/aae224.

Moore, Thomas, *A Religion of One's Own: A Guide to Creating a Personal Spirituality in a Secular World*, New York, Gotham Books, 2014).

Mullins, Aloysius, *Witchcraft: A Warning*, London, Catholic Truth Society, 1970.

Murray, Margaret Alice, *The God of the Witches*, London and New York, Oxford University Press, 1970.

——, *The Witch-Cult in Western Europe: A Study in Anthropology*, London, Oxford University Press, 1921.

Nesbit, Edith, *The Phoenix and the Carpet*, London, George Newnes, 1904.

Northage, Ivy, *Mechanics of Mediumship*, London, College of Psychic Studies, 1973.

——, *Mediumship Made Simple*, London, College of Psychic Studies, 1986.

Oldmeadow, Katherine Louise, *Princess Charming*, London, Collins, 1923.

Pausanias. *Description of Greece,* vol. 2, trans. Arthur Richard Shilleto, London, George Bell and Sons, 1886.

Pizzi, Rita, Andrea Fantasia, Fabrizio Gelain, Danilo Rossetti and Angelo Vescovi, 'Non-local correlation between separated human neural networks', in Eric Donkor, Andrew R. Pirich and Howard

Brandt, eds, *Quantum Information and Computation II: Proceedings of SPIE5436*, 2004, pp. 107–117.

Pratchett, Terry, *Small Gods*, London, Corgi, 1993.

——, *Witches Abroad*, London, Corgi, 1992.

'The priest and the black mass', *News of the World*, 2 February 1969, pp. 2–4.

Prinke, Rafał T., and Kamila Follprecht, 'John Dee and Edward Kelley in Cracow: Identifying the House of Enochian Revelations', *The Polish Journal of the Arts and Culture*, vol. 13, no. 1, pp. 120-137, 2015.

Radin, Dean, Marilyn Schlitz and Christopher Baur, 'Distant healing intention therapies: An overview of the scientific evidence', *Global Advances in Health and Medicine*, vol. 4, no. 1 (supplement), 2015, pp. 67–71, https://doi.org/10.7453/gahmj.2015.012.suppl.

Robertson, Olivia, *Field of the Stranger*, London, Peter Davies/The Book Society, 1948.

Roe, Chris A., Charmaine Sonnex, and Elizabeth C. Roxburgh. 'Two meta-analyses of noncontact healing studies.' *Explore*, vol. 11, no. 1, 2015, pp. 11–23. doi:10.1016/j.explore.2014.10.001.

Roerich, Helena, *Letters, Volume 2: 1935–1939*, New York, Agni Yoga Society, 1967.

Roxburgh, Elizabeth C., Sophie Ridgway and Chris A. Roe, 'Synchronicity in the therapeutic setting: A survey of practitioners', *Counselling and Psychotherapy Research*, vol. 16, no. 1, 2016, pp. 44–53, https://doi.org/10.1002/capr.12057.

Schrödinger, Erwin, *My View of the World*, trans. Cecily Hastings, Cambridge, Cambridge University Press, 1964.

Simard, Suzanne, *Finding the Mother Tree: Discovering How the Forest Is Wired for Intelligence and Healing*, New York, Knopf Doubleday, 2021.

Smith, Matthew, 'International Poll: Most expect to feel impact of climate change, many think it will make us extinct', YouGov [website], 15 September 2019, https://yougov.co.uk/topics/science/articles-reports/2019/09/15/international-poll-most-expect-feel-impact-climate (accessed 28 April 2020).

Steffen, Will, Jacques Grinevald, Paul Crutzen and John Mcneill, 'The Anthropocene: Conceptual and historical perspectives', *Philosophical Transactions of the Royal Society A: Mathematical, Physical, and Engineering Sciences*, vol. 369, no. 1938, 2011, pp. 842–867, https://doi.org/10.1098/rsta.2010.0327.

Suzuki, Shunryū, *Zen Mind, Beginner's Mind*, New York and Tokyo, Weatherhill, 1970.

Tam, Kim-Pong, Sau-Lai Lee and Melody Manchi Chao, 'Saving Mr. Nature: Anthropomorphism enhances connectedness to and protectiveness toward nature', *Journal of Experimental Social Psychology*, vol. 49, no. 3, 2013, pp. 514–521, https://doi.org/10.1016/j.jesp.2013.02.001.

Ulrich, Roger S., O. Lundén and John L. Eltinge, 'Effects of exposure to nature and abstract pictures on patients recovering from heart surgery' [abstract], *Psychophysiology*, vol. 30 (supplement 1), 1993, p. 7.

Villanovanus, Arnaldus, 'Rosarium Philosophorum', 1550/ c.1750, Alchemical Texts [website], https://www.alchemywebsite.com/rosary1.html (accessed 22 December 2020).

von Franz, Marie-Louise, *Alchemy: An Introduction to the Symbolism and the Psychology*, Toronto, Inner City Books, 1980.

——, *C. G. Jung: His Myth in our Time: Studies in Jungian Psychology by Jungian Analysts*, trans. William H. Kennedy, Toronto, Inner City Books, 1998.

——, *On Divination and Synchronicity: The Psychology of Meaningful Chance*, Toronto, Inner City Books, 1980.

Wahbeh, Helané, Lauri Shainsky, Angela Weaver and Jan Engels-Smith, 'Shamanic healing for veterans with PTSD: A case series', *Explore*, vol. 13, no. 3, 2017, pp. 207–217, https://doi.org/10.1016/j.explore.2017.02.003.

Webb, Mary, *Gone to Earth*, London, Constable & Company, 1917.

——, *The Golden Arrow*, London, Constable & Company, 1916.

——, *The Precious Bane*, London, Jonathan Cape, 1924.

Williams, Charles, *War in Heaven*, London, Victor Gollancz, 1930.

Winkelman, Michael James, 'A cross-cultural study of the elementary forms of religious life: Shamanistic healers, priests, and witches', *Religion, Brain & Behavior*, 2020, https:// doi:10.1080/2153599X.2020.1770845 (accessed 28 November 2020).

Wiseman, Richard, *The Luck Factor: The Scientific Study of the Lucky Mind*, London, Century, 2003.

Woodruff, Una, and Colin Wilson, *Witches*, Limpsfield, Paper Tiger/Dragon's World Ltd, 1981.

Woodruff, Una, and Lisa Tuttle, *Catwitch*, New York, Doubleday, 1983.

Yela, José Ramón, Antonio Crego, María Ángeles Gómez-Martínez and Laura Jiménez, 'Self-compassion, meaning in life, and experiential avoidance explain the relationship between meditation and positive mental health outcomes', *Journal of Clinical Psychology*, vol. 76, no. 9, 2020, pp. 1631–1652, https://doi.org/10.1002/jclp.22932.

Index